CONTESTED
CHILDHOOD

CONTESTED CHILDHOOD

Diversity and Change in Japanese Preschools

SUSAN D. HOLLOWAY

ROUTLEDGE • New York • London

Published in 2000 by
Routledge
29 West 35th Street
New York, NY 10001

Published in Great Britain by
Routledge
11 New Fetter Lane
London EC4P 4EE

Library of Congress Cataloging-in-Publication Data
    Holloway, Susan D.
    Contested childhood : diversity and change in Japanese preschools /
Susan D. Holloway.
        p. cm.
    Includes bibliographical references (p.) and index.
    ISBN 0-415-92458-8 (hb) — ISBN 0-415-92459-6 (pb)
        1. Education, Preschool—Japan. 2. Educational change—Japan. I. Title.
    LB1140.25J3 H69 2000
    372.21'0952—dc21   99-056428

Designed by Cynthia Dunne

For Bruce, Caitlin, and Dylan

CONTENTS

ACKNOWLEDGMENTS

I am deeply appreciative of funding from the Fulbright Scholar Program, which enabled me to make an extended visit to Japan in 1994 to collect data for this book. Professor Masahiko Minami helped me formulate the proposal that was eventually accepted by Fulbright. He and Hitomi Minami have been steadfast supporters of my interest in Japan. They translated most of the interviews after I returned from Japan, and assisted, along with Bruce Johnson-Beykont, in data coding. I benefited enormously from the involvement of Miyako Ueda who accompanied me on the majority of the interviews, serving as an interpreter and also a key informant. Together we engaged in the work that lies at the heart of this book— reviewing conversations, puzzling over meanings, and formulating questions for the next visit. Kazuko Narui also accompanied me on numerous visits to preschools and provided assistance not only in interpreting the interview data, but also in helping me develop a broader understanding of family and schooling in Japan. Both Miyako and Kazuko were wonderfully supportive of my family, providing food, shelter, and encouragement during the challenging times of transition between countries.

I am very grateful to Shigemitsu Kinoshita, President of Osaka Kyōiku Daigaku (OKD), for sponsoring my association with OKD during the fall of 1994. Noboru Takahashi, professor of psychology at OKD, was a key conduit to many of the sites I visited in Osaka and a major intellectual contributor to the ideas explored in this book. His students, Madoka Furukama and Mariko Uemoto, provided able assistance with several interviews. He introduced me to Masuo Fujikawa, who was very helpful in identifying and facilitating contacts with preschools in Osaka.

During my stay in Japan, I was also affiliated with Seiwa College, thanks to the hospitality of Vice-President Jitsuo Kuroda and President Tsugikazu Nishigaki. I gained assistance in locating research sites from Professors Emiko Ishigaki and Naomi Hiura. Ever since my first trip to Japan in 1981, I have drawn support and inspiration from Professors Hiroshi Azuma and Keiko Kashiwagi of Shirayuri College. Their wisdom and kindness have been invaluable resources.

I received able assistance at the University of California at Berkeley from Kazuko Behrens, who helped pull together government and private association statistics on preschools, provided feedback on drafts, and kept an eye on my Japanese. Valuable information about Japanese preschools was also provided by Kyōichi Ito, Masamichi Komata, Tomonaka Hiraoka, Mitsushige Akita, and the staff of the Japan Shinto Nursery and Kindergarten Association. Annette Holloway braved bad weather and cut-rate accommodations to help me lay the groundwork for my family's stay in Japan, and Jan Gelatti supplied much appreciated encouragement to undertake this book.

Bruce Fuller has provided steadfast support of my work in Japan over the past 20 years. He graciously agreed to spend his 1994 sabbatical in Japan, even though his own work at the time focused on educational policy in southern Africa. He has been pulled into countless discussions of Japanese preschools, participating with evident enthusiasm and bringing his deep theoretical understandings of cultural practices to bear on the specifics of my data. Caitlin and Dylan Fuller have visited many temples and eaten a lot of seaweed at my instigation; I am enormously grateful for their willingness to accompany me on this journey.

For reasons of confidentiality, I will not list the names of the staff at the preschools I visited, but they have my deepest gratitude for their gracious hospitality during my visits. Their deep caring for children and conscientious pursuit of excellence is truly inspirational.

CONTESTED CULTURAL MODELS OF SCHOOLING

The classroom at the Wakaba Preschool fills with the noise of 40 four-year-olds preparing for lunch. They talk animatedly as they put away their reading materials and wash their hands. With no direction from the teacher, they scrub down their desks and place them in groups of four. An aide staggers in with heavy plastic bins filled with food. The children give a cheer: it's McDonalds! The teacher plays a chord on the piano. The children scramble to their seats while a representative from each group fetches a paper bag containing the group's food. Each child spreads out a cloth napkin from home for a place mat, and places a hamburger carefully in the middle, with a drink at the top right corner. The group's representative puts out two small containers of french fries at the end of each table. The teacher begins to play a familiar song, and the children sing along without glancing at the food in front of them. A second song follows, this time with hand movements to accompany the lyrics. The teacher plays a chord and the children close their eyes, hands pressed together in prayer. "We will keep our feet together, we will sit up straight, we will eat everything," they say in unison. Then, "Itadakimasu—I gratefully take this food." At another chord they begin to eat, passing the french fries politely to their table mates, with no squabbles.

What does this scene reveal about cultural norms in Japanese pre-schools? At first glance, this scene in the classroom may seem "very Japanese." The children take responsibility for cleaning the classroom and serving the food. They work well together in a large group with little guidance from the teacher. They are polite, controlling their impulse to dive into the meal, and share with their classmates. Is there nothing Western in this scene besides the consumption of food from McDonalds? In fact, many features of the program are appropriated from Western sources. The large class size, which seems to epitomize "group-oriented" Japan, is a product of the Western restructuring of education subsequent to World War II. Before the war, small groups of children were educated under the guidance of a single teacher, who did not teach the class as a whole but, rather, supervised the students as they memorized and discussed important texts (Sato, 1998). And while preschool attendance is now virtually universal in Japan—far surpassing the rate of attendance in the U.S.—the notion of formal schooling for young children was introduced in the late 1800s by Japanese educators returning from study tours in Europe and the U.S., and by American missionaries, who established some of the first Japanese preschools. Many aspects of the preschool institution—including McDonalds—have been appropriated by the Japanese and given a purpose that is consistent with Japanese cultural values and the goals of each particular preschool director.

The preschool is a core institution in Japan, viewed as providing essential experiences that enable young children to obtain social and intellectual skills needed to function successfully in Japanese society. As such, it serves a conservative cultural function—both preserving and transmitting Japanese social values to the younger generation. Yet, as the lunch scene at Wakaba Preschool reveals, preschools are far from static. They do not merely reproduce a uniform cultural script; rather, each preschool is a vibrant, dynamic system whose participants engage in an ongoing, active process of perceiving, interpreting, and synthesizing beliefs and practices available in their cultural milieu. Although aspects of the Western preschool form the underpinning of its Japanese counterpart, these borrowed practices are afforded new meaning and are juxtaposed with other cultural elements, resulting in a setting whose connections to the Western prototype are often tenuous.

And this dynamic process of meaning-making also results in transformation of values and practices that are indigenous to Japan. In fact, what is "traditional" in Japan is not at all clear to the Japanese themselves. Many Japanese adults experience a deep nostalgia for the past, yet they disagree as to the distinctive qualities that made "old Japan" unique. In the process of attempting to recreate the "essential Japanese," they engage in a creative appropriation of beliefs and practices, resulting in a newly crafted set of cultural models deemed "traditional" (Tobin, 1992a). This activity is pursued most urgently by Japanese conservatives, who have the most faith that the old ways can be resurrected and reinvigorated.

Not only does the dynamic appropriation of symbols, beliefs, and behaviors result in historical change, it also results in considerable variation across institutions at any one point in time. The structured curriculum and strict discipline at Wakaba Preschool distinguish it clearly from the preschools described in previous work on Japan, where free play dominates the schedule and permissive teachers condone rowdy, boisterous behavior (Lewis, 1995; Peak, 1991). Yet each can be said to represent cultural values accepted by some members of modern Japanese society. The director of Wakaba, Mr. Waseda, argues that his curriculum encourages the development of traditional Japanese values such as diligence and self-sacrifice. Mr. Waseda argues that, while preschools that emphasize free play may now be "typical" in Japan, they have been too quick to incorporate Western values such as individualism and materialism.

MOVING BEYOND ONE-DIMENSIONAL PORTRAITS OF JAPANESE SOCIETY

In much of the work on education and child rearing in Japan, little emphasis has been placed on capturing the variation—and accompanying tensions and conflict—that characterize this society. Past studies have focused on identifying a canonical set of beliefs and practices that are endorsed and practiced by all but the most deviant members of society. In this book I am attempting to do something different. Since my first visit to Japan in 1980 as a graduate student, I have been more interested in the wide variation in behaviors deemed acceptable within Japan than in general contrasts between Japan and the United States. During that first trip, my naïve stereotypes were constantly challenged; for every person I encountered who displayed behavior consistent with the "typical" Japanese, I would meet two others who seemed to have completely missed these defining cultural directives. Yes, I did see Japanese businessmen running down the subway platform, as depicted in the famous *Time* magazine article on the Japanese work ethic, but I also encountered plenty of people who were quite relaxed, like the owner of a bed and breakfast establishment in Tokyo who preferred to lie on the tatami mat floor watching soap operas on television than straighten up the cluttered rooms in her home. And how could I reconcile the many descriptions of Japanese parents as invariably sweet and supportive with the father I saw fiercely hitting his young son on the head with an umbrella, as the mother looked on? Were these merely exceptions to the rule, or were the images I initially took to Japan far too simplified to convey the depth and nuances of this complex society?

While I continued to visit and write about Japan for the next decade, I did not have an opportunity to address this issue of diversity formally until 1993, when I spent six months in the Kansai area researching the experience of young children in preschools and child-care centers. My goal was to capture the variability that exists in the way Japanese children are cared for—without falling into a morass of noncohering details that pertain only to individual cases! During my stay, I spent a great deal of time in 32 preschools and child-care centers, observing in classrooms and interviewing directors and teachers about their educational philosophy and practices. I visited each school for a full day, then spent one week at each of three selected sites. The data obtained during that visit constitute the core of this book.

My theoretical framework for illuminating diversity, change, and contestation is drawn from recent work in cultural psychology. This emerging field builds upon insights from anthropology and cognitive science as well as social and developmental psychology. Its practitioners tend to look at a particular milieu as affording a variety of available pathways or cultural models. Cultural models refer both to people's beliefs—including ideas about how things work as well as how they *should* work—and the scripts or behavior sequences that they use to deal with routine situations (for a full discussion of this approach, see D'Andrade, 1992; Geertz, 1983; Holland et al., 1998; Holloway et al., 1997; Quinn & Holland, 1987; Shore, 1996). While cultural models are sometimes held by all members of broad social categories such as nation, gender, or social class, they are also formulated within more narrowly bounded social settings, including, for example, neighborhood or occupational niche.

When it comes to educating and rearing children, a number of cultural models are usually deemed acceptable in any given community. However, this cultural "pool" of beliefs and practices may contain elements that are in tension or even in fundamental conflict with each other (Kojima, 1986b, 1988). Because of their own experiences, social positions, and personalities, individuals within a community may appropriate particular cultural elements and synthesize them in a way that leads to disagreement with others in the community. Unlike parents, who often enact cultural models of child rearing without conscious reflection, teachers and preschool directors are typically aware of various theories and alternative strategies when it comes to educating children.

To thoughtful educators, the business of teaching young children turns quickly into an exploration of the type of human being that one hopes to create or at least to participate in creating. The goals and visions of educators are shaped by the cultural models available to them in their society. As Shore (1996) points out, cultural models provide us with a set of heuristics for conceptualizing and resolving these fundamental questions:

> Culture provides us with rhetorical strategies for making [ethical] choices in the form of clichés, proverbs, heroic models in myth, and other such cultural resources that help provide partial and temporary resolutions to what may be ultimately irresolvable predicaments. In this view, cultural systems do not invent values so much as they orchestrate rhetorical strategies, organizing the perception of value-laden situations with standardized and culturally acceptable formulations—what we call cultural models. (p. 304)

Much writing by American scholars and journalists on Japanese education and child rearing has failed to consider the varied and dynamic cultural models that characterize Japanese society and its institutions. Part of this is because Japan has remained ethnically and linguistically homogeneous, and its social class differences are less pronounced than in the United States and many other Western countries. Additionally, many Americans seem to have bought into the notion, also perpetuated by some Japanese, of Japan as the "unknown and unknowable." When a society is viewed as different from one's own, the tendency is to essentialize and exoticize it—to define it as possessing unique and static characteristics that give it its distinctive identity. Western writing not only essentializes Japan but adds a moral evaluation of the resulting portrait. Whether the spin is negative or positive depends on the writer's purpose as well as the political and economic climate of the times. For much of the period subsequent to World War II, the media characterization of Japan was negative (Zipangu, 1998). But along with Japan's rising economic power came more flattering portraits touting the Japanese work ethic, cooperative skills, self-discipline, and the like. As the economy began to slow down, the tide again turned, and culturally based notions such as group orientation are being portrayed in negative terms (e.g., Sayle, 1998).

The following stereotypes have circulated for decades through the popular and academic literature; each may contain a nugget of truth, but all fail to convey the complexity of children's lives in Japan.

Stereotype 1: Japanese Children Are Nerds Whose Days Are Spent Chained to a Desk Preparing for Entrance Examinations

The contrast between the hardworking Japanese student and his free-wheeling American counterpart has been satirized by cartoonist Garry Trudeau (1992), who compares fictional Yukio, a ninth-grader who spends his short summer vacation writing classical poetry, attending cram school, and going to the funerals of relatives who have died at their desks from overwork, with Johnny, an American adolescent who forms a short-lived heavy-metal rock band. The image of Japanese children as slaves to achievement is also pushed—*sans* tongue in cheek— in the mainstream media. For example, a hyperbolic headline in the *San Francisco Chronicle* announces "Battle for best schools reaches age 2 in Tokyo" (Efron, 1997). The attached article describes the plight of boy named Ko who goes to a cram school "with a tiny knapsack packed with his crayons, lunch box and a diaper." Such exaggerated reporting irritates writers like Lois Peak (1991), whose careful analysis of cram schools found that fewer than 1 percent of Japanese children take an entrance examination to get into elementary school, and among these, only a fraction go to examination preparation class. Furthermore, Peak found that most cram schools for this age of child meet for only an hour once or twice a week and focus on familiarizing children with the format of the test rather than drilling them on subject matter.

Like many stereotypes, however, this one contains a kernel of truth. Many leading Japanese educators have voiced their concerns about inappropriate academic pressure in the preschools, and in 1989, the Ministry of Education issued guidelines stating that preschools should be devoted primarily to free-play experiences, and should not provide instruction in reading, writing, or arithmetic (Ishigaki, 1991, 1992). How have schools responded? On the one hand, my research uncovered a number of very large schools that focused almost exclusively on teacher-centered academic instruction. While aware of the ministry guidelines, directors in these academically oriented schools were choosing to appeal to parents who wanted their children to get a head start in literacy, mathematics, and English.

On the other hand, several preschool directors I spoke with reported that they had loosened up their programs in response to the ministry, moving toward a more individualized curriculum that favors self-expression and creativity. In fact, some preschools I visited had done away with virtually all restrictions, permitting children to spend the entire day playing in any way they liked anywhere on the school campus. Recently, the abundance of freedom granted children in these loosely structured preschools has been cited as a cause of the epidemic referred to as *gakkyu hokai* ("collapsed classrooms"), in which elementary school children engage in rowdy, rebellious behavior that has supposedly driven unprecedented numbers of teachers into early retirement ("Nation of 'little emperors,'" 1999). The stereotype is far too simplistic; in fact, the preschool system continues to be characterized by a diverse array of approaches, ranging from the very tightly controlled to the exceedingly free and open.

Stereotype 2: Japanese Children Are Excessively Group-Oriented

For the last 15 years, the American media has been preoccupied with the phenomenon of *ijime*, or bullying. Incidents of bullying in Japan usually occur at the junior high school level, although the issue was frequently broached in my interviews with preschool directors as well. In the very worst cases, the bullied child is murdered by his tormenters or commits suicide (Lanham & Garrick, 1996). The tendency in American media reports is to attribute bullying to the pressures to conform in a group-oriented society—pressures illustrated by the only Japanese aphorism that many American journalists seem to know: "A nail that sticks out will be hammered down" (see Zipangu, 1998, for a critique of American media coverage of this and other social issues).

Certainly, bullying is recognized as a serious problem by the Japanese as well as Americans. Yet the American reports reveal more about our stereotypes of Japan than about the phenomenon of bullying itself. Rarely, for example, are the articles accompanied by any comparative data on bullying in the United States. Nor is it common to find a discussion of the important point that the rate of adolescent suicide is twice as high in America as in Japan (Feiler, 1991, p. 245). These articles go overboard in portraying Japan as a nation of groupthink, where individual rights count for little. One-dimensional contrasts—depicting the United States as individualistic and Japan as collectivistic—are increasingly found in the academic literature as well (e.g., Markus & Kitayama, 1991; Shweder et al., 1998). Western readers can easily gain the impression that Japanese children's individuality is stamped out during their school years, leaving them devoid of opinions and incapable of independent action.

In conducting my research on preschools, I found that the directors were intensely preoccupied with defining the notion of the "self"—and tried to achieve a balance between promoting children's self-expression and helping them exist in harmony with the group. Interested in the United States and in Western views of Japan, they manifested a metalevel awareness of the cultural values that underlie their society, and were motivated to reflect upon the similarities and contrasts between the two countries, particularly regarding individualism. I found tremendous diversity in the views of the directors as to the way that self and group could be brought into balance. Some, citing phenomena such as bullying as major concerns, advocated a move toward individual rights and self-expression. At the other end of the spectrum were those who were far more concerned about the negative consequences of individualism and who therefore desired to strengthen the group orientation of Japanese children. In the middle were the majority, who provided an articulate rendering of their philosophy on balancing the advantages of free expression with the rewards of close connections with group members. These thoughtful analyses quickly dispel the stereotype of a monolithic consensus-seeking nation.

Stereotype 3: Japanese Children Live Charmed Lives in which They Are Gently Enticed by Teachers into Stellar Academic Performance and Superb Social Skills

Interestingly, while the popular media have tended toward dark assessments of Japanese children's lives, academic writers have frequently highlighted the positive. Here, for example, is the remarkable conclusion in a recently published ethnography of a middle school: "Japanese children are happy at school; they learn a lot; they make friends with peers and learn to interact with them in culturally appropriate ways. What they learn at school academically and socially is useful to them in life after school; there are no major contradictions between the lessons of school and those of life in Japan, and they are appropriate at all social and class levels" (Benjamin, 1997, p. 222). Setting aside the question of how this sweeping generalization can follow from a study of a single school, it is also striking that the assessment is uniformly positive. Like many writers on the topic of Japanese education, Benjamin is interested in how Japan can serve as a model of excellence to stimulate American educational reform (e.g., Stevenson & Stigler, 1992; White, 1987).

Some academic writers choose not to examine the sacrifices that the Japanese system exacts from its students, and tend to dismiss Japanese educators' criticisms of their own system as an indicator of the high standards and perpetual self-analysis that are part of the Japanese success story. Professionals working for education reform in Japan have expressed to me their frustration at needing to counteract the optimistic analyses of foreign writers, whose work is accorded great prestige in Japan and therefore serves as a convenient shield for slow-moving bureaucrats in the Ministry of Education. When Japanese and American researchers convene to discuss child rearing and education, the Japanese researchers often spend a great deal of time attempting to rebut the rosy images of Japan that they read in the American academic literature (see LeTendre, 1999).

My own experiences with Japanese early-childhood education have made me wary of excessive rosiness. Although I have seen many preschools where teachers employ the gentle discipline techniques described by American academics, one of the first sites I observed in 1994 did not match this benign picture. Rather, I saw children being hit, shoved, yelled at, demeaned, and threatened with being locked in a closet. Perhaps most surprising was the fact that this went on in front of me—a visitor from America busily recording everything in a note-book—with no sign of hesitation or embarrassment on the part of the teachers.

Any serious account of Japanese cultural models about discipline needs to consider those pertaining to harsh discipline as well as those which advocate benign techniques. My conversations with preschool teachers occasionally brought to the surface the harsh, authoritarian thread that runs through Japanese society—a thread not always acknowledged in rosy academic portraits of children's lives. As one preschool teacher said to me, "In Japan we discipline children using *ame to muchi* (candy and the whip)." This cultural model of discipline was put into a political context by Gregory Clark, president of Tama University: "With each new scandal, the cry goes out for even stricter discipline from teachers and parents. Matching this is the call for something called *kokoro no kyōiku*, or education of the heart. *Ame to muchi*, sweetness and harshness, remain the conservative educational motto" (Japan's education dilemma, 1998).

Among various strict discipline strategies, the use of corporal punishment is the most carefully documented in Japan. Recent data from a variety of sources suggest that corporal punishment is part of the repertoire of many parents and teachers, and is directed to children of preschool age and beyond. For example, in 1996 the number of teachers penalized for inflicting corporal punishment increased by 37 percent, reaching the highest number since the statistics were first collected, in 1977 (Japan briefing, 1997). Kozu (1999) concludes a review of the literature with the following statement: "Corporal punishment of children by parents or even teachers is common to this day. Strong parental authority and tolerance for corporal punishment can blur the distinction between discipline and abuse" (p. 52).[1]

Stereotype 4: These Days, Most Japanese Children Are Deprived of a Normal Childhood

Unlike the other stereotypes, which are held primarily by foreign observers, the view of children as simultaneously deprived and overprotected is more common among the Japanese. Those who hold this view believe that urbanization has resulted in environmental and social changes that are damaging to Japanese children (see Kojima, 1986a, for a review). Children are depicted as virtual prisoners in their own homes, confined to small apartments in high-rise buildings with no other children to play with and nothing to do but watch television and play video games. Their mothers are viewed as either too selfish to pay attention to them or, more often, as highly insecure and overprotective. In a recent chapter on the history of childhood in Japan, Hara and Minagawa (1996) paint a gloomy picture of Japanese childhood, using the term "experiential deprivation" (p. 21) to describe the limited opportunities of children coming of age in contemporary urban Japan.

Gloomy pronouncements on the state of childhood—and unfavorable comparisons with family life in previous eras—are a staple of academic and popular writing across the globe. Too often these comparisons contrast selective, anecdotal images from current times with a romanticized composite of elements from unspecified historical periods (Coontz, 1992). Nearly every preschool director I spoke with voiced a pessimistic view of children's lives in modern Japan. They expressed great concern about the absence of the father from daily family life, the reluctance of mothers to provide adequate discipline and training in acceptable behavior, and the loss of grandparents as a loving and supportive presence. They regretted that urban Japanese children rarely encounter nature, are not allowed to play freely with friends, and are too sedentary.

My study did not focus on the home lives of children, nor did I assess their emotional development and peer relations. However, perceptions and concerns about the students' experiences at home formed an important part of directors' mental landscape and greatly affected how they set up their programs. Directors tended to see the preschool as one place where children could encounter adults with backbone, toughen up through vigorous activity, and engage in free-spirited, rough-and-tumble interactions with peers. Each director has devised a specific remedy to "cure" these perceived social ills. The interplay between perceptions of the problems facing Japanese children and the manner in which preschools were designed constitutes a dynamic property of that most cultural of institutions—the preschool.

WHAT CAN AMERICANS LEARN FROM STUDYING JAPANESE EDUCATION?

Better Understanding of Benefits and Costs to Students of Japanese Educational Practices. Little is gained by painting a simplistic portrait of Japanese education and airbrushing out the lines of tension and contradiction, or by rushing to judgment on its good and bad features. When the positive aspects of Japanese education and child rearing are exaggerated, we lose sight of the risks and sacrifices made by the students. No system is perfect, and choices must be made to prioritize certain values while sacrificing others. Many Japanese feel that their educational system, particularly in the older grades, requires too much conformity and a stifling of individual initiative and self-expression. These concerns deserve to be studied as carefully as have the academic high points, and so far this has not been the case.

Better Understanding of Causal Relationships between Preschool Attributes and Academic Achievement. By ignoring variation, we also run the risk of misunderstanding the causes of high performance in later grades because academic successes are wrongly attributed to preschool preparation in "typical" preschools. It is tempting to speculate that Japanese children obtain high scores on math tests in first grade *because* they attended play-oriented preschools, especially because some Japanese preschools resemble the American ideal of "developmentally appropriate practice" (e.g., Lewis, 1995, p. 34). But not all Japanese preschools are play-oriented. And since virtually no one has directly studied the effect of experiencing a particular preschool curriculum on later achievement, it is impossible to say whether it is the children who attend play-oriented preschools or those whose earlier schooling is more focused on academic skills who receive higher scores on achievement tests in first grade.

Fresh Perspective on the Long-Term Effects of a Market-Oriented Approach to Early Education. Another important reason to examine preschooling with an eye toward complexity is that the Japanese system can teach us important lessons about local control versus centralized administration of schooling. For the last decade, Americans have substantially diminished the role of the central state in determining educational policy and practices. At the K-12 level, for example, charter schools have been established to provide choices outside the usual public school offerings. Some states also provide parents with vouchers to enable them to send their children to the school of their choice. At the preschool level, similar battles are being fought. In the 1960s and seventies, child-care advocates who desired to boost child-care supply and improve quality called for government sponsorship—at the state or federal level—of child care (see Fuller & Holloway, 1996). However, these old remedies that call for a national system of child-care centers *à la* Sweden and Denmark are falling by the wayside. The new watchword is "parental choice"—fostered not by building child-care institutions but by giving parents vouchers that can be used to purchase care from relatives or a neighbor down the street as well as in more formal centers.

The Japanese preschool system is an interesting mixture of public and private institutions. Public preschools receive funding from the Ministry of Education, and while individual institutions are given substantial latitude in creating their own programs, the ministry actively attempts to shape curriculum to conform with current pedagogical expertise. There is also a large number of privately run preschools that subsist largely on tuition. The market for preschooling currently favors the consumer—the family—because the low birthrate in Japan has resulted in a declining number of children to fill available slots. The birthrate has declined steadily since the mid-1970s, and family size is shrinking as well (Ishigaki, 1994; Shwalb et al., 1992). Thus private preschools have to be responsive to families in order to stay competitive. As demand for preschooling diminishes, public preschools are closing down and leaving the field to the private institutions. Some cities, including Yokohama for example, have pulled out of the preschool business altogether. By looking at the types of programs that result from preschools driven by market pressure and comparing them to those that are structured by the Ministry of Education, we can anticipate some of the issues that Americans may face when schooling moves away from government oversight and develops a market orientation.

Clearer View of the Linkages between Cultural Models and Preschool Programs. A central conviction driving the move toward parental choice and local control in the United States is that child care should mirror—or at least be responsive to—community and parental values about rearing children. Once the sole province of the political right, this view now characterizes many leftist families and educators as well, particularly among ethnic minority groups who seek programs that reinforce their particular cultural models and child-rearing strategies. This viewpoint conflicts with the position of many mainstream early-childhood educators, who seek to develop a single definition of child-care quality that can be used to evaluate all settings (see Holloway & Fuller, 1999). For example, the National Association for the Education of Young Children (NAEYC) has drawn up a set of "developmentally appropriate" guidelines which it uses to accredit child-care centers (Bredekamp & Copple, 1997). The NAEYC's position is that children's developmental characteristics—rather than cultural values about how children should be raised—should drive the way programs are structured. The central goal of this book is to argue that cultural models inevitably form the basis of the way preschools are structured, and to show how these models are diverse, dynamic, and contested within the society. This should help American educators bring into focus the ways in which American preschools, too, are cultural institutions.

New Perspectives on Theoretical Links among Cultural Models, Educational Settings, and Macrolevel Social Structures. The longer I have worked on this project, the more social science disciplines I have incorporated into my analytic framework; theories from anthropology, psychology, and sociology are all brought to bear on this set of issues about early education. While working in this manner has been cumbersome and confusing at times, I have ultimately felt satisfied with the opportunities afforded by the coordination of multiple perspectives. I hope that this approach will inform others who venture into "multidisciplinary land." Given my focus on cultural issues, I draw upon the work of anthropologists and find the writings of cognitively oriented anthropologists such as Roy D'Andrade especially helpful (e.g., D'Andrade, 1992). In particular, I find the notion of a cultural model a good way to describe the beliefs and behavioral strategies available to preschool educators. While acknowledging the anthropological notion that cultural models are collectively generated, as a psychologist I am also interested in the way each individual appropriates available cultural models. I use the individual—in this case a teacher or a director—as the basic unit of analysis, looking at how he or she interacts cognitively with the available cultural models, interpreting, evaluating, altering, and synthesizing (Holloway & Minami, 1996).

But I needed to move in the direction of sociology as well. Much of the current work in anthropology tends to view culture as an exogenous variable that causes people to behave in certain ways—without considering how elements of culture are themselves shaped by social institutions. Influential anthropologists such as Clifford Geertz focus on a world of symbols, usually embodied in elements of "high culture," ignoring or downplaying the role played by history, biology, economics, and politics in the construction of those symbolic worlds (e.g., Geertz, 1983). I found much value in the work of those sociologists who are interested in the ways that broad social structures are reflected in everyday interactions between children and adults at home or in school. In particular, the work of Annette Lareau (1989) has shown how research focusing on "microlevel" interactions can illuminate the ways in which "macrolevel" class differences manifest themselves and are partially reproduced in subsequent generations.

A primary goal of this book is to look at the culturally patterned ways in which large-scale structures shape the ideas and strategies available to educators of young children. I have selected three such macrostructures: the social class of the families served by a preschool, the linkage of a school to a religious organization, and whether the school is public or private. I examine how these institutions and their accompanying ideologies supply cultural models for the care and education of children. The following quotation from Kuper (1999) aptly summarizes the need for a dual focus on institutions and cultural models:

> No worthwhile theory of change can exclude objective economic interests and material forces, the social relations that constrain choices, the organization of power, and the capacity of the people with guns to impose new ways of thinking and acting on those without them. It is equally the case that no historian can afford to ignore the ideas that motivate and inform actions. The sensible if unexciting conclusion is surely that one does not have to accept either extreme position. Culture does not provide scripts for everything, but not all ideas are afterthoughts. (p. 199)

THREE FUNDAMENTAL APPROACHES TO EARLY EDUCATION

The original purpose of my project was to examine how preschools were implementing new guidelines from the Ministry of Education that urged a move toward individualized instruction. Eventually, I broadened this objective to include a more general look at the varied philosophies that directors held about the fundamental nature of the child, their ideals about relations among people, and about the balance between the individual and the community. I wanted to see how these basic beliefs would then play themselves out in specific actions the directors took to shape their programs, including their decisions about the issue of individualization.

This new goal was relatively easy to implement. With little effort on my part, I found myself moving among programs whose directors differed radically in their views on all these questions. Many of them made my life even easier by offering to contrast their views with those of other institutions, and argued for the validity of their own position. The majority of them easily identified two major types of preschool— a strict (*kibishii*) type and a relaxed (*yasashii*) type. According to their view, in the strict type, sometimes referred to as "spartan," there was a greater emphasis on teacher-directed activities and discipline was strict. The relaxed type was thought to feature a play-oriented curriculum and pleasant, warm relations with teachers. While these perspectives were enlightening, I ultimately decided to move beyond this two-part typology. I identified three types of preschool, each characterized by distinctive beliefs on the part of the directors pertaining to the basic nature of the child and to the relation of the self to others. The directors within each of the three types utilized distinctive images and metaphors to describe young children and advocated a particular approach to activities, materials, and social relations. Table 1.1 characterizes the three contrasting patterns in terms of their instructional structures, use of procedures and routines, preferred modes of behavioral control, the relative importance of emotional attachment to teacher and peers, and general philosophy about balancing individual needs and group demands.

Twelve preschools (two public, ten private) in the sample could be characterized as *relationship-oriented.* The overall goal of the staff was to provide an enticing introduction to group life that focused on building the children's ability to form relationships with peers and on learning basic classroom routines. Teachers in these schools try to pull children gently out of the warm cocoon of family life and entice them with the rewards of being part of a larger group.

The children at relationship-oriented preschools alternated between activities that were structured by the teacher and those that are relatively free of teacher direction. During their free playtime, children were encouraged to play with others and avoid solitary activity. There were relatively few play materials available, which focused the children on interactions rather than object-mediated play. Art materials were usually

TABLE 1.1

CLASSROOM PRACTICES AND STRUCTURES IN THREE TYPES OF JAPANESE PRESCHOOL

Classroom Practices & Structures	TYPES OF PRESCHOOLS		
	Relationship	Role	Child
Structure of instruction	Mostly large group	Large group	Individual and small group
Verbal participation structure	Teacher to group	Teacher to group	Teacher to individual child
Use of routines	Strong focus	Strong focus	Moderate focus
Modes of control	Diffused	Authoritarian	Diffused
Focus on emotional attachment to peers	High	Low	High
Conceptions of self and group	Relational	Coexistence	Mutually reinforcing

provided by the teacher only when it was time to engage in a specific activity. Much of the teachers' time and effort were spent helping children master the routines of group life: managing their possessions (for example, unpack schoolbag, remove shoes before entering classroom), greeting adults properly, using polite table manners, and participating in occasional group performances with their classmates. Teachers attempted to foster warm relationships with the students by being friendly, relaxed, and nonauthoritarian, but did not engage frequently in prolonged interactions with individual children. The relationship-oriented preschools are characterized at greater length in Chapter 3.

A second type of school has roots in more conservative Japanese traditions, including Buddhism. At the six *role-oriented* preschools in the sample (all private), the basic curriculum consisted of group instruction in academic skills rather than low-key art and music projects as in the relationship-oriented schools. Children in role-oriented schools were learning to read the complex characters (*kanji*) that form the basis of the Japanese writing system (but that the Ministry of Education does not recommend teaching until first grade). Children in these schools also learned how to write the simple syllabary (*hiragana*), engaged in pattern recognition and memory-building activities, played musical instruments, and received instruction in drawing and painting. Other subjects, including English, tea ceremony, traditional Japanese dance, choral singing, and gymnastics, were often taught by specialists once a week. These schools were popular; four of the six had more than 400 students.

I call these schools *role-oriented* because their goal was to strengthen children's capacity to fulfill the requirements of the role they occupy in a given situation. Unlike the relationship-oriented schools, where the emphasis was on having fun and learning the pleasures of group life, children in role-oriented schools were expected to acquire self-discipline through experiencing physical challenges and mastering the demanding curriculum. Children's time was completely structured, with little or no opportunity for individual choice. School rules were enforced with a variety of strict discipline strategies, including threats, identification of potential troublemakers, and shaming. This type of preschool is described at length in Chapter 4.

A third type, which I call *child-oriented* schools, bore a superficial resemblance to American play-oriented preschools. Compared to the other types, the nine child-centered schools (four public, five private) in the sample tended to be small. Most of the day was devoted to free play, with few group activities and no direct instruction. Unlike the relationship-oriented schools, where children's materials were distributed only for use in a particular activity, the child-oriented schools tended to set up activity corners with materials for children to use when they wanted. The children had access to manipulatives and a variety of art materials, as well as supplies for fantasy play. The teachers in child-oriented schools were warm and cheerful, as they were in the relationship-oriented schools, but they had a more individualized approach. They engaged in long conversations with individual children, in contrast to the rather minimal verbal exchanges in the other types of schools.

Some staff in child-centered programs reported that they were attempting to create a feeling of *amae*—warmth, dependence, and informality that typically characterizes mother-child relations in Japan (Doi, 1986). The child-centered preschools seemed to be appropriating *amae* relationship dynamics found in home settings and adapting them to a group program. Child-oriented schools are discussed in Chapter 5.

My decision to describe the schools in terms of three patterns was not taken lightly. An alternative would have been to focus on particular pedagogical dimensions, such as the use of whole group instruction, and discuss variation across the sample on each distinct dimension. I decided against a dimensional analysis for two reasons. First of all, the dimensions were not independent. Those preschools that made frequent use of whole group instruction, for example, also emphasized academics, offered little time for free play, made few manipulatives available, and incorporated physical challenges in the curriculum. If each dimension were considered in isolation, it would be very difficult to convey what it felt like to be a student in a particular school. Secondly, I believe that each dimension takes its meaning in relation to the context in which it is placed. Diana Baumrind pioneered the use of typologies in describing parental discipline practices, arguing that, for example, physical punishment by a parent takes on a different meaning if it is utilized by a parent who is otherwise warm and supportive, compared to one who is cold and rejecting (Baumrind, 1989). Anthropologist Fredrik Barth makes a similar argument in favor of clustering cultural models, noting that cultural pluralism can be captured by describing "streams" of cultural traditions, "each exhibiting an empirical clustering of certain elements in syndromes that tend to persist over time. . . ." (Barth, 1989, p. 130). I think a similar argument holds for preschool programs, and I believe that qualitative methods are particularly well suited for this type of analysis.

Table 1.2 contains a list of all the preschools in the sample, categorized according to their membership in one of the three types. Overall, it was relatively easy to conduct this classification, although some schools fit more neatly into a category than did others. Classification was more difficult in two or three cases when the description provided by a director of school objectives did not seem to be implemented by the teachers, or when a school was in the process of changing its approach. These instances are discussed in detail later in the book.

TABLE 1.2
CHARACTERISTICS OF THE PRESCHOOL SAMPLE

Name	Location	Auspice	Enrollment (at time of data collection)
Relationship-Oriented Preschools			
Nada	Osaka	Private: Nondenominational	114
Okayama	Kobe Suburb	Private: Nondenominational	135
Bunka	Osaka	Private: Shinto	281
Izumo	Osaka	Private: Shinto	228
Kitano	Osaka	Public	139
Akita	Osaka	Private: Nondenominational	90
Hirano	Osaka	Private: Nondenominational	200
Otsubo	Osaka	Private: Buddhist	200
Matsushima	Osaka	Private: Nondenominational	250
Ogura	Osaka	Private: Nondenominational	93
Kitamachi	Osaka	Private: Nondenominational	200
Kuriyama	Osaka	Public	58
Role-Oriented Preschools			
Sannomiya	Osaka	Private: Buddhist	550
Wakaba	Kobe suburb	Private: Nondenominational	411
Tennoji	Kobe suburb	Private: Buddhist	600
Suma	Osaka	Private: Buddhist	188
Taisho	Osaka	Private: Nondenominational	585
Mito	Osaka	Private: Nondenominational	329
Child-Oriented Preschools			
Hanna	Kobe suburb	Private: Christian	150
Takenoko	Tokyo	Private: Nondenominational	180
Fukui	Kobe suburb	Private: Catholic	250
Arima	Kobe	Private: Christian	55
Aizawa	Kobe suburb	Private: Christian	125
Nikko	Osaka suburb	Public	41
Higashimachi	Tokyo	Public	42
Nishimachi	Osaka	Public	170
Maeda	Kobe suburb	Public	93

SOCIAL STRUCTURE AND CULTURE: MOVING BEYOND THE "AVERAGE NATIVE"

Over the last 20 years, the notion of "culture" as represented in traditional ethnographies has been criticized as being "essentialist," ahistorical, and apolitical. Current work in anthropology tends to pay most attention to the "discourses" and strategies used by competing interest groups and political actors within a population (Holland et al., 1998; Shore, 1996). In describing recent developments in the fields of anthropology, Bradd Shore (1996) has written that "the agents of culture are no longer hypothetical or average natives but look like real individuals with specific histories, particular interests, and concrete strategies" (p. 55).

There is still a substantial body of work in the fields of education and psychology, however, that attempts to portray societies as united in their adherence to particular overarching cultural models. In such work, little attention is paid to the possibility of diversity—much less conflict—within a society. And, in spite of increasingly strident outcry by foreign scholars (e.g., Azuma, 1996, p. 222), countries as different as Japan and China are frequently lumped together in describing "Asian" beliefs about child rearing, education, and other topics. A major example of this approach is the recent efforts by several influential scholars to revive the global dichotomy of individualism versus collectivism. In their contribution to the prestigious *Handbook of Child Psychology*, Shweder and colleagues argue that "the individualistic model of the self . . . is an obvious and natural model for European American researchers. . . . Another model of the self stands in significant contrast to individualism, but is generally characteristic of Japan, China, Korea, Southeast Asia, and much of South America and Africa. According to this perspective, the self is not and cannot be separate from others and the surrounding social context. The self is experienced as interdependent with the surrounding social context" (Shweder et al., 1998, p. 899). Furthermore, the individualistic-versus-collectivistic distinction is seen as a key to understanding the development of children from ethnic minorities in the United States and a guide in developing educational programs that are "culturally sensitive." For example, Greenfield proposes that "a value orientation stressing interdependence would characterize the cultural and cross-cultural roots of socialization practices and developmental goals for the [following] minority groups . . . : Native Americans, African Americans, African French, Mexican Americans, Asian Americans and Asian Canadians" (Greenfield, 1994, p. 7).

Proponents of these formulations largely ignore the fact that foundational schemas such as individualism may be contested within a society, or that they may be defined and implemented quite differently within and across communities (Hermans & Kempen, 1998). Furthermore, they frequently focus exclusively on the variable of "culture" and exclude consideration of how cultural models are shaped by societal institutions. Politics and economics are ignored as major forces that bring certain cultural models into play and suppress others.

As I talked with directors in various preschools, I began to get a sense of the institutional forces at work behind the three types of schools. Each of these forces—social class, religious affiliation, and public versus private auspice—provided certain kinds of material resources and ideological guidance that helped to shape a school's program. In the second half of this book, I examine how these three forces express themselves and are intertwined within the preschool institution.

In Chapter 6, I take a closer look at the issue of social class as it pertains to Japanese preschool education, comparing a preschool that serves children from elite families in Tokyo with one that has existed for years in a working class area of downtown Osaka. Japanese society is often touted as remarkably lacking in class-related variation. However, while income and education levels may not vary as widely in Japan as they do in the United States, there are other powerful indicators of social status at work in Japan. Mouer and Sugimoto (1986), for example, have challenged the frequent assertion that the group orientation of Japan is a function of a culturally shared ideology. They point instead to the dynamics of power within Japan, arguing that the myth of collectivism serves the desire of the elite to maintain their resource base and squelch dissent from the disenfranchised. In the field of education, evidence of social class differences in child rearing and education is found in a small body of work (e.g., Rohlen, 1983; Vogel,

1963). At the preschool level, however, little work has been done to document the types of preschool experiences available to children from different social-class groupings. I found that preschools serving wealthier children were more likely to adopt a child-centered approach than those in working-class communities; they had the resources to keep class sizes low and could provide extensive space and materials for teacher-guided free play. Teachers in the wealthier schools were also aware of how little time the children had for free play at home, given that many attended music and language lessons after school. Children in less opulent surroundings received less individual attention and were more often expected to suppress their interests and fit into a group structure.

A second important influence on the preschool programs I visited was religious auspice. While Japanese people are often described as less religious than Americans, the major religions have been unusually active in the area of early education. In Chapter 7, I examine how Buddhist, Shinto, and Christian ideas were represented in the preschools that were affiliated, respectively, with each of those religious institutions. Christian schools tended to emphasize the importance of the individual and developed programs that were child-centered, while Buddhist schools were more oriented toward teaching children to perform their role in the group context. Directors in Shinto schools tried to focus on developing a sensitivity to living things and celebrating the traditional rituals; their programs tended to be relationship-oriented.

In Chapter 8, I compare public and private preschools. Public schools have access to the intellectual resources of the Ministry of Education, which in turn is oriented toward Western early-childhood education. Additionally, because they are government-funded, public schools are somewhat protected from market pressures, even as the decreasing birthrate continues to cause lower enrollments (Ishigaki, 1994). Many public schools continue to operate even with class sizes as low as 10 or 15. These combined factors make it more likely that they will operate child-focused programs. Private preschool directors, on the other hand, are free to develop an educational philosophy that is entirely unique and unfettered by accountability to any central government agency, but they must maintain a higher enrollment to remain viable economically. Some directors that I interviewed resolved these issues by creating a highly structured, role-oriented program, while others opted for the more familiar relationship-oriented approach that many parents themselves experienced as children.

The final chapter of the book examines the implications of these complex patterns and relationships. In particular, I challenge the current predominant emphasis on the single criterion of "developmental appropriateness" as a benchmark for determining the quality of a program. As growing numbers of children spend increasingly long hours in preschool and child-care institutions, addressing the articulation among the cultural models present in the school, home, and community becomes a pressing task. How should early-education institutions respond to the cultural models favored in diverse social classes and ethnic communities? How are these institutions shaped by the moral vision embodied in the teachings of organized religion? And how can professional knowledge about effective practices be used to guide program development at the same time these other influential forces are recognized? By examining these questions in the context of Japan, I hope the issues confronting Western educators will become clearer as well.

2

CARING FOR YOUNG CHILDREN IN JAPAN

THE COOPERS AND THE NOMURAS: A SNAPSHOT OF WORK AND FAMILY LIFE IN TWO CULTURES

When Mrs. Cooper gave birth to Sophie, her first child, she and her husband decided they could afford to live on one salary, so Mrs. Cooper quit her job and stayed home to care for the new baby. Sophie's first school experience did not come until she was enrolled in kindergarten at the age of five. The same year Sophie began kindergarten, her brother Jason was born. With the added expenses of a second child, the family found it impossible to survive on Mr. Cooper's wages, so when Jason was three months old, his mother took a full-time position as a receptionist in a law office. She left Jason in the care of Mrs. Kent, whose family day-care home was just down the street. Mrs. Kent cared for one other infant besides Jason, and two toddlers. Jason remained with Mrs. Kent until he was three, at which point Mrs. Cooper decided that he needed a structured program to prepare him for elementary school. She enrolled him in a child-care center, where he stayed until he was five. He then entered a full-day kindergarten program at the local elementary school.

For Mrs. Nomura, there was no doubt that she would leave her position as a secretary in a large Tokyo manufacturing company when she became pregnant with Kimiko. Kimiko remained at home until she was four, at which time she entered the neighborhood preschool that her mother had attended as a child. Housed on the site of the elementary school, the preschool accommodated four- and five-year-olds; at the age of six the children moved into the first grade. When Kimiko was four, her brother Jun was born. He was an active, outgoing toddler, and by the time he was three Mrs. Nomura felt he was ready for a group experience. Since the public school had no class for three-year-olds, Mrs. Nomura enrolled Jun in a local private preschool, where he remained for three years before entering the first grade of elementary school.

These contrasting portraits of fictional families illustrate some of the differences between Japan and the United States in their respective systems of early childhood education. The preprimary experiences of the Cooper children is representative of the diversity and complexity of American early-childhood education. In 1995, 41 percent of American preschoolers aged five or under were cared for only by their parents. The remaining children were also cared for by relatives (17%), in centers (26%), in family child-care homes (13%), or at home by baby-sitters (3%) (U.S. Department of Education, National Center for Education Statistics, 1998). As American children grow older, their parents are increasingly likely to enroll them in center-based care, as opposed to less formal arrangements. Thus many American children enter kindergarten with no previous experience in preschool, while others have already participated in a variety of different types of care.

In Japan, virtually all children attend some form of preprimary school for at least one year, the vast majority attend for two years, and roughly half attend a full three years. Compared to the diverse types of care used by American parents, the majority of Japanese preschoolers are placed in either preschools or child-care centers. *Yōchien*, or preschools, are operated under the auspices of the Ministry of Education, Science and Culture, and serve children aged three through five.[2] *Yōchien* are intended primarily to provide social and educational stimulation for children whose mothers are not employed full time outside the home. The program in most private and public *yōchien* lasts for five hours a day or fewer (Morigami, 1993).

While subject to ministry oversight, the majority of preschools are actually run as profit-making enterprises by private organizations or individuals. According to Ministry of Education figures from 1994, 42 percent are public, 47 percent are operated by private educational organizations, 5 percent are operated by religious organizations, and 6 percent are owned by individuals (Morigami, 1996). Private preschools tend to be larger than those that are public. Figures from 1998 indicate that 79 percent of children enrolled in *yōchien* attended private facilities (Morigami, 1999). In contrast to the public preschools, private schools often have classes for three-year-olds, as well as for children who are four and five.

A second system, operated by the Ministry of Health and Welfare, is intended to serve children of working mothers. *Hoikuen* provide full day care six days a week for children aged six and younger. Historically, *yōchien* and *hoikuen* were developed for different purposes; the distinction between them is similar to the historical differences between nursery schools and child-care centers in the United States, with the former a middle-class institution designed to provide social interaction and cognitive stimulation, and the latter focused more on safety and cleanliness. *Hoikuen* have evolved from providing custodial care to offering educationally oriented programs similar to that of *yōchien*. The ministry guidelines for the two types of programs are similar. While some observers argue that the allocation of children to *yōchien* and *hoikuen* is no longer associated with family status (Boocock, 1989), others maintain that *hoikuen* are more often utilized by lower-income families, plus a small percentage of professional women who need full-time care for their children (Shwalb et al., 1992; Tobin et al., 1989). In addition to the *hoikuen* and *yōchien* systems, there are several other child-care options that are used by a small percentage of families for children under the age of three, including grandparents, unlicensed-center care, and baby-sitters (Shwalb et al., 1992).

Educational requirements for staff are similar for *yōchien* teachers and *hoikuen* providers. The majority of *yōchien* teachers are graduates of two-year colleges. About 11 percent have degrees from four-year colleges, and fewer than 1 percent have graduate degrees (Morigami, 1999). About 80 percent of *hoikuen* providers are certified to teach in *yōchien* as well. Professional training in early-childhood education generally consists of at least six credits in general education and child development, 12 credits in curriculum and teaching methods, and five in a practicum course that includes four weeks of practice at a school site (Japanese National Committee of OMEP, 1992; Peak, 1992). Unlike their American counterparts, Japanese preschool teachers are paid a salary comparable to similarly educated peers working in other settings (Center for the Child Care Workforce, 1999; Peak, 1992).

Japanese caregivers tend to be young; a 1991 survey found that 39 percent are under 25, 39 percent are between 25 and 39, and only 22 percent are 40 and over (Morigami, 1993). Largely because of societal expectations that women should leave the labor force following the birth of their first child, average tenure of teachers is short (Peak, 1992). Japanese teachers tend to remain within the same institution until they leave the profession, so the children in any given class experience consistent care. In the U.S., with a turnover rate of 31 percent per year, many children experience one or more changes of caregiver in a given year (Whitebook et al., 1998).

Child care is fairly inexpensive for Japanese families because much of the cost is subsidized by national and local government. Large class sizes also function to keep costs low. For *hoikuen,* working expenses are divided roughly evenly between parents and government, and about 75 percent of the costs of building, remodeling, and equipping *hoikuen* are borne by national and prefectural governments. Some metropolitan and municipal governments subsidize *hoikuen* beyond these legal levels (Boocock, 1989). Both public and private *yōchien* are subsidized by the national and prefectural governments. Parents pay tuition directly to the schools, whose fees vary considerably. In 1997, the average cost of attending a private *yōchien* (excluding equipment fees) was 259,828 yen annually (roughly $2,142); the average cost of attending public *yōchien* was 69,842 yen annually (roughly $576) (Morigami, 1999).

THE DISCOVERY OF DIVERSITY

In 1992, when I began to prepare for this investigation of preschooling in Japan, I felt that Western and Japanese academics had provided a thorough outline of the educational system. One accepted fact about schooling in Japan is that the older the children, the more uniform the curriculum. The diversity of the preschool gives way to a national elementary curriculum, but one in which local schools have substantial latitude to develop their own materials and approach to teaching. By middle school, the pressure to prepare for high school entrance examinations constrains the options for local control. The "hands-on," constructivist approach often favored in elementary school is replaced by a more traditional lecture format, which is carried through into the high school (LeTendre, 1999).

While many sources I consulted in 1992 agreed that diversity characterizes Japanese preschools, there was almost none that actually distinguished among different types of programs in a detailed manner (see DeCoker, 1993, for one of the few exceptions). The goals of the "first generation" of research on preschools had been to document the type of school that is seen by Japanese as "ordinary," or to examine practices in elite institutions such as those under the auspice of the national government or in "escalator" schools whose pupils remain at the same school from preschool through university (Hendry, 1986; Lewis, 1995; Peak, 1992). Furthermore, the comparative framework utilized in some work focused on global cultural patterns of child rearing and pedagogy rather than intranational diversity (e.g., Tobin et al., 1989).

My curiosity about the diversity among preschools had been piqued by conversations with preschool directors I had encountered on previous visits to Japan who expressed their great sense of challenge in understanding the notion of "individualization" (*koseika*), which was one of the goals articulated in the revised educational guidelines issued by the Ministry of Education in 1989. As I listened to these directors wrestle with the interpretation of *koseika* in the context of Japanese preschool education, I thought that their deliberations would provide a very interesting window on Japanese views of the self and human relations. The Japanese Fulbright Association was also interested in the implementation of the new guidelines, and I was awarded funding for a six-month stay in Japan.

Early in my stay, I had several experiences which would shape the focus of the project. On a particularly hot summer day, I was out on the playground at a child-care center observing a group of four-year-olds splashing around in an above-ground swimming pool. Several toddlers emerged from their classroom and stood on the balcony overlooking the playground and pool. One of them carried a box of tissues, and he and his classmate began pulling tissues from the box and throwing them over the railing onto the playground below. I smiled knowingly, thinking how similar this incident was to a scene from a videotape on Japanese early education that I show every year in my class on culture and social development. In that video, when children fling playing cards off a balcony, their teacher continues calmly sweeping the floor, ignoring rather than attempting to stop this behavior (Tobin et al., 1989). This incident is portrayed as representative of the nonauthoritarian approach to discipline preferred by Japanese teachers, who are said to rely on peers and other indirect means to encourage children's good behavior.

However, the teachers at Akebono Child-Care Center had a different reaction from those at the child-care center featured in the video. Miss Shimahara, the tall, vigorous teacher supervising the pool area, glanced up and saw the tissues floating down to the playground. She jumped out of the pool, ran over to the tissues, and began snatching them off the ground. "Hey, cut it out" (*Shinai no, yo*), she yelled with an angry look. The chubby toddlers looked at her solemnly and headed back into their classroom.

That incident was just the start of an eye-opening experience. In the two weeks that followed, as mentioned in Chapter 1, I saw Miss Shimahara and other teachers at Akebono yell at children frequently, push them against their cubbies, cuff them on the head or leg, roll them up in futons briefly when they were disruptive at the beginning of nap time, and threaten to lock them in the supply closet. During my last day of observation at that site, I watched a teacher stuff noodles into the mouth of a four-year-old who had stated his intention not to finish his lunch. In spite of the long chopsticks poking into his mouth, he did his best to blow all the noodles back out just as fast as she pushed them in.

I initially dismissed the teachers' authoritarian behavior as a stress reaction to the stifling August heat, and was unwilling to see it as anything other than an anomaly. But when I reported my observations to Japanese friends and colleagues, they did not express a great deal of surprise. One friend, who conducts Parent Effectiveness Training Seminars with Japanese mothers, said that she was aware that mothers often yelled at and spanked their children—after taking the precaution of closing the windows so that the neighbors would not hear. Another woman, a college student, reported that a friend who taught preschool in a remote area near the Japan Sea was sometimes so hoarse from yelling at the children that she could barely make herself heard on the phone and eventually had to take a medical leave in order for her vocal chords to heal. When I presented my preliminary observations at a graduate seminar in early childhood education, several Japanese students brought up incidents from their own childhoods to illustrate cases where adults had identified them as having a bad character and had punished them severely. Of course, these reactions and anecdotal accounts did not constitute definitive data, but they did give me some confidence that if I pursued the issue of diversity among Japanese cultural models of rearing and educating young children, I would likely uncover new and interesting material.

CAPTURING IMAGES OF PRESCHOOLS:
A NOTE ON METHODS

During my six-month stay in Japan, I conducted observations and interviews at 32 sites (27 preschools and five child-care centers) in the Kansai area of Japan. These sites were located with assistance from faculty at local universities and from a preschool director affiliated with the regional private preschool association. I asked them to help me identify equal numbers of urban and suburban schools, and to over-sample on private schools, which are attended by the majority of Japanese children. I emphasized that I was not conducting a study tour of exemplary schools and was interested in all types of schools. These individuals contacted preschool directors and arranged the particulars of my visit. Thus, while the sample was not randomly selected, it was obtained in a way to maximize the representation of different philosophies and approaches.

Each visit typically began with a tour of the school, followed by observation in a classroom serving four-year-olds. During all interviews and observations, I was accompanied by a native Japanese speaker who was either a student or a professor in the field of early childhood education or developmental psychology. These individuals were well versed in Japanese and English languages, as well as educational concepts and terminology. I have moderate proficiency in comprehending Japanese, but relied on my colleagues to provide precise instantaneous translations during the observations and interviews. All interviews were also tape-recorded and later translated into English.

During the observations, I took detailed notes on the physical characteristics of the site and kept a running record of teachers' actions and verbalizations. These observations were used to inform the subsequent interviews with preschool staff. In every preschool, I interviewed the director and at least one teacher. For the most part, I attempted to keep the interviews rather informal. While I asked a number of general questions to structure the conversations, I did not follow a rigid interview protocol, preferring to bring up questions when they seemed to fit naturally. I encouraged the participant to take the conversational lead as much as possible. By letting the respondent bring up topics of interest, I hoped to capture the "emic" or insider point of view rather than focus solely on issues defined as important by Western early childhood educators.

During these conversations, I was particularly interested in having teachers and directors describe their goals—to reveal what they were trying to accomplish in their schools. For example, I asked how important it was to them that children be prepared for the academic work they would encounter in elementary school. I also tried to get a sense of the strategies they used to attain those goals. Sometimes the conversation focused on the concrete and definable: the daily routine at the school, activities that were offered, and kinds of children served. But the staff also described the types of relationships that they tried to foster among the children and between the teacher and the children. I tried to stimulate this line of thinking further by asking questions about interactions. What sorts of discipline practices were used? How did teachers react when children got into fights? How did teachers motivate children to learn? I also asked about barriers that made it difficult for the directors to attain these goals—obstacles such as resource issues, for example—as well as opportunities that helped them reach their objectives.

The themes that emerged from these conversations constitute the core of the data that I present in this book. These cultural models—or clusters of beliefs and practices—penetrate to the heart of what it means to be a person in Japan. The directors and teachers offered their speculation on a variety of existential questions: What is the nature of the child? What is the meaning of self? To what extent is there an essential self and to what extent is the self created by and within the social milieu? What is the nature of relations between the self and group—

family, the peer group, the preschool? And what is the role of the preschool in shaping someone who will become a successful adult in the Japan of the twenty-first century? To provide directors with an opportunity to discuss their views in greater depth, I returned to three preschools—two private and one public—for a full week each. In each school, I spent most of the day observing in a four-year-old classroom, interspersed with additional interviews with teachers, administrators, and consultants in charge of special programs such as English and gymnastics. As part of these routine observations, I attended rehearsals for performances, went on field trips, and observed parents' drop-off and pick-up time. These periods of extended observation helped me to understand how the philosophy articulated by the staff was actually implemented at each site.[3]

How, then, to analyze and present this material that consumed hours of conversation and resides on hundreds of pages of transcriptions? I sought in these data what Valsiner and Litvinovic (1996) have characterized as "rule-governed heterogeneity." In other words, I wanted to remain sensitive to the variation—the heterogeneity—across the different preschools. Yet, in accordance with the notion that meanings and practices are developed by communities of actors rather than constituted *de novo* by a single individual, I wanted to understand how cultural models were shared and by whom, and to note patterns or distinctive clusters of models. This search for patterns was a way of discovering the "rules" governing the association among beliefs and practices.

To accomplish these objectives, I had all the interviews translated and transcribed by a bilingual Japanese doctoral student in education. The original Japanese terms used for child rearing and educational concepts were retained, along with the translated equivalents. A coding system was developed that permitted sections of the interviews to be tagged with category labels (for instance, goals, activities, teacher-child relations, discipline, role of the parent, and issues of individualism and group orientation).

The final stage of analysis involved a number of activities. First, all passages associated with each category were examined to obtain a sense of the variation that existed within the category. Next, the entire body of transcripts and field notes was reviewed to learn how the categories fit together at each school. I created a large matrix listing the central findings pertaining to each category for each preschool. These steps resulted in the confirmation of earlier hypotheses about the ways that cultural models clustered together, shared by subgroups of teachers and directors. These clusters of models were often signaled by key phrases; for example, the goal of "strengthening the child's weak points" was frequently cited by directors who favored a didactic, large-group format rather than an individualized approach. I also wrote brief case studies of particular schools to use as a point of discussion in informal interviews with Japanese informants—including parents, parent educators, and faculty in departments of psychology and early childhood education. Reactions and commentary from these informants, as well as field notes and written material provided by the preschools (curriculum guides, parent newsletters, and promotional materials) were used to refine further my understanding of the material.

In the book I provide translated excerpts from my interviews. For key phrases, the original Japanese term is also included in parentheses. I use ellipses to signify that I have omitted a portion of the passage in order to eliminate redundant or unclear statements. At various points in the book, I also quote passages from my field notes. I have used pseudonyms for everyone I quote or describe, as well as for the school names.

3

RELATIONSHIP-ORIENTED PRESCHOOLS:

Fun and Friends

A PORTRAIT OF KITAMACHI PRESCHOOL

It is only December 4, but Christmas preparations are in full swing at Kitamachi preschool. In the "Kitten"class, children are gluing cutouts of Christmas trees to sheets of construction paper. "After you glue your Christmas tree onto the dark background, you can decorate it any way you want," explains the teacher to her class of three-year-olds. Meanwhile, a class of four-year-olds is also learning about the art project of the day. The teacher distributes cutouts of reindeer faces to the boys and Santa faces to the girls. Each child receives a second sheet of paper for designing eyes, nose, and mouth. They are supposed to cut out the facial features and glue them on the face. The teacher demonstrates how to draw a big eye, saying, "You can draw big eyes or small eyes. Whatever you want. My Santa's nose is going to be like this . . . big and round."

In the five-year-olds' classrooms, the project is substantially more complicated. The children in the "Tiger" class listen attentively as their teacher explains how to complete the nativity scene that each child is constructing from origami paper. This project has taken several days. They had to learn first how to create human figures and barnyard animals from origami paper, then a stable (with doors that actually open) and the two small buildings on either side of the stable. Today, the goal is to cut out and fold a cross, which will be attached to the roof of the stable. Then they will glue the people, animals, and buildings onto black construction paper. The teacher holds up a piece of gold paper that measures only about two inches by one inch. She demonstrates how to cut the paper prior to folding it into a cross shape. Like the other teachers at Kitamachi, she gives the children some latitude in executing the details of the project: "There are several ways to get a cross shape. Let's see which one you like. You can draw lines on the paper if you want to."

In addition to making these art projects, the teachers are preparing a Christmas party for the children, where they will have cake and receive presents from the *yōchien* staff. Later, they will attend a puppet show given at a concert hall downtown, and they will give a Christmas performance for the parents. The performance will include singing as well as orchestral music, and will feature their marching band.

Why is Kitamachi pulling out all the stops in their celebration of Christmas? Is this a Christian preschool? "Oh no," asserts the director, Mrs. Wada, "we don't do religious activities! Christmas is a time for pleasure." The Christmas activities are directly in the service of the primary goal of Kitamachi, which is to help children realize the enjoyment to be had in participating in group experiences. As the Kitamachi brochure states, "The task of Kitamachi preschool is to observe and support children who are excited and whose hearts are pounding." Relationship-oriented preschools like Kitamachi approach their objective of preparing children for enthusiastic participation in group life by focusing on three essential experiences: having fun, learning routines, and forming friendships with other children.

Kitamachi, which I describe in detail to illustrate the characteristics of relationship-oriented programs, was founded in one of the older residential sections of central Osaka in the early 1950s. The school primarily serves working-class families. Most of the fathers of Kitamachi children are involved in running small businesses. Some of the mothers work in convenience stores or other local shops. A few of the fathers are professionals; there are one or two doctors as well as a couple of middle-management employees of large firms. The director of Kitamachi, Mrs. Wada, is proud of the fact that a number of the parents are themselves Kitamachi graduates.

The preschool building contains seven classrooms—three for five-year-olds, two for four-year-olds, and two for three-year-olds. The narrow play yard features a large three-story climbing structure with attached slide and enclosed spaces for pretend play. Outside, children have access to balls, hoops, stilts, jump ropes, and a sandbox with buckets and shovels.

The classroom decor and furnishings of Kitamachi and the other relationship-oriented preschools are fairly standardized. Generally, most of the floor space is occupied by tables that accommodate four or six children each. In many schools, these tables can be easily folded and stowed away to accommodate whole-group activities such as dancing or band practice. All classrooms have a piano or an organ, and teachers are proficient in playing songs as well as using musical chords to signal classroom transitions. The walls are usually covered with teacher-made artwork on a seasonal theme; cartoon animals are very popular. In many schools, at least one wall is devoted to a display that incorporates each child's name and birth month. At Kitamachi, for example, the teacher in a four-year-old class had designed a train with 12 cars, each labeled with the name of one of the months. A cheerful, anthropomorphized squirrel, rabbit, or deer sits inside each car, and the names of the children whose birth date falls within that month is written in *hiragana* just above the animal's head.

Compared to most American classrooms, there are relatively few play materials in relationship-oriented schools. Most have a few crates of wooden or Lego-type blocks, and a crate of dolls or stuffed animals. Some schools have a bookcase. In most schools, each child has a small box containing basic art materials that can be used during free play. The classroom materials tend to be stored out of sight rather than on open shelves but are occasionally brought out during free play, particularly when it is too cold or rainy to go outside.

Creating a Fun, Happy Atmosphere

Let's take a closer look at the cultural models that govern the curriculum at Kitamachi. A major objective was to create an exciting, fun experience. One way this was accomplished was by keeping the tone light and happy. School materials, from wall decorations to the pamphlets and notes that parents receive, are replete with drawings of happy woodland creatures. The brochures advertising the schools feature many photographs of laughing children, often with captions in which children are saying things like: "I have so much fun with my friends at school." While many societies associate early childhood with innocence, sweetness, and gaiety, there is a special intensity to the efforts in these Japanese classrooms.

Having fun is also emphasized during the many special events that the relationship-oriented preschools organize each school year. The Christmas activities at Kitamachi are one example. The extent to which Japanese preschool teachers will go to create a memorable experience for the children is illustrated in the following excerpt from fieldnotes taken during a visit to a different private school:

> On the day of the Christmas party, each child is allowed to decorate his or her own individual cake, which had been baked earlier by the teachers. The children are brought two at a time to "Santa's workshop," where they can adorn their cakes with items from five trays, including little Santa Claus figures, sugar replicas of ivy and Christmas trees, and an assortment of colored candies. The decorated cake

is then wrapped in clear plastic wrap and festooned with a red bow. Each child's portrait is taken—with his or her cake—in front of a wooden backdrop depicting snow-laden trees and an elf, which was constructed and painted by the teachers.

After the cake-decorating, the teachers perform a Christmas play for the children. Then a "messenger from Santa Claus" pops in with ice-cream cones. After a round of active games and dancing to Christmas music, the time for presents has arrived. Each child is given ten tickets. Each ticket has a small picture on it that designates a place in the preschool where a gift can be found. The children are supposed to go to each area, give the appropriate ticket to the teacher in that area, and take their gift. So, for example, in one area there is a large Christmas tree hung with miniature flashlights for the children. The children spend an hour or so running to the ten areas, collecting their gifts and putting them in the festively decorated bags designed by the teachers. This is followed by a farewell ceremony with their parents, and departure.

The importance of special events like these was highlighted for me during a discussion with members of the "Mothers' Club" at a relationship-oriented preschool. The mothers asked me which holidays are celebrated in American preschools. I replied that most holidays are not celebrated because the schools try to avoid favoring any particular religious or ethnic affiliations. A palpable sense of disappointment hung over the room. After a moment of silence, a mother asked: "What do the children have to look forward to?" I tried to convey my sense that high-quality American preschools supply a steady daily progression of interesting experiences and projects, whereas in Japan there seemed to be a more noticeable cycling between the somewhat low-key events of ordinary days and the very elaborate activities of special occasions. But I was reluctant to imply that the ordinary days in some Japanese schools may be less exciting than those at American schools, and I am afraid the mothers left the meeting with a feeling of pity for American preschoolers growing up in a "ritual-poor" culture (Tsuda, 1994).

Four-year-olds practice a song-and-dance routine that they will perform for parents.

The behavior management style of the Kitamachi teachers was consistent with their overall goal of making school a place that children would find fun and exciting. They avoided hard, authoritarian control and relied on indirect methods such as observation, low-key responses to misbehavior, and peer sanctioning. Teachers tried to head off potential problems by remaining alert for warning signs that a child was not in a good mood or was having a bad day. As one teacher at Kitamachi put it:

> I have a daily work plan, the first step of which is observation. When the children come in the morning, I closely observe their behavior to see whether they are happy or whether they are sad . . . because of something that happened at home. I try to talk to the ones who look down. I also try to observe the children's complexions. If a child looks ill I try to pay particular attention to that child that day.

In many cases, misbehavior was simply ignored. For example, one rainy day I spent the afternoon in the four-year-olds' class at Izumo preschool. The children were restless, having spent the whole day indoors. The teacher was trying to get them to practice a puppet show that they were going to be performing for their parents in the coming week, but they were not paying much attention. After one run-through, she had the children sit down. Shige, a large, very active boy who is mildly mentally retarded, was pacing restlessly around the perimeter of the room. The teacher asked him to come and sit on her lap. He did so, but swatted her face playfully three or four times. She said nothing, but took hold of his hands. Meanwhile, the children were talking loudly among themselves. She called out a few children's names, asking them to calm down. When it was relatively quiet, she asked, "Is it all right for me to say something?" "Yes, we are ready," some of them responded. Meanwhile, Shige slid off her lap and moved to the wastebasket, dumping its contents on the floor. She followed him, and picked up the trash. "Next time, I want another group to practice the play," she continued. "Please do it better than today. Remember when the mice [characters in the play] appear. So, next time you can do it well." Some of the children nodded, while others watched Shige, who was pulling papers off the bulletin board. At no time during the afternoon did she appear exasperated, and in a subsequent interview, she confirmed that there was nothing particularly difficult about managing a class of 32 children that included a boy with significant disabilities.

While Shige's teacher ignored his disruptive behavior, she did use some strategies to bring order to the rest of the group. An important part of creating a fun, enticing experience was maintaining control so that activities could be undertaken—without directly confronting or contradicting the children. The skillful ways that some Japanese teachers can manipulate good behavior from children has been described by Peak (1991) and Lewis (1995). Sometimes this may include giving them credit for good intentions even when the desired behavior is not yet in evidence. Azuma refers to the deliberate socialization of a "good child" (*ii ko*) identity: "A child who accepts that he is a good boy, or a child who has an *ii ko* identity, thinks how a good boy should behave when a new situation arises and selects the behavior pattern accordingly"

(1994a, p. 65, translated from Japanese). The reinforcement of an *ii ko* identity is exemplified in the following quotation from a teacher of four-year-olds, who talks of praising a child's effort even when he or she is not actually making much effort at that precise moment:

> If the children refuse to do a [required] activity, we try to talk to them and encourage them, saying something like: "Please show me what you were working so hard on." And although they may not agree to complete the project they may at least say: "I will try."

In some cases, when teachers felt that ignoring one child's misbehavior would encourage other children to try the same thing, they intervened with stronger measures. For example, the head teacher at Okayama Preschool described an incident in which one boy insisted on having more milk at snack time. When the teacher said no, the child hit his cup and spilled the milk, became even angrier, and started crying. The head teacher described the staff response as follows:

> We took him to the teachers' room and talked to him about what he had done. We explained that he had caused a lot of trouble for other children. We asked him to apologize to his classmates as well as to the teacher. But soon he did the same thing again. Even if we admonish him, it doesn't mean that he will start behaving. We need to keep admonishing him. Other children are watching the teacher's response to that child's misbehavior. If the teacher ignores the misbehavior and does not do anything, other children will conclude that such misbehavior is acceptable.

While teachers sometimes worried that misbehaving children will set a bad example for others, they also expected much of the learning about social rules to occur in the context of peer play. Although the teachers at Kitamachi carefully monitored the children to prevent bullying, they also expected some conflict and felt that letting children resolve disputes was an important learning experience (see also Tobin et al., 1989). The assistant director at Sannomiya Preschool expressed this very directly:

If a teacher scolds three-year-olds, they will not understand why she scolds them. But they do understand that if they do whatever they want to, other children will not accept them. After all, every child wants to play with other children. Therefore children learn how to behave in a group.

This teacher was referring primarily to the fact that children will react negatively toward a child who is disrupting their play or otherwise behaving in a way that bothers or inconveniences them. Additionally, in my observations, it seemed that most children realized that they were supposed to help enforce the school rules, and so they did speak up when they saw any sort of rule infraction, whether or not it bothered anyone else. For example, one day toward the end of the lunch period at Bunka preschool, I saw one small boy ask a large boy with a big lunch if he would share his last bite of omelette. The large boy thought for a second, and agreed to share. But a third boy who overheard the conversation told him that food sharing was not allowed. The teacher then came over to the boys and confirmed the rule, stating that each person should eat his own lunch.

Another use of peers is the nearly ubiquitous practice of assigning daily monitors to supervise classroom cleanup, lead the class as they say grace before lunch, and undertake other minor responsibilities. This practice is continued in elementary school, where the monitors take on increasing responsibility for enforcing classroom rules when the teacher is not in the room (Lewis, 1995). Children are also encouraged to perform such tasks as monitoring whether everyone has brought a clean handkerchief to school. While it may shift responsibility for control off the teacher, some American observers report feeling discomfort at this practice of handing over so much responsibility to peers (Lewis, 1995). Interestingly, ambivalence was voiced by some of the directors in relationship-oriented schools in my sample as well. The director of Bunka Preschool, for example, felt that by expecting children to align themselves with the teacher and report on their classmates, they sacrificed the closeness that children feel when they participate in something forbidden:

When children engage in different kinds of play, they get rid of the stress that they feel. Moreover, they can find with their peers a sense of making something together and of hiding something. There is a Japanese phrase "*sune ni kizu o motsu*" (literally, "having a wound on one's leg"), which conveys the idea of having a bad conscience or feeling of guilt. Children nowadays do not have such a shared sense of guilt. When I was a child, there were farms and rice paddies in this area. I admit that I stole strawberries and watermelons with my friends. We shared a sense of guilt, knowing "we were thieves." This allowed us to drop our masks. Children nowadays do not have such experiences and because of this they cannot drop their own masks. This is a strength as well as a very serious weakness.

The nonauthoritarian control structures found within the relationship-oriented preschools are common to other Japanese institutions as well. The tendency of these teachers to downplay their authority and invest considerable power in children themselves corresponds to an analogous structure often observed in Japanese businesses and other social institutions. Rohlen refers to this as a "polycentric" system of power and distinguishes it from the authoritarian use of power that is more a direct descendent of institutions affected by Confucian principles of hierarchy: ". . . Japanese tend to distinguish their own thought from the Chinese in terms of mutability, diffuseness, and emptiness at the center" (Rohlen, 1989, p. 18). Rohlen has noted that both types of control—the authoritarian and that which is "empty at the center"—still exist in Japan, although the latter seems to be gaining in popularity.[4] In the next chapter, we deal at length with preschools that make use of a more authoritarian style of controlling children's behavior.

Encouraging Good Work Habits and Mastery of Routines

According to the teachers at Kitamachi, children must learn how to engage in the specific behaviors that are needed to complete tasks in a group setting. During daily structured activities—usually art projects—

the teachers encouraged children to think before they started working, to use materials carefully, and to continue until the project was completed. At the same time, they tried to allow some opportunity for individual choices within the general framework provided. These activities were designed to give children the opportunity to practice certain skills, but not at the expense of some degree of self-expression and fun. This dual focus is well illustrated in the daily curriculum plans developed by each teacher. For example, the objectives of the Christmas art project at Kitamachi, as stated in the daily lesson plan for the "Kitten" class, were: "1) work happily; 2) avoid excessive use of glue; and 3) listen carefully before starting work." At dismissal time, the stated objective was "to create an atmosphere so that the children have positive expectations about returning to school tomorrow." The lesson plan for the "Bear" class stated the following objectives:

Children copying a model of a Christmas scene provided by the teacher; they have some opportunity to make choices concerning colors and other details.

"1) encourage neat work; 2) use a variety of types of paper to make what they want; 3) allow each individual to go at his or her own pace, but pay attention to what the whole group is doing without anyone being too slow or too fast."

Teachers at Kitamachi also sought to develop children's ability to follow routines and to acquire regular habits in areas of daily life outside the structured art projects. For example, all children learned the correct way to unpack and set up their box lunch—spreading out the place mat first, positioning the thermos at the top right corner and chopsticks to the side, then removing the tops from the containers and waiting without tasting anything until everyone was ready and had said grace.

The emphasis on routines seems to be a rather distinctive Japanese practice. Even in the child-oriented preschools, where there was more emphasis on such issues as exploration, discovery, and self-expression, teachers felt it was important to teach the children proper habits and routines. In one child-oriented school, I noted that the children had one set of clothes for traveling between home and preschool, and another set to wear in the preschool. This meant that the children put on their traveling uniforms at home, changed into their "gym uniform" at school, then changed back into the traveling uniform before going home, where they presumably changed out of their school uniform into play clothes. When I asked the teachers why they set aside approximately 20 percent of the school day for changing clothes, they said that this activity has always been required in this preschool, but that the purpose of the activity had changed as the school became less structured. In the past, the focus was on acquiring the skill of changing one's clothes for its own sake, whereas now the goal of the same behavior is "helping the child have an enjoyable life." One teacher provided the following elaboration:

> One objective [of having them change uniforms] is for them to learn to button up their clothes. Also, by putting on a school uniform, the child feels that he is going to school. . . . It provides the motivation

to come to school. . . . The third reason is so that the school uniform does not have to be washed so often. . . . I think we used to see this as a matter of training. But now we pay a lot of attention to children's feelings. So now the purpose [of changing clothes] is more for the children to have the pleasant feeling of being clean.

The strong attempts by schools to dictate the routines of daily life have been noted in elementary school as well. For example, Lewis (1995) writes that: "Schools provide rules governing students' use of time over vacations and weekends, asking, for example, that students rise early, exercise daily, and stay away from video parlors. Schools also regulate how students come to school (in neighborhood walking groups that arrive well before school actually begins), suggest an appropriate

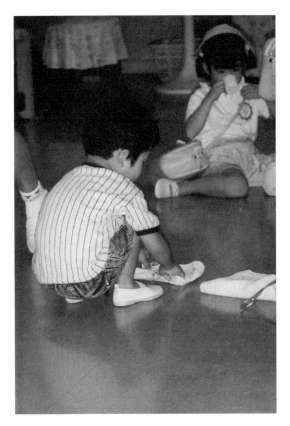

A four-year-old carefully folds his hand towel as he packs up his schoolbag prior to departure at the end of the day.

bedtime and wake-up time for students, and even suggest the appropriate timing of bowel movements (before school)" (p. 142). In middle school, there is even more emphasis on conforming to strict behavioral regimens in school and at home, as Feiler (1991) notes in his description of a middle school practicing for an upcoming field trip to Tokyo Disneyland:

> The school had tried to anticipate every possible problem, beginning with the coordination of two hundred students and five rented luxury buses. This potential bottleneck was considered so severe that on the day before the trip, the teachers set up chairs in the gymnasium in the shape of a bus to allow students to practice getting in and out of their seats in an orderly fashion. This rehearsal was followed by another, in which students practiced running in and out of formation for the class photograph when they heard the sound of a whistle. (p. 264)

Although adherence to regular routines and habits appears to permeate many institutions in Japan, the way in which these routines are taught and enforced differs from one site to the next. In relationship-oriented schools, the focus is on showing the rewards to the individual child of performing the routines, rather than emphasizing the negative consequences of failing to observe them. In the role-oriented schools, the need for self-discipline is purposely highlighted and enduring minor hardship for the sake of conforming to the rules of the group is seen as character-building.

Nurturing Children's Capacity for Social Relationships

The teachers in relationship-oriented preschools emphasized that a successful group experience hinges on the acquisition of social skills, including cooperation, empathy, and the ability to play together. The three-year-olds' teacher at Kitamachi told me that the purpose of free play was to provide children with an opportunity to improve their relationships with peers:

> I try to encourage the children to play with others. But in sand play, for example, the children tend to play alone. I would like to avoid

solitary play and encourage children to play together. After all, three-year-olds learn the existence of certain rules even in play. . . . They learn what they should not do. They also learn that they can hurt other children's feelings by taking certain actions.

Other relationship-oriented schools also emphasized the importance of learning the competencies that enable children to form close, enduring ties with others. When I asked the director of a small private preschool in Osaka about the overall philosophy of his school, he focused on the acquisition of sensitivity to others:

> First of all, we hope that children will be healthy. Making friends is also important. We ask children to observe what is going on around them in their daily routines. Seeing and observing are different. If the mother observes something with her child, saying something such as, "This flower is beautiful," the mother and child share the same feelings. That kind of sensitivity or insightfulness is important. The same is true of listening. We ask children to think about these profound issues in preschool.

Like the teachers at Kitamachi, this director explicitly recognizes that nonverbal skills (for example, observing) are part of successful relationships. His program focuses squarely on improving children's language skills, particularly their receptive language, or, as he put it, "developing children's sensitivity through rich language." Three times a week, each class listens to a 15-minute storytelling program on the national public radio channel. After each episode, the teachers lead a discussion of the material, helping the children summarize what had happened in the story. Additionally, the teachers read the children fairy tales, including those by Hans Christian Anderson, Aesop, and the Brothers Grimm. The teachers try to elicit children's reactions to the story, particularly "to appreciate what the authors were trying to say." Unlike the child-oriented schools, where children are encouraged to put their own thoughts and feelings into words, this school focused its communication activities on fostering children's ability to capture the thoughts and feelings of the speaker.

Tensions between Individualism and Social Relations

At Kitamachi, the teachers were constantly seeking a way to teach children the skills and routines of group living while recognizing that each child has unique characteristics that deserve recognition. In other relationship-oriented schools, the issue of individualization was considered less important. For instance, the director at Ogura Preschool stated: "We don't put a particular emphasis on individualization. That aspect is left to each individual teacher's discretion." But in most schools, staff were less dismissive and openly grappled with the two goals of respecting the individual but encouraging children to think of others and participate in the rhythms of group life. This struggle was sometimes revealed in disagreements between staff members within a single school. For example, here is a dialogue between the director and assistant director of Sannomiya Preschool, a private preschool in a wealthy suburb:

> *Assistant Director:* The primary goal of this preschool is to create individuals who can adapt to society.
> *Director:* We want to raise individuals who do not make trouble for others.
> *Assistant Director:* This is not the sole issue. We point out what constitutes antisocial behaviors . . . but we also want to provide children with as many types of opportunities as possible so that they can find what they like.

At another point, the assistant director at Sannomiya reflected on the difficulty of balancing the two foci:

> Appreciating each individual's characteristics is important, but teaching the importance of maintaining good relationships among individuals in a group is also important. Some teachers may neglect the importance of individual characteristics and force all children to do the same activity. Other teachers tend to leave outsiders as they are. Balancing these two factors is the most difficult task.

Some directors felt that they were in agreement with the ministry's call for increased individualization, and had moved confidently in that direction. Others expressed uncertainty about how to implement this idea and reported having difficulty persuading their teachers that it was a good idea. This sense of being somewhat at a loss was apparent at Kitano, a public preschool perched on a hill just south of Osaka, where rice paddies and small orchards coexist with concrete apartment buildings. The director contrasted the current emphasis on individualization with the older days, when the school day was much more structured:

> We used to actually teach children. Now the more frequently used words are "support" and "help." In olden times we used to sing a song with the words: "A sparrow's teacher teaches with a whip." [She sings the melody.] Then education changed to: "Who is the teacher, who is the student?" [She sings.] . . . In this preschool we had a reputation for children's picture drawing. Now it has changed, but in those days, six or seven years ago, we had many winners in art competitions. But now we try to see whether children are willing to draw pictures by themselves.

Later in the afternoon, this director showed us a multipurpose room where an exhibition of the children's art was being prepared for a visit by parents. Many types of projects were carefully arranged on tables throughout the large room. The director paused in front of a table laden with small ceramic mushrooms. They all looked the same—a large cap covered with colored spots, perched on a columnar stalk. The only variation was the color and size of the spots. The director sighed, and commented:

> The projects in this class tend to be similar to each other because one child makes something and then the others imitate it. Another class has more creative projects because the teacher is young and encourages them to do what they want. With the older teacher, the children ask, "Is this right? Is this right?" It is easy for a teacher to give the children a pattern and have them all make the same thing. This teacher needs to make more effort to bring out the children's creativity. She isn't thinking about the children's individuality.

CONCLUSION: DIVERSE FACETS OF
COLLECTIVISM

The relationship-oriented preschools can be characterized as operating in what Kim (1994) refers to as the "relational mode," which is characterized by "porous boundaries between in-group members that allow thoughts, ideas and emotions to flow freely. It focuses on the relationship shared by the in-group members" (Kim, 1994, p. 34). To operate in the relational mode, the individual must be able to feel and think what others are feeling and thinking, absorb this information willingly, and help others satisfy their wishes and realize their goals. In a word, the relational model emphasizes "oneness" rather than "sameness."

In relationship-oriented preschools, the goal of "oneness" is apparent in their prioritization of social goals over individual development. To be sure, staff at these schools identified certain self-oriented goals, such as "building on one's strong points" or "identifying one's individual characteristics." But they were always described as being in balance with—or in the service of—learning to enjoy the rewards of friendships with other children and participation in group life. The staff modeled the characteristics that they wished the students to attain. They emphasized their multisensory attempts to feel and understand what the children were experiencing, not just through verbal interaction but also by continual careful observation. As was illustrated by the elaborate Christmas parties in two preschools, the teachers in relationship-oriented preschools often worked extremely hard to create an environment that would be not just enjoyable but truly memorable for the children. The emotional tone of this socialization—light, cheerful, and nonauthoritarian—was calculated to engender in the children a sense of the fun and rewarding nature of participating in group life. It was important to the teachers that children willingly join in without being forced to do so. Another way they achieved "oneness" was by aligning children's behavior through the use of behavioral routines, from the way that art projects were conducted to the strategies for managing personal belongings.

This is a type of collectivism, therefore, that highlights the psychological closeness that results from empathy and interindividual attunement. It depends on sincere commitment to the welfare of others but is seen as personally rewarding as well. And it is achieved through opening the self to all modes of understanding the thoughts and feelings of others—through verbal communication, careful observation, and synchronizing one's actions with those of the other.

4

ROLE-ORIENTED PRESCHOOLS:

Sweetness and the Whip

When Haruko Koreyasu's parents made the decision to move to the suburban town of Minamimachi, they talked about how best to prepare Haruko and her younger brother for the educational pressures they would encounter in their new school system. They were happy that Mr. Koreyasu had been able to start a small auto parts store in their new town, but they aspired to something better for their children's future. Therefore, when they heard of a preschool that was teaching the four-year-olds to read *kanji*, they decided to enroll Haruko there. On registration day, in order to be sure that Haruko would get a place, Mrs. Koreyasu awoke at 5 A.M. and joined a small group of mothers lined up in the rain outside the school gates. Her diligence paid off, and Haruko was accepted at Wakaba. Mrs. Koreyasu was not surprised to read in the paper later that month that two small preschools in the town had closed due to declining enrollments. Like the Koreyasus, most of the upwardly mobile parents in this working-class community wanted to give their children a head start on academic learning, and Wakaba appeared to fit the bill perfectly. The other preschools had allowed the children to play all day, and how was that going to help prepare them for school?

The Koreyasus are a fictional family, but Wakaba Preschool is real, an example of the type of preschool that is giving officials at the Ministry of Education nightmares. It is perhaps inevitable, given the emphasis the Japanese place on educational attainment, that the preschool is viewed by some parents as the starting point of a long preparation for the high school examinations that determine college placement and later employment opportunities. Many Japanese educators have the perception that more and more preschools are responding to parental concerns by engaging in formal academic instruction. To counteract this trend, the Ministry of Education's most recent guidelines specify that the basis for the preschool curriculum should be play rather than lessons (Ishigaki, 1991, 1992). Yet, in spite of these attempts by the ministry, there are a significant number of preschools that provide an early introduction to reading, writing, and mathematics. The directors of these schools are sometimes openly critical—if not contemptuous—of the Ministry of Education, and some claim to be purposely ignorant of ministry guidelines. In these schools, in addition to studying reading, writing, and mathematics, children are given lessons in such areas as English, art, tea ceremony, gymnastics, swordsmanship, and traditional Japanese dance.

In this chapter, I focus primarily on three secular schools oriented toward academic learning. Three others, run by Buddhists, are described in detail in Chapter 7. It is difficult to know how common these academic preschools are among the general population. A director active in the regional private preschool association estimated that approximately 30 percent of private preschools have adopted an academic curriculum (Hiraoka interview, December 6, 1994). This may underestimate their actual influence because academically oriented preschools tend to be quite large, and hence serve a large proportion of children who attend private programs.

A TYPICAL DAY AT WAKABA PRESCHOOL

Wakaba Preschool is located in a new development of small single-family houses. The town's commercial center is adjacent to the train station, separate from the residential area. The silent streets, with wide, empty sidewalks, contrast sharply with the mixed commercial and residential pattern of the big city, where tiny stalls crammed with goods coexist with throngs of pedestrians and cyclists. The preschool occupies a new two-story building. It is freshly painted with cheerful colors. Large windows stretch from floor to ceiling, admitting lots of light even during the rainy season. The playground is large and bordered along one side by a well-tended garden.

The children at Wakaba are engaged in structured, teacher-directed activities from 9 A.M. until 2 P.M., with a one-hour break for lunch and a half-hour of free play time. An ordinary day's schedule for the four-year-olds is as follows:

9:00	Arrival
9:00–9:30	Gymnastics instruction
9:30–9:45	School meeting and group exercises
9:45–10:00	Classroom meeting: singing, vocal exercises, repetition of poetry and proverbs
10:00–10:15	Mathematics instruction using abacus
10:15–10:30	*Kanji* (Chinese characters) reading instruction
10:30–11:05	*Hiragana* (Japanese syllabary) writing instruction (by specialist teacher)
11:05–11:12	Free drawing
11:12–11:25	Memory exercises using pattern blocks
11:25–12:30	Lunch
12:30–1:00	Free play
1:00–1:45	Teacher reads aloud to children
1:45–2:00	Preparation for dismissal
2:00	Dismissal

This schedule is sometimes amended when the class is practicing for one of their numerous musical performances. Special classes such as gymnastics and writing are given once a week, alternating with English, art, choral music, and instrumental music. Parents may also sign their children up for optional classes in tea ceremony, martial arts, and drawing, which are given during the free-play period.

EDUCATIONAL PHILOSOPHY OF WAKABA PRESCHOOL

The central conviction expressed by Mr. Waseda, director of Wakaba, was that children must be brought up to perform their role in life with diligence, confidence, and competence. To illustrate the notion of role dedication, he drew upon the image of the traditional Japanese artisan (*shokunin*). These craftsmen—typically gardeners, carpenters, sushi chefs, and the like—have an honored role in Japanese society. They are seen by many Japanese as pure and honorable by virtue of their single-minded dedication to their craft. Simple and direct, their taciturn demeanor serves to indicate that they eschew all that is superficial and insincere. Mr. Waseda hoped that the children in his school would develop the focus and self-discipline necessary to undertake this difficult but honorable approach to life. Because of their strong focus on role dedication, I have labeled these as "role-oriented" preschools.[5]

Mr. Waseda took pains to clarify that he did not see the artisan as a conformist who obliterates the unique self in order to fit in the group. He believed that role identification is compatible with maintaining one's individuality (*kosei*):

> We need to create a feeling of harmony (*wa*) among people but not simply conformity (*dō*). With harmony we can communicate but our individual identity remains clear. With conformity we overlap and blend together too much. Agreement exists with doubts. To get harmony we need to have a clear understanding and acceptance of our role. If one person is clear who he is, he can join with another to create something new. If he is wishy-washy about who he is, he can't

synchronize with anyone. . . . We need to revive the idea held by traditional artisans who have a strong feeling of responsibility toward their trade and pride in their skills. . . . It is good to have the artisanal spirit *(shokunin katagi)*. We need the strength to find and go our own way.

Time and again he emphasized how knowledge of one's role can lead to self-knowledge—not just correct behavior. He tried to convince the teachers that achieving clarity concerning their own identity and their own feelings was crucial to embracing their role: "She [a teacher] must know her own feelings. If she has the feeling of being quiet, it will come through to the children. The feeling behind the words is important." In other words, the self and the role have to be blended and harmonious, not in conflict.

Mr. Waseda sought to dampen teachers' desire for recognition, and urged them to focus instead on appreciating the contributions of others. He emphasized the importance of performing one's role even when one operates "in the shadows," that is, when one's actions take place behind the scenes rather than in the bright light where they are more easily acknowledged:

> One phrase we repeat often here concerns the importance of helping others, without saying anything. In doing so, our own mind becomes brighter. By doing this, children will feel thanks to their parents, and will do things for others. This gets below the surface and helps them learn the deep lesson of helping others. Some people work very hard behind the scenes, like trash collectors for example. They are "in the shade" and may not be seen. People like this are very important. There is a Buddhist saying: "We bless from the bottom of our feet." It refers to the fact that the undersides of your feet—which are in the shade and cannot be seen—are crucial because we cannot stand without being strong there. These days people only want to look at the bright things that are in the light. We need to have feelings for things that are below the surface and do things without being seen by others. Don't be conscious only of the parts you can see.

The intertwined elements of role obligation and individual initiative expressed by Mr. Waseda have been noted by DeVos (1996):

> In Japan one learns increasingly to put off immediate gratification, but with a defined collective future social purpose and an awareness of the satisfactions to be gained from future social and occupational mastery. Such a sense of future-oriented mastery means that Japanese self-development is *defined within one's prescribed social role.* One is not simply taught to remain passive to avoid conflict, but to sense internally an *active* potential to be exercised in the future. One seeks individually to enhance an active locus of control within, even while one's overt behavior may remain docile in appearance [emphasis in original text]. (p. 62)

The directors of academic preschools believed that the increased materialism, permissiveness, and individualism of today's young adults have led to the weakening of the Japanese people and to the decline of Japan as a world power. As one director said, "After World War II, the Japanese people made the mistake of seeking only freedom. We misunderstood that there is a strict aspect of freedom. Freedom is not easy." According to Mr. Waseda, learning to fulfill the requirements of one's role requires a great deal of effort and self-discipline. Success is not achieved simply by passively accepting the rules dictated by society. Only by actively committing oneself to one's role-dictated responsibilities can the individual become strong.

THEORIES OF PEDAGOGY

The classroom teachers in role-oriented preschools were given extensive training in the school's method for teaching *kanji*, mathematics, and music. The method used at Wakaba for teaching *kanji* recognition was developed by Mr. Waseda, who drew loosely upon ideas from American educator Glen Domon and Japanese educators Shinichi Suzuki and Isao Ishii. He used textbooks developed by an educational publishing company that specialized in academically oriented material for preschools. The basic approach was to include key vocabulary in the context of an interesting story, followed by the presentation of the *kanji* for those select words, and ultimately by the removal of contextual cues. Here is a description of one lesson I observed in a classroom of four-year-olds:

The children are seated on the floor in front of their classroom teacher, Ms. Watanabe. She writes the name of this week's story in the simple syllabary script (*hiragana*) on the board. Below it she has taped a *kamishibai*—a paper scroll with pictures illustrating the story. She then begins telling the story from memory. The story is a lively account involving a band of monsters and their escapades. She creates a feeling of drama and excitement by using a distinctive voice for each monster and maintaining eye contact with the children. When she comes to a key vocabulary word, she takes out a card bearing that word written in *kanji* and tapes it to the blackboard. Because the class reviews the same story (and accompanying *kanji*) every day for a week, by Wednesday the children anticipate the story's events and call them out in advance. They appear to be interested and are following closely. By the end of the story there are 20 *kanji* on the board.

The teacher removes the *kamishibai* and uses a long pointer to indicate each *kanji*. She reads it and asks the children to repeat. She then removes all but five of the *kanji* and asks a question about the story. The children raise their hands to answer. She selects one girl, who moves to the board and selects one *kanji*, the one that she think represents the word that answers the question. The girl turns to the class and asks: "Am I right?" Those who think she has picked the correct word make a large circle above their heads with their arms; those who think she is wrong make an "X" by crossing their arms in the air above their heads. "She is wrong," the teacher says, and the girl runs back to her seat. A second child comes up and picks a card, again asking for and receiving feedback. He too is incorrect, but the third volunteer picks the correct card.

This process continues for another five minutes. The teacher is relaxed and smiling. When the children are incorrect she gives mild feedback and encouragement. When they are correct she praises them briefly: "Great! You did it!"

At the end of the session, the teacher selects two cards that are confusing because the *kanji* are similar. She holds one behind her back and shows the other, getting the children to repeat the correct word, then reverses cards. She compliments them on doing such a good job that day, and indicates the lesson is over.

While Wakaba focuses on teaching *kanji* within the meaningful context of an interesting story, other schools used flash cards to help the children memorize individual unrelated *kanji*. However, despite some differences in teaching techniques the directors of these schools all shared a number of cultural models about learning that were reflected in their pedagogical practices. These elements included evalu-

A teacher drilling her class of four-year-olds in kanji *(Chinese characters) recognition by showing them flash cards.*

ation and strengthening of pupil weaknesses, downplaying individual preferences and opinions in deference to the teacher's superior knowledge and experience, and enduring hardship to strengthen and improve one's character.

Explicit Evaluation and Strengthening of Pupil Weaknesses

The teachers at Wakaba provided explicit feedback concerning the accuracy of the children's responses. As we saw in the *kanji* lesson, children were also corrected by their peers, who signaled with hand movements whether a child had correctly answered the teacher's questions. Evaluation was not limited to academic subjects, but was also used during music and art lessons. For example, when giving a lesson on the keyboard (*pianica*), Ms. Suzuki, a teacher in a classroom for four-year-olds, mixed evaluation, praise, and criticism:

> "Listen to your weak points. Let's do it together—try to feel it in your heart (*kokoro*) while I am clapping. Let's all do it the same way. We must match my heart and your heart together." The class plays the piece again, and this time she moves around the room, correcting individual children. She has them play the song a third time, this time commenting on the group's performance, "You're too loud. Let's make the sound smaller." One child plays a few notes on his own, without a cue from the teacher. She chastises him, "You are playing selfishly. You don't need your *pianica*" and makes a motion as if to take it away. She soon relents, however, and moves back to the front of the class. The children play several more songs. They are getting restless. She ends the lesson, telling them they did a great job (*sugoi*).

In this example, the teacher encourages the children to evaluate their own performance and take responsibility for correcting their "weak points." She urges them to use empathy to synchronize their hearts (*kokoro*) with that of the teacher. Lebra (1992) has argued that conscious activation of one's empathy is a common Japanese strategy for creating a connection between the egotistical private self and the public self that is in harmony with the actions of the group.

Downplaying Individual Preferences

One element common to all schools is the notion that children should be exposed to many experiences rather than participating primarily in activities that they already like. Directors in the relationship-oriented schools tended to talk about the importance of building upon children's strengths. In the role-oriented schools, directors were more concerned with strengthening the children's weak points and filling in the gaps in their knowledge:

> Many people criticize me because I lack a focus on individuality. If a child likes drawing pictures then it is his or her choice to do that. But drawing pictures and doing nothing else is utterly wrong. Children should establish solid basics, then each individual's particular characteristics will grow. Energy and persistence should be nurtured. . . . Our motto is that they should come to like everything. I certainly believe that strengthening the areas children [already] like is education. But I believe that helping children overcome dislikes is education in the real sense. . . . A group helps individuals overcome their dislikes.

This director drew a connection between strengthening a child's weak points and situating instruction in the context of a group. He rejected the Ministry of Education's move toward individualized instruction, believing that it will cause children to persist in a narrow range of behaviors and ways of thinking. He argued strongly in favor of group-oriented education:

> Our basic principle is group education. The teacher does not raise individual children. Instead children learn from the group. Therefore it is essential to create a good group, and from the good group good individuals grow.

A corollary to this emphasis on group-oriented education is that the teacher plays a salient role in structuring the group experience. The writing specialist at Wakaba preferred to control the students' experience by requiring them to write a symbol only at the precise time dictated by him. He did not permit free writing, for the following reason:

Three-year-olds at a role-oriented school practice for an upcoming musical recital for parents.

With my method, even the slow children can follow. The three-year-olds are at different levels, but by the age of four they are all the same. If I were to let them write freely, the low-ability children would be left behind.

In the relationship-oriented schools, children were also encouraged to engage in new activities and learn new skills. But far less time was devoted to mandatory participation in teacher-directed learning, and the goal was to master a few basic skills such as using scissors or managing time effectively. In the role-oriented schools, the curriculum was ambitious, and children were expected to make substantial progress in the subject areas. Another difference was that in the relationship-oriented schools, the activities were made as fun as possible. Children were enticed rather than compelled to participate. In the role-oriented schools, directors set aside little time for pure fun and focused on creating an atmosphere of earnest, energetic, and focused study.

Creating Conditions of Challenge or Hardship

One of the principles stated in the Ministry of Education guidelines is that the school environment should be warm and supportive, encouraging a child to express him or herself confidently. This principle was endorsed by many relationship-oriented directors, some of whom used the term *nobi-nobi* or "carefree" to characterize the type of atmosphere they hoped to create in their preschools. The academic preschools did not appear to be guided by the *nobi-nobi* principle. As we have seen, children at Wakaba were expected to sit for long periods of time and to perform activities dictated by the teacher rather than personal choice. They were also challenged to train for marathons, run obstacle courses, or perform other demanding tasks. Similarly, at a large role-oriented preschool in Osaka, numerous physical challenges were purposely created; for example, the annual three-day field trip took the children "into a wilderness that is full of danger . . . where the children ford a river and climb a steep mountain." The director explained why experiences of hardship were needed in preschool, and explicitly distinguished his point of view from that of the easy going (*yasashii*) preschools:

> Today's affluent and free society robs children of their independence. Adults intervene in children's activities and try to protect them too much. . . . Early-childhood education in Japan tends to analyze children from the adult's viewpoint; they analyze them and try to protect them. . . . They spoil children's inherent energy. . . . [In the past] children used to grow up without as much parental care. The environment was suitable for children's growth, in terms of nature as well as society and home. For example, hard domestic labor was a good environment for children. Hard circumstances such as many siblings, poverty, and less parental attention caused severe competition among siblings. Although there was less parental care there was an abundant amount of nature.

The views of these directors are rooted in the traditional notion that experiencing hardship (*kurō*) is an essential part of moving from the self-centeredness of childhood to the social responsibility of adulthood.

Children in a large role-oriented school lined up for morning exercises.

Children are expected to become mature as a result of experiencing 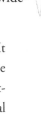 some hardship as they learn the role of student. Kondo (1990) argues that enduring hardship is a well established cultural model with widespread application in Japan:

> The process [of becoming a mature person] is an arduous one. It means having to undergo hardship, *kurō*, for only in this way will the hard edges of immaturity be planed into the roundness of adulthood. *Kurō* can be found in carrying out the requirements of a social role, whether it be the role of bride, mother, or worker. The hardship of a young person in "training" for the university entrance examination can be a form of *kurō*. So can economic hardship. So can the efforts of a beginner in the Zen arts. (p. 235)

Historical analyses bear up Kondo's claim about the centrality of this cultural model. In his review of child-rearing advice between the mid-seventeenth and mid-nineteenth centuries, Kojima (1986b) has found that Japanese physicians as early as the eighteenth century made use of the Chinese saying: "Thirty percent hunger and cold makes a child healthy." During that period and subsequently: "to expose older children to mild deprivation and hardships was thought to express parents' true consideration for them because it would enable them to endure hardships when they were called upon to perform adult roles. As indicated earlier, enabling a child to work hard to perform his assigned task faithfully was one of the basic goals of training and education" (p. 325). As this quotation makes clear, the experience of hardship was explicitly connected to role performance; by lessening children's expectation of special treatment and coddling, the adult strengthens their ability to endure the demands of a particular role.

MODELS OF CONTROL

It has often been noted that many Japanese mothers and preschool teachers avoid overt expressions of their authority. They are likely to ignore misbehavior or to rely on peers to sanction a classmate. In case of serious transgressions they may try reasoning or gentle, persistent persuasion; their goal is not to achieve behavioral compliance but to help a child understand the benefits of good behavior. Peak has likened teachers to "an army of friendly shadows" who appear to yield to the child's desire but eventually win by prolonged, good-natured cajoling (Peak, 1991). Many Japanese teachers shy away from labeling children as "problems" and avoid isolating or chastising them. The permissiveness of Japanese mothers relative to Western mothers has been described in ethnographies and by quantitative researchers (Conroy et al., 1980; Smith & Wiswell, 1982; Vogel, 1996).

The teachers at Wakaba avoided coercive discipline strategies much of the time. They were usually cheerful, smiling, and energetic. They generally tried to encourage the children to participate by presenting material in a very organized manner, maintaining a snappy pace, and persistently encouraging children who were slow or unwilling to go along with the program. However, their task was a challenging one, given that the academic schools required children to sit at desks for long periods of time and afforded little opportunity for free play, talk-ing, or physical movement. These restrictions sometimes led the chil-dren to become restless and disobedient. On these occasions, teachers threatened to leave the classroom, asked misbehaving children to leave the room or sit alone, or took away their materials. These actions seemed to have a strong effect on the children, as the following inci-dent reveals:

> It is time for free drawing. Ms. Watanabe is passing out drawing paper. The noise level rises as children begin to chat with each other while waiting to get their paper. She admonishes the students for being noisy, and tells them that anyone who is talking will not receive paper. A few minutes later, as the children begin to draw, one boy is sitting quietly at his desk, with tears running down his face. The teacher asks what is wrong, and several children near him say: "You didn't give him any paper." Apparently, he thinks he is being punished. The teacher says that it was an accident and that she did not mean to punish him. He says nothing, sniffles, and accepts paper from her.

It is not clear whether this boy had been talking or not when the teacher made her threat, but his reaction suggests that he may have felt he was in the wrong. Even though the teacher's reaction suggests that she did not actually expect to withhold paper from anyone, whether or not they were talking, he clearly took the threat seriously.

The mildly coercive strategies employed by the classroom teachers contrasted with the more heavy-handed, authoritarian behavior of the administrative staff and a few of the specialist teachers at Wakaba, who used surveillance, physical punishment, criticism, and labeling to maintain order. All of these practices are illustrated in the following excerpt from an observation of the special teacher in charge of choral music instruction:

> The music specialist, Mr. Yamagi, comes once a month to instruct the children and teachers in choral singing. We enter the classroom

after he has begun a lesson with a class of four-year-olds. The children are warming up with vocal exercises. Mr. Yamagi darts from one child to the next, crouching before each one for a few seconds and listening with an exaggerated look of intensity on his expressive face. He races to the front of the room and leans sharply to the right, cupping his right ear with his hand. He urges that side of the room to sing much more loudly. When they oblige with deafening volume, he shifts abruptly to the left side and repeats his exhortations.

Mr. Yamagi catches sight of us when we enter the room, and, motioning for the class to stop singing, he makes his way back to greet us with a bow. In a loud voice, he tell us that this room contains four "problem children" whom he then points out. He indicates that their names were provided to him by the school administrators, who feel that these students are "in need of observing" (*yō kansatsu ji*). He runs over to one of the four and pulls him in front of me, saying: "He doesn't have any energy so it's hard work to give him energy. It's important to educate him." He turns to the boy for confirmation: "Right?" The boy shifts uneasily and mumbles. Mr. Yamagi pulls the boy to the front of the class, and grabs his hand, uncurling the fingers and raising it straight into the air. "Say 'Yes!' like this," Mr. Yamagi yells enthusiastically, still holding the boy's hand up in the air. "Yes!" says the boy in a high-pitched voice. "You see," says Mr. Yamagi, "we have to train them how to answer."

He then moves back to the group, and separates the boys from the girls. He asks the girls to sit down, and lines the boys up along the front of the room. "The boys will sing and you tell me which is the best," he says to the girls. The boys sing a few bars and he stops them, then marches along the line holding his hand over each boy's head for a few seconds while the girls clap tentatively. Mr. Yamagi pushes some of the boys back to their seats and allows four to remain, proclaiming them "the best." They then sing a few more bars to the rest of the class.

The lesson is over for this group. Still a whirlwind of motion, Mr. Yamagi rushes to another class of four-year-olds. They are sitting cross-legged on the floor, silently awaiting his arrival. As he crosses the threshold, the classroom teacher strikes a chord on the piano, an indication to the children that they should bow. Mr. Yamagi bows crisply, then strides over to a child whose bowing has displeased him, saying: "If you don't bow correctly you may leave." He asks him to bow again, then cuffs him on the cheek. He turns briefly to us and adds an aside: "A good class of children doesn't say anything." Turning back to the class he says: "If you sing very nicely with big, open mouths, I will take your photograph." He pulls out an old camera and holds it, poised to take pictures. As the children proceed through the lesson, he occasionally "takes" a picture, although it is clear to us that the camera contains no film.

A number of Mr. Yamagi's pedagogical techniques were similar to those used by the regular teachers at Wakaba. He was very organized and lively, and created a routine, which he repeated with little alteration from one lesson to the next. He created a feeling of energy and drama, projecting commitment and authority as a teacher and a talented musician. He also gave explicit feedback concerning the quality of the children's performance. These pedagogical techniques were accompanied by a panoply of strategies more directly aimed at controlling children's misbehavior including careful surveillance, humiliation, criticism, shaming, and physical sanctions. Because these techniques differ so profoundly from the methods used in the relationship-oriented preschools, it is worth taking a closer look at them.

Surveillance, Criticism, and Shaming

Surveillance was frequently used by Mr. Yamagi and the staff to keep the children under control during their music lessons and practices for performances. The children who received the most surveillance were those identified as potential troublemakers. In the field notes quoted earlier, we saw how the school provided a list of three or four children in each class who "needed observation," and Mr. Yamagi was not reluctant to identify these children publicly when we visited his class. This practice reveals quite a different attitude from the teachers in relationship-oriented preschools, who are very reluctant to label children as being troublesome (see also Peak, 1991).

At Wakaba, it was not only the problem students who were subject to surveillance. The director, Mr. Waseda, spent a great deal of time observing teachers and students, making corrections when behavior did not meet his expectations. The assistant director also patrolled the grounds, monitoring the ongoing activities. Both these staff members maintained a stern demeanor, dressing in dark clothing and refraining from smiling or casual conversation. During the morning meeting and exercises in the school yard, they walked up and down the lines of students, pulling stragglers into formation, and tapping the shoulders of those who weren't standing up straight. When the children returned to classes, the dark figure of Mr. Waseda could frequently be seen passing by the windows along one side of the classroom, glancing briefly into each.

At music rehearsals, which sometimes lasted almost two hours, constant monitoring and correction were used to keep the children quiet and attentive. At one rehearsal, I observed the regular classroom teachers crouch down unobtrusively and shuttle along the lines of singing children, correcting their posture, straightening the lines, and silently mouthing the words to the song, all the while smiling in an exaggerated manner and motioning for the children to do the same. Mr. Waseda also patrolled the rows, shaking a finger at children who were talking and occasionally removing a particularly rowdy child from the room for a scolding.

Are these behaviors characteristic of only a few colorful individuals like Mr. Yamagi, or do they represent more widespread cultural models of child rearing and pedagogy available in the "pool of ethnopsychological ideas" in Japan? I would argue that the practice of regulating behavior by calling attention to the fact that others (*seken*) are watching and judging behavior is found in many areas of Japanese life and that failing to behave appropriately under public scrutiny leads to a feeling of shame (Clancy, 1986; Lebra, 1992). More specifically, regarding the use of surveillance in educational settings, Mouer and Sugimoto (1986) report that principals in some areas submit lists of problem children to the city government, dividing the group into children who are currently troublesome (*mondai ji*) or potentially troublesome (*mondai yobi ji*). Furthermore, surveillance of students is considered part of teachers' responsibilities both outside school as well as in class. Teachers in high schools sometimes check students' book bags for cigarettes and makeup, and even administer nicotine tests to those suspected of smoking (Rohlen, 1983).

Fukuzawa (1994) illustrates the use of surveillance and interrogation in a very powerful description of how staff at one middle school handled the problem of illicit candy-eating on campus. All the students in the grade where the problem was occurring were asked to confess whether they had either eaten candy or given candy to others. If they had given candy to others, they were asked to report the names of all recipients. The teachers mapped out this information on a large grid, enabling them to identify students who reportedly received candy but who had not confessed to getting it. These children were called in for questioning in front of a group of teachers and the chairman of the guidance department. They were scolded harshly, including those whose offense had been to bring in cough drops for sore throats. For example, a group of girls was told the following by the guidance counselor: "You have both a good heart and a bad heart. This time you listened to the bad one. A murderer is the same; he listens to the bad one. You all haven't gone that far, but you're fueling the growth of the bud of a bad heart. . . . Get rid of that budding evil in yourself. In your life now you probably do lots of things half-heartedly—cleaning at school, committee duties. You have not been concentrating on what you have been doing. Mend your sloppy ways now. For your sake we are angry with you today" (p. 316).

Punishment

Mr. Yamagi's cuff to the cheek of the "problem child" is surprising in light of the voluminous writing on the indulgent, affectionate attitude of Japanese adults toward young children. In my week of observing at Wakaba, I saw no other instances of children being hit, although I did see them handled in a rough physical manner by teachers seeking to move them into line or remove them from the classroom if they were misbehaving. In most of the other preschools I visited, the staff did not use corporal punishment or used it rarely (with the exception of one child-care center, described in Chapter 1, where I saw teachers hit and push children).

While my data do not permit any inference about the prevalence of corporal punishment in preschools, I surmise that it is not as taboo as some writers would suggest. The fact that some teachers used physical methods of controlling and punishing children when I was openly observing them suggests that they did not perceive a strong social sanction against it. In the later grades, it appears that harsh corporal punishment is widespread, in spite of being outlawed some 50 years ago. In his autobiographical account of a year he spent teaching in a Japanese middle school, Feiler (1991) describes numerous instances of children being hit by teachers at his school:

> In Sano I regularly saw teachers force students to sit on their knees for long periods of time; other teachers slapped offenders on the head. Teachers who occasionally pushed students, kicked them, or shoved them away are common. But often the line is blurred between gentle reminders of who is in charge and more serious efforts to inflict pain on students. In a notorious 1986 incident, a teacher in the south of Japan beat a student to death for bringing an outlawed blow dryer on a school excursion. At least one teacher I knew in Tochigi kept two hollow bamboo sticks under his desk for more serious transgressors. (p. 246)

Feiler (1991) also cites a survey of Japanese teachers in which three quarters of the respondents reported using corporal punishment on students.

Reflections on Behavioral Control in Japanese Preschools

Throughout the last century there have been conflicting reports about the relative harshness of Japanese parents toward their children. On one hand, some observers have noted the permissiveness with which Japanese adults treat young children. For example, in an ethnographic account of village life in Kyushu in 1935, Smith & Wiswell (1982) report the following observations: "One cannot say that the children are bad. It's because they never hear 'no' that they behave the way they do. While still babies they are not allowed to cry, for they are promptly picked up and fed or rocked or quieted. When older, if they say anything in baby talk, everyone praises them. If they ask for something, no matter how busy she is, the mother will usually get it for them. 'Mother, come here!' a kid will yell, and his mother will come in from the kitchen to see what he wants" (p. 220).

On the other hand,[6] some elderly Japanese believe that parental permissiveness is a relatively recent product of Western individualism. This was certainly the view of some of the preschool directors I interviewed, especially those who believed in more strict methods of behavioral control. Their impression that Japanese parents have not always been so lenient is supported by historical analyses. Historian Kathleen Uno (1991a) found that adults of the period from 1600 to the end of the nineteenth century used "patient persuasion, cajoling, moral lecturing, and silent example to train children, but also resorted to harsher means, such as scolding, physical punishment, confinement in dark storehouses or cages, locking children out of the house, and, for extremely intractable children, moxa cauterization (burning dried vegetable powder on the child's skin)" (p. 396). During those times, children were viewed primarily in terms of their utility to the household (*ie*), and adults believed that "an excess of sentiment could lead to overindulgence and lax discipline, resulting in a spoiled, willful child who refused to subordinate personal desires to *ie* interests" (p. 397).

It is perhaps misleading to focus exclusively on the role of mother as disciplinarian, since other family members were clearly involved, especially in earlier times. In a community, both permissive and strict styles may coexist, although balanced differently depending on the character-istics of the community at a particular period of history. As one direc-tor mentioned in remarks cited earlier, when Japanese society was primarily rural, the exigencies of farming life ensured that negative consequences would befall children who did not fulfill their work obligations. Children also spent more time with peers, away from adults, and were thus subjected to the "frontier justice" of the peer group. These more harsh forms of control may have offset the relatively more permissive behavior of mothers. It may also be that men are now—and have been in the past—more strict than women. I found that male directors tended to be more strict than women in their approach to discipline.

Thus most evidence suggests that many Japanese children are exposed to discipline that combines "candy and the whip" (*ame to muchi*). And while many preschools and contemporary parents have tended to focus on the "candy" side of behavioral control, the "whip" element is still evident in some quarters, such as at Wakaba. The key elements of the stricter approach have also been identified in cram schools (*juku*) for middle and high school students, and at after-school sports clubs. As Rohlen (1983) notes, "The shaved heads, the harsh lectures, the raised voices of the leaders, the strict discipline, the constant challenges, the focus on competitive spirit, and the friendly pat on the back from the coach belong to both [cram schools and sports clubs]" (p. 192).

At Wakaba, the relatively permissive styles of the teachers and the strict approach of the administrators combined to create a powerful system of control, familiar to Americans as a "good cop–bad cop" routine. A glimpse of how this dynamic operates in contemporary middle schools is provided by LeTendre (1996), who contrasts the warmth and sympathy provided by the school nurse at one school with the strict disciplinary style of the chairman of the student guidance committee. The school nurse describes the system in the following terms: "The chair of student guidance does the strict (*kibishii*) guid-ance, I do soft (*yasashii*) guidance" (p. 281).

Ultimately, in Japan as in the United States, the effects of a behavioral strategy such as corporal punishment depend on the meaning that the strategy has for the user and the recipient. In the American research literature, some writers try to distinguish parents who use corporal punishment based on a conscious theory of guidance implemented in the child's best interest from those who lash out due to stress, rage, or a desire to denigrate the child (e.g., Baumrind, 1989; Chao, 1994). What is the meaning of corporal punishment when it occurs in Japanese schools and families? Is it analogous to the "Zen master rapping young monks to instill determination" (Feiler, 1991, p. 43)? It is clear that strict discipline practices are rooted in long-standing cultural models that are still viewed as legitimate by some Japanese. Conversations with the role-oriented directors suggest that strict methods are implemented as one element of a complex system that must be studied in its entirety for its effects to be understood.

TENSION, CONFLICT, AND RESISTANCE IN ACADEMIC PRESCHOOLS

In the metaphor favored by Mr. Waseda, the solitary artisan accepts the culturally derived and approved *kata,* the acknowledged way to make delicious sushi or create a beautiful garden. The individual artisan then finds a way to perfect his own personal style within the essential dictates of that *kata.* The goal is a synergistic fusion between the accepted form and the artisan's vision, not an ongoing battle of domination and subordination. In the real world of preschools, this attempted fusion is messy and riddled with ambiguity. At stake is who gets to prescribe the *kata,* the ideal way to create and implement a program. Those at the top of the hierarchy—the Ministry of Education—are moving away from the values held by the directors in role-oriented schools. As a result, these rather conservative directors are in the ironic position of being dissidents—and they are engaging in a subversive call for a renewed respect for adult authority! In my conversations with Mr. Waseda, it became quite clear that he was angry and frustrated with many elements of contemporary Japanese society. One of his primary opponents was the Ministry of Education, particularly because of the ministry's efforts to convince schools to individualize instruction, nurture creativity and personal expression, and promote an international perspective. Mr. Waseda viewed these objectives as Western, and strenuously resisted the idea that Japanese should dilute their national identity by accepting American values. In his opinion, many current problems in Japanese society could be traced to the relinquishing of traditional ideas and practices:

> I want to reestablish the real Japanese culture. We need to find the one straight path (*ikkansei*) for the Japanese. If you are in a culture with a strong religion you can establish a strong philosophy of life. But the Japanese don't have a strong religion. Japan needs to find its *ikkansei* in order to be respected. We should stop being wishy-washy like Japanese politicians these days. We need a strong pole.

As we saw in the preceding pages, directors like Mr. Waseda rejected the authority of the ministry but acted strongly to enforce their authority over the teachers and the students. During my observations of academic preschools I became aware of a number of tensions within the organization, expressed in disagreements between the director and mothers of students, underlying tensions between the staff and the director, and covert resistance by some students against the teachers.

Disagreements between Directors and Mothers

Mr. Waseda expressed strong criticisms of the mothers whose children attended his school. Like most of the school directors I interviewed, he was convinced that Japanese mothers were overly permissive and either neglectful or overprotective of their children. Some directors were contemptuous of mothers who were spoiled and self-centered, or too insecure to raise their children properly. Others acknowledged that mothers no longer received the support and guidance formerly provided by fathers, grandparents, and other extended family members. Almost all shared a deep pessimism about the fate of the Japanese family.

In light of these criticisms and perceptions, they could not imagine much possibility for a meaningful partnership, nor did they see their roles as complementary with those of mothers. Most felt the only realistic solution was to ignore parents and attempt to influence the children as profoundly as possible through the daily school program.[7] The following quotation from the head teacher in a role-oriented preschool is typical:

> Mothers are young and have a lot of information about early-childhood education. They want to educate their children in the way they believe works best, but this way may not fit well with Japanese classrooms. Since they each have a particular view, there is no clear consensus and they make a variety of requests. They are very enthusiastic about after-school programs and lessons like violin and tea ceremony. However, they tend to ignore the importance of discipline. They seem to assume that preschool teachers discipline their children. They want to enjoy their own lives and they have jobs. They think they can buy discipline.

Surveys of mothers tend to back up the directors' perception that Japanese mothers feel very insecure about their parenting abilities (Bornstein et al., 1998; Shand, 1985; Shwalb & Nakazawa, 1999). On one hand, they have lost the immediate support provided by extended family in earlier times when child rearing was considered a household responsibility, not solely a maternal one (Uno, 1991a). On the other hand, they are still subject to criticism from elders that leads them to blame themselves for problems that could justifiably be attributed to structural changes in the family and corporate practices that limit fathers' opportunities to participate in child rearing.

An interesting analysis of a year's worth of advice appearing in a daily column in a national newspaper illustrates the pressure that can be applied to Japanese mothers by outside observers (McKinstry & McKinstry, 1991). The authors analyzed 180 letters written by adults (mostly women) about family problems, as well as the responses given by one of five primary advice givers. Those who reported problems with their children were usually blamed for somehow causing the problems and were charged with solving them single-handedly, as in this response to a mother who asked for advice about a son who continues to "bum around" with his old friends even after a one year stint in a juvenile detention center:

> I had to gasp at astonishment at this boy who, instead of enjoying the innocent pleasures of a person fresh out of school, indulges himself in such indecency. I believe your boy has lost faith in adult life due to the severe blow to his spirit caused by your divorce when he was just becoming adjusted to junior high school. But he is only seventeen years old. There is hope for someone of that age. . . . Just as something you once did fundamentally disturbed him, you have within you the deep store of ability to touch him again in a vital way. . . . Doesn't this give you more power over the situation than anyone else? . . . With undaunted resolve, with no thought of fatigue, with the strength of love that only a mother can bring to a task, you must keep at it until you reach his heart. There is no other medicine for his sickness. (McKinstry & McKinstry, 1991, p. 191)

The tendency of preschool teachers and child-care providers to criticize parents has been well documented in the literature on American preschools as well (e.g., Joffe, 1977; Zinsser, 1991), particularly when the staff is of a higher SES or educational background than the parents (Kontos, et al., 1983; Kontos & Wells, 1986). However, the field of early-childhood education in the United States is gradually changing its rhetoric about parents, as evidenced in the shift from the patronizing term "parent education" to new phrases like "partnership with parents" and "parent empowerment" (Holloway & Fuller, 1999; Powell, 1994). It will be interesting to see how Japanese early-childhood education policy moves in regard to parent involvement. While Japanese mothers have apparently begun challenging directors in small ways, they often lack the confidence necessary to have a strong impact on the programs.

Tensions between Directors and Teachers

What about the relations between Mr. Waseda and the teachers? Following the usual practice, Mr. Waseda avoided hiring teachers who had worked in other preschools, preferring to draw from the pool of young women who had just received their college degree. The rationale for this practice was that an inexperienced teacher could be more easily trained in the methods used at Wakaba and would be more likely to follow them than would a teacher familiar with an alternative system.

Heavy demands were placed on the teachers at Wakaba by the school administrators. Ms. Watanabe, the teacher I observed most extensively, reported that she arrived at school by 7:30 A.M. and never left before 6 P.M. In addition to her regular teaching duties, she had a number of peripheral responsibilities. For example, each day one teacher was responsible for leading a discussion among the teachers on an article from the day's newspaper. Like most Japanese preschool teachers, Ms. Watanabe was responsible for creating the material displayed on the walls of her classroom, as well as some routine cleaning. Failure to meet these demanding standards could result in the same sort of criticism that was meted out to the children. The music teacher's visits seemed to be particularly stressful for the teachers. The following example is taken from my field notes:

> Toward the end of the session, Mr. Yamagi asks the teacher to lead the children through a song they had been practicing for several weeks. The teacher starts playing the piano, but after a few bars Mr. Yamagi abruptly motions for her to stop. Looking at me, he says loudly: "This teacher is talented but very weak-minded and passive." He turns to the class and said sternly: "You are five years old but you don't act like it. In Korea, teachers are more strict and the children are better behaved." He moves to the door and, at a musical signal from the teacher, the children bow. The bow does not meet Mr. Yamagi's standards, and he demonstrates how to bow more fully and more crisply. The teacher apologizes to him, but he replies curtly, "Do not apologize. You are weak-minded."

How did the teachers feel about this treatment? In my view they were not treated as professionals, in spite of the fact that the role of preschool teacher is said to carry more prestige in Japan than in the States. Perhaps this somewhat disrespectful treatment can be attributed to the fact that although they are relatively well trained and well paid, Japanese teachers are likely to be young women with, as mentioned earlier, little work experience outside the setting of current employment. Like many of the mothers, they seemed to lack confidence in their knowledge and abilities, and this was particularly true in the role-oriented schools. I found the teachers in these schools noticeably reluctant to offer an opinion to me about even very inconsequential matters.

In spite of great curiosity on my part, it was difficult to find out what Wakaba teachers perceived about their working conditions. One of the difficulties I experienced in talking to the teachers at Wakaba and the other role-oriented schools was that the director was usually present during the interview, making it very difficult to get candid evaluations of the school program. In my conversations with her, Ms. Watanabe expressed considerable anxiety and doubt about her own teaching skill. She worried about her ability to control the children, and asked me for advice on how she could improve her teaching. She did not offer any criticism of the school or the director.

I heard concerns about the program from only one teacher at Wakaba. After making several positive comments about how much children learn, this teacher offered the following criticisms of the program:

> Children here don't have any time to play or to be with their teacher. They are never encouraged to think. And the teachers get in trouble if they ever let the children talk or do what they want. [Referring to a lesson in which she threatened to leave the room if the children didn't stop talking] I don't like to tell the children I'm going to leave them like that.

It is difficult to conclude from this sparse data whether other teachers at Wakaba agreed with the views of this teacher. I simply did not have the time or the opportunity to develop the degree of trust that might lead teachers to reveal their inner thoughts and feelings, particularly at Wakaba, given the close surveillance to which all staff were subjected.

Resistance by the Children
In contrast to the boisterous activity that characterized the other types of preschools, academic schools like Wakaba were usually quiet and orderly. The children's behavior during transitional times was particularly striking. At several points during the day, the small tables they used as desks had to be dismantled and stowed along one wall. This was accomplished quickly and efficiently by the children with no direction from the teacher. They also responded very quickly when the teacher called an end to their free-play time. For example, on one rainy day, the after-lunch recess was held inside. A group of five or six boys pulled out a large container of Legos. They did not have much time to play, and wasted no time deciding on a project. They worked rapidly, but before the structure was complete the teacher called for them to put everything away. They instantly responded by tearing down their creation and heaving the Legos back into the container.

However, as has already been noted in the section on behavioral control, there were occasional eruptions of misbehavior. Underneath the external appearance of general compliance existed a second set of norms and behaviors that were independent of or contradictory to the teacher's expectations. Over the five days I spent observing in the "Rabbit" class, I noticed that, one child, Kohei, was frequently involved in subversive incidents. His ready smile and the slight swagger to his step reflected his confident and enthusiastic approach to life. Kohei used humor and daring to entrance the other children, and often succeeded in charming the teacher even as he was doing something mischievous. For example, one time the children were in the middle of a writing lesson when one of the other teachers came in with a message for Ms. Watanabe. The children looked up in surprise because visitors were rare, but only Kohei called out, saying, "Minagawa! You are a robber!" The children laughed and Ms. Watanabe looked flustered. She softly reprimanded him for using an impolite form of address: "You should say Miss Minagawa!"

One of Kohei's primary roles in the classroom was to mediate disputes among the children. The following excerpt from my field notes illustrates how Kohei managed the underground world of peer relations, where small dramas were enacted as a subtext beneath the official world of learning:

> Ms. Watanabe is explaining an art project to the class. Each child will receive a paper with an oval shape drawn on it. They will be asked to fill in the facial features of their own fathers. She passes out paper and the children begin to draw. After ten minutes, Miki starts crying and leans over to cover her paper, hiding it from view. The others at her table look concerned and I hear them whisper: "Get Kohei." Someone finds Kohei and explains that Noboru has made fun of Miki's drawing. Kohei listens, nodding briefly. He walks over to Noboru, slugs him on the arm, then turns to pat Miki briefly on the head. Then he strides back to his table. The children watch him go, apparently satisfied that justice has been done. The teacher is busy with children on the other side of the room and hasn't responded to any of this.

Kohei's behavior helps us remember that even in tightly controlled classrooms, children find small spaces of resistance (Tobin, 1995). At Wakaba, except for the lunch break and subsequent recess period, the children are really not supposed to interact with each other *at all*, unless specifically invited to do so by the teacher. The teachers and staff at Wakaba monitored and regulated children's group behavior and also gave some control to children in the form of the *tōban*, or daily monitors. However, the children themselves created an alternative, hidden layer of control that enabled them to manage interpersonal disputes without relying on adults.

The various levels of tension and conflict at Wakaba illustrate how resistance to authority can occur simultaneously with submission to authority, even in environments where cultural models for behavior are clearly articulated and enforced. Western writers have tended to classify individuals as *either* accepting norms mandated by authority *or* rejecting those norms, or they have tended to develop neat categories of action, such as resistance, coping, and consent. Kondo (1990) argues that in complex social settings: "people consent, cope and resist at different levels of consciousness at a single point in time" (p. 224). Japanese individuals are sometimes portrayed as outwardly submitting to authority while inwardly resisting it. From examining the role-oriented schools, we see that resistance can be fragmented and situationally differentiated, and that it is often combined—within the same person—with endorsement and incorporation of dominant norms and practices.

CONCLUSIONS

In the role-oriented preschools, as exemplified by Wakaba, the directors sought to skirt the dangers of individualism and indulgence by creating a very structured, rule-governed environment which required children to engage in a wide variety of activities proposed and organized by adults. The ultimate goal was to move children toward a "mind of appreciation," a sense of their obligation to their teachers and to parents that could be repaid only through hard work and dedication to one's appointed role. The beliefs and practices of the role-oriented directors spring from cultural models with deep roots in Japanese society and are an important part of the story of socialization in Japan.

The view of social relations espoused by Mr. Watanabe and his colleagues at other role-oriented preschools resembles what Kim (1994) calls the "coexistence mode" of social relations. Like the "relational mode" characterizing the relationship-oriented preschools, the coexistence mode emphasizes the fundamentally social nature of human beings. But it views the nature of these social relations as *antagonistic* to the desires of the individual. As Kim (1994) argues, "The coexistence mode separates the private self . . . from the public self. . . . The public self becomes enmeshed with collectivist values, such as family loyalty, in-group solidarity, and national identity. It coexists with the private self, which maintains individualist values of self-cultivation and personal striving" (p. 36). The connection between this type of duality and role enactment is clear:

> In public situations, social norms and roles dictate the behavior of individuals. Collective actions need to be orchestrated cooperatively and harmoniously. If an individual's aspirations are not compatible with social demand, he or she is likely to be asked to sacrifice his or her personal interests for group harmony. This does not imply that individuals necessarily agree with the existing social norms. The cultural expectation is that if there are conflicts, individuals must suppress their own desires, locate them within the private domain, and not display them in public. Individuals have particular statuses and roles, and they must fulfill them in socially prescribed manners. (Kim, 1994, p. 37)

For the role-oriented directors, the task was to strengthen children's ability to fulfill the demands upon the public self. The existence of a private self was acknowledged but not deemed to warrant cultivation during the preschool years. The directors hoped to foster a sense of responsibility for maintaining the welfare of the group rather than a preoccupation with the desires of the private self. They believed that if the private self was not overly indulged in the early years the hard work of fulfilling one's role—including the occasional need to ignore one's selfish desires—would become a source of reward rather than an unpleasant obligation.

As we saw in Chapter 3, the relationship-oriented directors believed that social harmony depended on cultivating one's interpersonal skills, particularly empathy. These skills were thought to emerge and become refined in the context of relationships. This orientation was not totally absent from role-directed classrooms, where teachers implored children to use empathy in the service of such group activities as playing music together. But the role-oriented directors more often focused on one's responsibility to assess the requirements of a situation and accommodate one's behavior appropriately. Like the solitary artisan, the children were expected to work hard at their studies and they were given few opportunities to form relationships with peers or teachers. In this way, they were expected to make a contribution to a smoothly running classroom, a successful school, and a strong society.

Role-oriented directors were very comfortable wielding their authority and created a clear hierarchy within the preschool organization that specified the behavior expected by each member *vis-à-vis* all the others. While they themselves rejected the authority of the national government, they expected full compliance with their own policies from the teachers and students. I noted elements of resistance among the less powerful members of the preschool community, but they were fragmented and difficult to discern. More extensive participant observation would be needed to explore fully how organizational authority—as well as power linked to gender—interact to create layers of cultural models that may be at odds within the same organization.

5

CHILD-ORIENTED PRESCHOOLS:

Strong Individuals, Good Groups

Mrs. Kusumoto doesn't bat an eye when Shoji insists on being a dog ninja. She merely pulls out a white sheet of paper and hands it to him with a suggestion: "Why don't you cut out some ears and we'll tape them to your headband?" He jumps off the tall tower of blocks that he and the other diminutive ninjas have been using for a fortress, finds his scissors, and flings himself on the floor. Within minutes, two floppy ears are drooping from his wide blue headband. He stands proudly while the other ninjas examine his full costume: headband with ears, short black robe formed from a plastic garbage bag held in place by a bright blue ribbon, yellow sword constructed of origami paper, and bare feet. Whooping wildly, the boys run up a wooden plank to the top of their fortress and jump to the floor below, narrowly missing a boy who is quietly constructing a village by taping together old milk cartons. Shoji and Takase fight a duel with their paper swords, running around the classroom yelling loudly and bumping into furniture and other children. Mrs. Kusumoto says nothing, but keeps an eye on them while she helps a group of girls make maracas by filling plastic bottles with small beans.

"I need a ninja throwing star (*shuriken*)," Shoji announces and runs over to a small table set up with many colors of origami paper. The other boys cluster around, select paper, and begin making *shuriken*. Some have clearly mastered the correct sequence of folds, while others are floundering. Mrs. Kusumoto watches them for a few moments, then says, "If it is too hard to make an origami *shuriken*, you can do it another way." She disappears for a few moments and comes back with a large sheet of thick cardboard. "This is a different way to make a *shuriken*. You can trace and cut it out if you don't want to do origami. Which kind would you like to do?" A few boys opt for the cardboard method and run to get their scissors. When they return, Mrs. Kusumoto cuts out a *shuriken* to use as a template, and hands it to one of the boys. "When you trace the shape, be sure you don't move the template," she cautions, and leaves the room. For the next 15 minutes, the boys work hard to create a small arsenal of *shuriken*.

The preschool attended by Shoji and the other ninjas is an example of a "child-oriented" program. At these schools, most of the day is devoted to free play, with optional art activities introduced by the teacher to individual children or small groups. Unlike the role-oriented schools, there is no explicit instruction in literacy or other academic subjects. Compared to the relationship-oriented schools, there is a greater availability of materials to be used alone or with classmates. Sports events, as well as music and dramatic performances, are kept simple and preceded by short, relaxed practice sessions.

When I first visited schools like Higashimachi, I assumed that their directors had been strongly influenced by Western early-childhood education. Indeed, some of them did report that they had adopted a more individualized approach in response to guidelines from the Ministry of Education, which are viewed by most directors as reflecting Western values. All of the Christian preschools I visited were child-oriented, which also seemed to suggest the influence of Western thinking. But I gradually began to see that these programs were not merely replicating American practices, and that their philosophical underpinnings were different from the culturally based assumptions that underlie definitions of good practice in the United States.

To illustrate the ideas and activities found in child-oriented preschools, I will focus on two schools—Higashimachi, the public school attended by Shoji, and Hanna, a Christian preschool in a suburban town outside Kobe. In spite of their different institutional connections—one to the Ministry of Education and the other to the Protestant Church—the directors and teachers at these schools shared a similar view of the goals and methods of educating preschool children. In this chapter, I will show how teachers scaffolded children's interactions with peers during free play and group activities to foster competencies—both personal and social—necessary for engaging in rewarding relationships with other children and adults.

Only 42 children were enrolled at Higashimachi when I visited there, 21 in a class for four-year-olds and 21 in a class for five-year-olds. This number represents a 50 percent decline from previous years. Because enrollment is so low, the school has plenty of space, in spite of occupying very expensive land in a wealthy section of the city. Each classroom is large, and the two classes share a huge multipurpose room. This school shares its campus with an elementary school. There is one principal in charge of both the preschool and the elementary school, but the day-to-day business of running the school is handled by an outgoing, middle-aged woman named Mrs. Kimura.

Located in the hills of a suburban community between Osaka and Kobe, the second school, Hanna Preschool, has served neighborhood children for over a hundred years. Hanna has a Christian orientation, although children from any background are welcome.[8] Although larger than Higashimachi, with 150 children, Hanna has also suffered a loss of enrollment in previous years. Unlike the public schools, private schools like Hanna—whether religious or nondenominational—have an economic incentive to maintain a certain level of enrollment. So far, however, the staff at Hanna has resisted the temptation to change their program just to attract new students.

FOSTERING STRONG INDIVIDUALS AND EFFECTIVE GROUPS

One cultural model that emerged as a leitmotif of both schools was the notion that each child is an individual worthy of respect. As Ms. Takeda, assistant director at Hanna, put it: "When you observe each individual child you will find that he has a particular individual nature (*kosei*). I believe that education begins when we receive children as they are." This thought was echoed by Mrs. Kimura at Higashimachi, who described personal experiences with her own daughter that led her to a professional realization about the importance of individualization:

> I personally believe that children will be best served if there is a min-
> imum of five and a maximum of 15 children in a class. . . . The big-
> ger the number, the more orders and prohibitions the teacher tends
> to use. The bigger the number, the more the teacher is likely to rely
> on her power. Bringing out the best in each individual child is
> important, and having each individual child express his or her char-
> acter is important. Also having each individual child have confidence
> in himself or herself is important. To tell the truth, my daughter . . .
> has had eating disorders for three years. . . . As a preschool teacher, I
> had been very involved in education and tended to control my
> daughter too much. I now regret that I tended to ignore her individ-
> ual characteristics.

A second important cultural model was the notion that "strong" children were able to contribute their skills to create "good" groups. The staff at the child-oriented schools believed that by developing their own skills and defining their own interests, children became more able to contribute to the group's welfare. Ms. Takeda described group processes in terms of relationships and exchanges among individuals. In the following statement, she explained her focus:

> A group consists of individuals. If each individual grows, the entire
> group becomes better. We do some group activities. One way to do
> them is to form the group first, and then tell them what to do. The

other way is for each individual to propose different ideas and then integrate those ideas. The end results may be the same but the processes are different.

In her ethnography of a Japanese elementary school, Nancy Sato (1996) also found that the teachers saw "individual-capacity building" and "group-community building" as complementary: "I discovered uniformity as the starting point for diversity, standardization as a catalyst for creativity, and individualization as a means to become group oriented" (p. 120). In the school she observed, "individual development is both bound and enhanced by membership in mutual learning communities, and those same communities, in turn, are strengthened by increased individual capacities; they complement one another toward reciprocal growth" (pp. 121–22). This emphasis on enhancing the complementary relationship between individual competence and group strength aptly characterized the child-oriented preschools in my sample of preschools. In contrast, the staff at role-oriented schools assumed that individual characteristics would blossom naturally—but probably not until adulthood—after a solid, common base had been established from engaging in group activities. In their view, the artisan develops a unique style only after years of apprenticeship in which he masters the required forms. And in the relationship-oriented schools, teachers acknowledged the existence of individual differences among children, and accommodated them if possible. But cultivating children's interests, deepening their communication skills, and helping them identify their emotions were not identified by the teachers in relationship-oriented schools as major elements of the curriculum. In the child-oriented schools, these were all important goals.

In order to implement their goals of "individual-capacity building" and "group-community building," the teachers in child-oriented preschool programs blended long periods of free play with a number of group activities. This balance was similar to the relationship-oriented schools, but one difference lay in the extensive use of materials for art, construction, and fantasy play in the child-oriented schools. At

Higashimachi there was a diverse array of materials accessible to children throughout the free play period in a number of loosely organized activity areas. Child-sized couches and a bookshelf defined the reading area, and musical instruments occupied their own space. There was an area devoted to origami, as well as a housekeeping corner. Numerous labeled shelves held art supplies, and there were many large bins containing recycled household materials like egg cartons, milk cartons, cardboard tubes, and scraps of cloth. Over a hundred large blocks—some as long as four feet—were stored in the multipurpose room where children spent hours making forts, houses, obstacle courses, and other constructions. Children's artwork covered the walls, unlike in other types of preschools where teacher-created art predominated.

Varied materials such as these characterized the classrooms at Hanna as well. One day, I observed the four-year-olds at Hanna circulate among stations containing blocks, art materials, and manipulative toys. I saw children create a nearly life-sized bowling alley out of blocks, make origami figures to decorate the bulletin board, create collages with pieces of felt, use simple looms to weave strands of yarn, and paint a large cardboard box to be used as a puppet theater in the upcoming sports-day festivities. All of these materials were available to every child throughout the morning.

A basic pedagogical strategy underlying the curriculum at the child-oriented schools was that children should be free to select activities and materials that suit them as individuals. It was the role of the teacher to make sure that the materials were interesting and appropriate. As Ms. Takeda said:

> We should arrange environments considering each individual child's interest and desire as well as developmental stage. We would like to arrange environments in which as soon as the child comes to school in the morning, he or she can play with interesting materials. We consider free activity (*jiyū katsudō*) to be very important. Children are interested in different activities and materials depending on their age, interest, and desire.

These children playing in the sand have access to a wide variety of materials for their activities.

The curriculum was planned in advance in the child-oriented schools, but it was customized daily to meet the needs of the individual children. This process was described by Ms. Takeda:

> It is important for us to observe carefully and notice what the children are interested in. We have to check and see whether they are satisfied with the materials. It is also important for us to understand what children want to do next. Understanding children is our task.

In relationship-oriented preschools, the teachers tended to follow the daily curriculum plans developed at the beginning of the year, which specified certain common activities for all the classes. In child-oriented preschools, the teachers appeared to act more directly upon feedback they obtained from their observations of children as they engaged in activities, providing materials that reflected children's current interests and extended their skills. At Hanna, different activities were going on in each of the various classes for four-year-olds.

Scaffolding Children's Social Skills

In reading these descriptions of how materials were used to deepen play, Western educators may be tempted to conclude that the teachers held the goal of fostering children's cognitive development. But the teachers I spoke with did not view the purpose of these activities as stimulating cognitive outcomes. Rather, they saw themselves facilitating *social* cognitive skills—such as empathy—as well as related social behavioral competencies such as cooperation. Every time I asked about their motivation for scaffolding children's actions and interactions during free play as well as group time, the teachers brought up the importance of these social skills, as in the following statement by Ms. Takeda:

> During free play the child interacts with peers who have different ideas. Through such interactions the child understands that these differences exist . . . and he or she gradually develops an understanding of living together with others.

The following two anecdotes illustrate how teachers worked with two socially isolated children to build up their capacity to engage in relationships with peers. At Higashimachi, I observed Mrs. Kusumoto repeatedly scaffold a shy girl's attempts to play with other children:

> Fumiko is sitting by herself, watching a group of girls play house while she dreamily shakes a maraca (plastic bottle filled with small beans) that was part of an earlier class project. Mrs. Kusumoto notices a few beans leaking from the bottle, and helps Fumiko seal it with tape. She sings a song to Fumiko, demonstrating how to shake the maraca in time to the music. At that point her attention is diverted by requests from other children. Fumiko follows her around, shaking the maraca but not engaging with any other children. Mrs. Kusumoto helps Fumiko put a cha-cha-cha tape in the portable cassette player, and calls a second girl to come over and join them on a small stage made of blocks. The two girls and Mrs. Kusumoto stand on the stage, singing and shaking their maracas. Then Mrs. Kusumoto steps down and faces them, singing along and encouraging them to continue. After a few minutes she attempts to

melt away. The girls continue singing briefly, but when the song ends the second girl runs off, leaving Fumiko alone and unoccupied. She looks for Mrs. Kusumoto and begins following her around again. Mrs. Kusumoto approaches a small group of girls who are playing house, asking them: "Would you like to invite this girl over for dinner? After giving the concert, she is very hungry." One of the girls nods silently. Fumiko smiles and enters the "house." She stands there uncertainly, saying nothing. Mrs. Kusumoto inquires, "Fumiko-chan. Have you had your dinner? Why don't you join us? Don't you want something to eat? It looks good." Fumiko nods and the girls bring her a couple dishes of clay "food." Mrs. Kusumoto looks on briefly, then moves quietly out of the scene.

This anecdote reveals only a small portion of Mrs. Kusumoto's repeated attempts to help Fumiko become more able to play with other children. Her strategy was to pick up on something that Fumiko was doing, even if it was the absent-minded shaking of a maraca, and to build it into an activity with a peer. She often modeled the desired behavior, then encouraged Fumiko to do it with her. Once Fumiko was engaged, she would step aside and let Fumiko try to interact with peers independently.

The teachers in the child-oriented preschools also encouraged children to verbalize their thoughts and feelings. This objective was not emphasized in the role- and relationship-oriented Japanese preschools, where I rarely saw verbal exchanges between the teacher and an individual child that lasted more than one or two turns. But in the child-oriented preschools, the teachers engaged in long dialogues with the children. These often occurred at lunchtime, when the teachers would sit for as long as an hour while the children ate and chatted in leisurely manner. Here is a sample of a lunchtime conversation between Mrs. Kusumoto and Koichi, a bright boy whom the teachers viewed as immature and socially inept:

Mrs. K: Koichi, how big was the dragonfly you caught the other day?

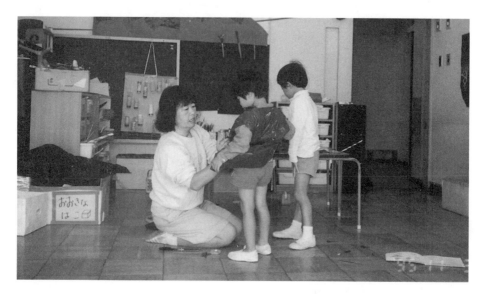

A teacher helps two boys design a costume from plastic garbage bags.

Koichi:	It was a [technical name] dragonfly.
Mrs. K:	So how big was it?
Koichi:	[Indicates size with his hands.] I'm going on a car trip tomorrow.
Mrs. K:	Where are you going?
Koichi:	I am going to be sitting next to my daddy.
Mrs. K:	What about your mother?
Koichi:	She is going to be at home. I'm going to see a lot of insects.
Mrs. K:	That is wonderful. Can you come back to school and let us know what you saw?
Koichi:	Maybe I can catch a grasshopper.
Mrs. K:	If so, can you bring it back and we'll keep it here?
Koichi:	I know where there are a lot of grasshoppers.
Mrs. K:	Is it where you went for summer vacation this year? The ground may be covered with snow by now.
Koichi:	Someone I just talked to found a cricket there.

Throughout this exchange, Mrs. Kusumoto made use of information that she already knew about Koichi, including his interest in insects and where he spent his summer vacation. As in her interactions with Fumiko, she provided a scaffolding—structuring the conversation so that it had shape and coherence, but allowing Koichi to participate to the extent of his capabilities. She ignored the fact that some of his responses were non sequiturs, choosing instead to build on his statements whether they were connected to her previous remarks or not. She also tried twice to connect his personal experience to school life by asking whether he would share his findings with the class. She later explained to us that Koichi had an extensive vocabulary about scientific and technical matters but little ability to hold a conversation. Much of his interaction with other children consisted of hitting, screeching, and making strange noises. So she tried to talk with him as often as possible to help him build up a vocabulary and skills for everyday conversation.

A crucial point here is that Mrs. Kusumoto was building on Koichi's personal interests in the service of helping him develop the skills to communicate effectively with other people. Her strategy of scaffolding during her conversations was not so different from what one might find in many American preschools. But the goal was to help him build his skills for relating to others, not to extend his personal interests in insects or to achieve any other cognitive objectives, which may have been more salient to American teachers.

Helping Children Identify and Express Emotions

Throughout each day, Mrs. Kusumoto took many opportunities to encourage children to think about their feelings and express them. In the case of arguments between children, the teachers in other types of schools often allowed children to experience the consequences of their behavior without adult mediation (see also Tobin et al., 1989). But the child-oriented teachers more frequently intervened to help children identify their own feelings and reactions in particular situations. In the case of serious disagreements, Mrs. Kusumoto would mediate, encouraging both children to tell their sides of the story. She would sometimes sum up the case made by each child, but avoided dictating the terms of a settlement. She tried to help them identify and articulate their feelings in any situation where they might be experiencing anger, jealousy, or other strong emotions:

> Mrs. Kusumoto has organized a Rochambeau ("rock-scissor-paper") tournament. Several pairs of children play at a time, and the winners of each dyad go on to play each other. The bout between the two finalists is dramatic. All the children crowd into a circle to cheer on their favorite player. Upon winning this final match, Sayuri throws her hands into the air and staggers across the room in delight. Mrs. Kusumoto claps and cheers with the class. She says: "How come Sayuri is such a good Rochambeau player? Raise your hand if you are jealous of her!" The children's hands shoot up. "Raise your hand if you want to win all the time!" Laughing, children raise their hands again. "Sayuri, how can you be so good at Rochambeau?" Mrs. Kusumoto asks. Some of the children drift away to other activities. Mrs. Kusumoto begins playing Rochambeau with those who remain. She somehow manages to "lose" every one of the matches.

Mrs. Kusumoto and Ms. Takeda did not particularly worry about conflicts among peers or view occasional aggression as a sign of serious disturbance. They saw these phenomena as learning experiences, arguing that when children do not get what they want they realize that their own feelings are different from those of others. According to these teachers, such realizations lead the children to think about the diversity of individual feelings and experiences and ultimately to an acceptance and understanding of others:

> In preschool life, getting into fights is important. Fighting takes place because you [i.e., the child] want to have your own way. Fighting also takes place because you do not understand others' positions. In these kinds of experiences you might get hurt not only physically but also mentally. You may feel physical as well as emotional pain. You might understand the fact that there are a lot of peo-

ple who are different from you. Still, however, you understand that they are your friends and you love those people. This may sound a bit too general, but through understanding each other and fighting with each other you might realize that there are a variety of types of people. I consider this realization to be very important.

At Higashimachi, the teachers were even willing to provoke squabbles by limiting the number of toys available for play:

> In the period when children are increasingly aware of others, we purposely do not provide an adequate number of toys, and we have children fight with one another to get a toy. By doing so, we try to have children understand that what you want may be what others want. . . . The bottom line is the understanding of the existence of the feelings of others.

Helping Children Learn to Manage Materials and Persist with Challenging Tasks

When teachers allow free play to dominate the curriculum, there are implications for the problems that arise, and the strategies that are used to resolve those problems. As we have already seen, the teachers in child-oriented schools tried to "scaffold" children's conflicts, protecting children from harm while encouraging them to experience the consequences of conflict and figure out constructive ways of resolving it. In the child-oriented schools, the sheer amount of material available for free play meant that a substantial amount of the teacher's effort also went into helping children use the materials appropriately, keeping them somewhat organized, and cleaning up when they were finished playing. To do this, the teachers relied on praise as well as mild reminders. For example, at one point after a group of children had spent nearly an hour cutting and pasting, the floor was covered with little scraps of paper. Mrs. Kusumoto said, "I see a lot of little pieces of paper on the floor. Let's see if we can clean them all up." As the children began doing so, she worked with them, occasionally complimenting those who were especially diligent: "Good job (*erai*). Great, the floor is becoming nice and shiny again. Look at Madoka-chan. She is trying to carry as much as possible. Good job!"

When children blatantly ignored her suggestions about cleaning up, Mrs. Kusumoto tended to react mildly. For example, the following incident occurred after she had announced that it was time to clean up the multipurpose room:

> Mrs. Kusumoto begins dismantling the numerous wooden block structures that fill the room. Some of the structures are over five feet high and occupy as much as 40 or 50 square feet. The larger blocks are quite heavy and can barely be managed even by an adult. A few children help Mrs. Kusumoto as she begins lugging blocks back to the storage area, but several continue playing or drift away to the other room. She does not admonish them. Two boys begin an argument, and one approaches Mrs. Kusumoto, saying: "Teacher, Toshio says he doesn't like you." Mrs. Kusumoto replies mildly, "I am sorry to hear that," and continues to put away blocks. She says nothing else, even though the boys leave the area, continuing their argument rather than assisting with the clean-up efforts.

The emphasis on individualization in these schools did not preclude the existence of rules and encouragement to improve on one's skills or behavior. One of the most important was the notion that a child should not give up easily or on a whim, but rather should learn to be persistent and continue to exert effort even when a task becomes difficult or unpleasant. The cultural importance placed on effort and perseverance—expressed in the term *gambaru*—has been noted by many observers of Japanese educational settings (e.g., Holloway, 1988; Holloway et al., 1986). Indeed, nurturing perseverance was a primary goal of the directors in the academic preschools. The role-oriented directors tend to emphasize that effort is associated with self-denial and strict discipline, although it eventually results in the honing and perfecting of the self. But the widely accepted cultural model concerning the importance of perseverance is subject to varying and contested interpretations, and it existed in a different guise in the child-oriented preschools. Mrs. Kimura, at Higashimachi, believed that it was important for children to persist upon encountering a challenge, even if one was not immediately inclined to do so. In describing a student named Yuta, who often disobeyed his teacher, Mrs. Kimura reflected on the need to accept a child's individual nature while encouraging him to stretch beyond his immediate comfort level:

> In my experience as a preschool educator I have often heard teachers say to a child: "You have to behave better because you are in the older classroom." But Yuta always moves at his own pace. We should not flatly refuse [to accommodate his pace] according to adults' standards or convenience. It is important to consider what he thinks and how he has been raised. And it is important to observe his individual characteristics. It is important to allow him to do what he wants to, as long as his behavior does not bother others. . . . He does what he is interested in. He once said to his mother that he would not be a company employee. That makes sense to me. He will work freelance. But I say to him: "In some cases, please give it your best effort."

Strengthening Peer Relations through Group Activities

While free play formed the core of the curriculum in these schools, there were times when the class gathered together as a group. Generally, group activities took the form of discussions facilitated by the teacher. I observed two variations of this basic activity. In one variation, children would gather to discuss the artwork generated by each children in the preceding art period. Such a discussion will be described in detail in Chapter 7 in the context of Christian preschools. A second variation took the form of a planning session for an upcoming event or project. The goal of these activities was to provide an opportunity for each child to "understand differences between him or her and others," in the words of Ms. Takeda. The teacher's role was to stimulate a discussion so that "the child may discover what is wonderful about others, and also what others consider good about him or her."

The following anecdote pertains to a planning session held in a classroom of five-year-olds. The children were discussing the details of how to construct a baseball-toss game for sports day. In a previous group meeting, they decided to create a target by cutting a hole in the side of a large packing box. Players will try to throw balls into the hole. Mr. Matsumoto opened the new discussion by asking how the box should be decorated. One child suggested that the box be decorated as a face, with a hole for the mouth. This idea was generally received with enthusiasm; one after another, children suggested particular facial features that could be added. The following exchange ensued:

Child 1: Make it a body, and put waving hands on the sides.
Child 2: But how would the hands move?
Child 3: I know, put someone in the box to move the hands!

(Several boys jump out of their chairs and get into the box. Mr. Matsumoto laughs and playfully pretends to try and lift the box, groaning with exertion.)

Child 4: But the person inside will get hurt when people throw the baseballs in there.
Teacher: Well, it's a good idea to put someone in there, but since we're throwing balls at it we do risk hurting anyone. Any other opinions?
Child 3: Use a stick to move the arms from the outside.
Child 5: Make the arms out of paper. When you move the box, the arms will move.
Teacher: Why don't you try that idea tomorrow?
Child 6: Tomorrow let's only make the hands because if we make the whole thing and the arms don't work it will be ruined.
Teacher: Maybe you can attach the box to a pole. The pole could be used to move the box. So tomorrow, those who want can work on the box, and others can make flags.

This brainstorming session shows how skilled these four-year-olds had become in coming up with creative ideas as well as considering and building upon the ideas of other children. They were also able to give—and take—constructive criticism of their ideas. They demonstrated a variety of problem-solving skills, including thinking through the implications of their decisions and taking the initiative to resolve glitches rather than relying on the teacher. These skills will come into play with increasing frequency in elementary school; in her observations of elementary classrooms, Lewis (1995) has noted that teachers often encouraged "a sustained, relaxed focus on a single major issue over one or more entire class periods [with] plenty of 'invitations' to connect the lesson with personal experiences [and] activities that engaged children (often physically and emotionally as well as intellectually) with what was being studied" (p. 177).

UCHI AND SOTO: SORTING OUT THE DEMANDS OF HOME AND SCHOOL

The staff in child-oriented and relationship-oriented schools carefully considered the needs of the individual child as well as the benefits of becoming a group member, but they were different in how they prioritized and actualized these sometimes competing goals. In relationship-oriented schools, brief structured activities were designed to teach the child how to accommodate to the goals and pace that had been set by the teacher. Free play was seen as helpful in building social competence and as something fun, a motivator that helped children tolerate the more structured activities. In child-oriented schools, play was seen as a means for deepening self-knowledge and for expressing individual feelings and thoughts. Through their relationships with peers, children gained social skills as well as important knowledge about themselves. Group activities were also part of the curriculum, but were more open-ended and participatory than in the other schools. The goals and features of the activities emerged through extended discussions among children that were carefully scaffolded by the teachers. As we saw, the teachers were well aware of, and respectful of, children's personal characteristics. Mrs. Kusumoto built upon her knowledge of Koichi's interest in insects to involve him in a prolonged dialogue. And she skillfully built upon Fumiko's small initiatives to bolster her abilities to engage in peer play. In child-oriented preschools, the needs and characteristics of individual were accentuated, yet individual development—and the expression of that individuality—was firmly bound up with membership in collective structures.

There has been so much emphasis on the collectivistic side of Japan in the popular and academic literature that the reality of Japanese individualism may need compensatory highlighting (see also Hofstede, 1994). The issue is not whether or not individualism exists in Japan but how individualism is expressed and responded to (Mouer and Sugimoto, 1986, p. 193). As we saw even in the role-oriented preschools, the existence of individuality was not itself contested, but the opinion was strongly held that cultivation of that individuality at school was unnecessary and even harmful until the basic attributes shared by all could be firmly established.

One reason that the child-oriented directors felt comfortable encouraging children to express themselves freely is that they saw the preschool as an informal, somewhat homelike setting. In Japan, very different sorts of behavior are expected in *uchi* (home or homelike) settings and *soto* (public) settings. In many public settings, people experience a great deal of pressure to behave in an appropriate manner. They are expected to exhibit *enryo*, or reserve, and to refrain from acting in a way that will bother others or that will appear strange or unconventional. However, there are safety valves built into this system, so that everyone has some opportunity to escape the pressure of external standards at some time. In *uchi* settings, which are intimate and informal, it is possible to loosen up and express oneself openly without a great deal of regard for the perceptions and evaluations of others.

Is the preschool an *uchi* setting or a *soto* setting? Joseph Tobin (1992b) has argued that preschools contain elements of both *uchi* and *soto*:

On the road to adulthood Japanese children must learn lessons more complex than simply distinguishing inside from outside, front from back, public from private, and family from strangers. To have a proper, two-tiered Japanese sense of self one must learn to make much more fluid and subtle distinctions, learn to step back and forth across the gap dividing *omote* [front] from *ura* [rear] in the course of a single conversation. . . . Thus the most crucial lesson to be learned in the Japanese preschool is not *omote*, not the ability to behave properly in formal situations, but instead *kejime*—the knowledge needed to shift fluidly back and forth between *omote* and *ura*. . . . I suggest that the Japanese preschool helps children develop and integrate this twofold selfhood not by offering a world completely unlike the world of mother and home, but instead by offering a world that is simultaneously home (*uchi*) and not home (*soto*), front (*omote*) and rear (*ura*), a world of both spontaneous human feeling (*honne*) and prescribed, formal pretense (*tatemae*). (pp. 24–25)

To this basic argument, I would add that the various types of preschools have developed their own recipes for combining the elements of *uchi* and *soto*. The role-oriented schools required a child to operate almost entirely in the public (*soto*) world. In these schools, children were never pampered or indulged. They were encouraged to study hard, master challenging physical skills, avoid sweet food, wear minimal amounts of clothing in cold weather—all without complaint. There was no encouragement of a mother-like relationship with teachers. The relationship-oriented schools, on the other hand, provided dollops of *soto* against a general background of *uchi*. All day long children made transitions back and forth between very structured routines and nearly total freedom. They arrived in the morning and changed clothes according to precise guidelines, then ran outside for an hour of play with minimal supervision from teachers. This cycling continued throughout the day, ending with a final bit of structured time before returning home. Tobin's description applied best to relationship-oriented schools.

In the child-oriented schools I visited, there was clearly a strong *uchi* element. Class sizes were small, making it possible for each child to get a lot of attention from the teacher. Teachers often made use of their empathic skills (*omoiyari*) much as a parent does, anticipating the child's desires and sometimes acting on them without the child having to verbalize anything at all. Through careful observations, teachers in the child-oriented schools sought to adjust the materials in the environment to accommodate the current interests and developmental level of each child in the classroom. For example, when Mrs. Kusumoto noticed that some children were having trouble making origami throwing stars—without their saying a word about it—she offered them an alternative suggestion along with the necessary materials.

However, it would be inaccurate to conclude that the environment was entirely *uchi*-oriented in child-oriented schools. In a truly *uchi* situation, the individual is free to "let it all hang out" and do as little as he or she pleases. In the child-oriented schools, the teachers were constantly monitoring the children, looking for opportunities to deepen and extend their activities. Whether it was free play, lunchtime, or a group discussion, teachers were constantly concerned with helping children gain the competencies needed to relate successfully to other children and to function appropriately in the classroom.

FINAL COMMENT ON THE THREE TYPES OF PRESCHOOLS

While most of the preschools that I visited could be rather easily categorized into one of the three types, there is nothing magical or definitive about that number. I believe that this taxonomy characterizes preschools in the Kansai area rather well, but it may be less applicable in other parts of the country. Even within this sample, there were some schools that were not clear exemplars of a category. In some cases, the director may have had a vision that did not seem to be fully implemented by the teachers, leading to a more hybrid approach. Director and teachers may have sometimes been prevented by material constraints from realizing their philosophy, creating a disjunction between the stated philosophy and the actual curriculum. And a few schools were in the middle of a transition toward a more individualized curriculum but were not yet entirely clear on their new vision.

In general, however, I was more surprised by the orderliness of the data than by the few schools that seemed to jump back and forth between categories. I think that the general willingness of teachers to implement the director's vision faithfully usually lead to schoolwide consistency; the fact that the teachers received intense on-site training and tended to remain at one school for their entire career made them relative "purists" as far as embodying a particular orientation toward curriculum and relationships. In a broader sense, the characteristics of each preschool were clearly informed by cultural models that have been circulating in Japan for a long time. While that pool of models is varied, it is not limitless. What I saw over and over again is the appropriation of basic models, which were then customized by the directors according to their own experiences, viewpoints, and pragmatic goals.

In the next several chapters, I take a closer look at the societal structures that gave rise to—and continue to support—these cultural models. While some folk theories may simply float around the pool as cultural flotsam and jetsam, most are attached to some structural component of a society, such as social class or religious institution. Three societal elements emerged as major contributors to directors' pedagogical views: social-class milieu, religious affiliation, and whether the school was public or private. These form the core subjects for analysis in Chapters 6, 7, and 8, respectively.

6

PRESCHOOLS AND SOCIAL CLASS:

Early Experiences in a Stratified Society

Critics of capitalist America are fond of comparing the salary range among employees in American corporations with the analogous range in Japan. While the highest paid CEOs of American firms may pull in as much as 500 times the annual income of the lowest paid worker, Japanese CEOs, who rarely claim extravagant salaries and stock options, typically differ from the lowest paid worker by a factor of 15. Another oft-cited difference between the countries is the relative absence in Japan of severe poverty, chronic unemployment, family disintegration, crime, and drug addiction. While these observations may be basically accurate (although with Japan's economy faltering, unemployment and crime are rising, especially among youth ["Japan's lingering recession," 1999]), they do not tell the whole story of social-class differences in Japan. The economic differences among social strata in Japan are not as stark as in the United States, but there are significant class-related patterns in family practices and educational opportunities that serve to perpetuate young children's class position. In this chapter, I contrast two preschools that serve families from different ends of the social-class spectrum. The schools are strikingly different in appearance, philosophy, and activities. The comparison may provide some hypotheses concerning the role of early experiences in contributing to later social class differences in school attainment.

A HISTORICAL OVERVIEW OF SOCIAL STRATIFICATION IN JAPAN

Social-class differences are deeply rooted in Japanese culture. During the years from 1600 until the 1850s, the rulers of Japan supported a rigid class system. The imperial family and court nobility were at the top, and below them, in descending order of status, were the samurai, peasantry, artisans, and merchants. Outside and below these official four castes were the outcasts (*burakumin*). Within each of the four castes there existed numerous subdivisions; members within the subdivision were ranked, with little chance for social mobility. Extensive laws dictated the lifestyles, customs, work practices, and privileges of each caste (Hunter, 1989). Children's activities were dictated by their caste; sons and (to a lesser extent) daughters of wealthy families were often allowed to attend school, whereas the children of farmers, merchants, and artisans were expected to sustain the household economy by working at home or in the households of wealthy families (Uno, 1991b; Walthall, 1991).

In the early part of the nineteenth century, the caste system began to break down, as occupation and wealth became less closely linked to formal class status. In the political upheaval subsequent to the forced "opening" of Japan by European merchants, the Tokugawa shogunate was overthrown by a small group of low-level samurai who declared an end to all class divisions. To maintain social control, the government strengthened the moral and economic functions of a long-standing social unit, the *ie*, or household. The *ie* consisted of an extended family grouping extending across generations which served the purpose of preserving household property, occupation, name, and status (Uno, 1991b). As a social structure, the *ie* itself was arranged in a strict hierarchy, with each individual carrying out a prescribed role.[9] During a nationalistic period in the early 1900s, the government reinforced and even increased these structural forms of social control in order to bolster its political power. Subsequent to World War II, mandatory reforms by Occupation authorities dissolved the legal authority of the *ie* and instituted a variety of reforms designed to create a democratic state, including reforming the elitist educational system (Hunter, 1989; Reischauer, 1981).

SOCIAL CLASS IN CONTEMPORARY JAPAN

While social connections may still benefit a few members of old aristocratic families (Hunter, 1989, p. 77), class differences today are largely based upon educational attainment and type of employment. Social-class differences in family lifestyles during the immediate postwar period are extensively documented in Vogel's study (1963) contrasting the "salaryman" with men engaged in traditional, nonprofessional work. Salarymen who worked for large companies received higher wages than their counterparts engaged in independent business activities, and were guaranteed lifetime employment. The families of salarymen could therefore afford to participate fully in the materialistic surge that accompanied Japan's economic development in the 1950s. Numerous ensuing changes significantly affected family relations in the new middle class: fewer households contained extended family members, mothers spent more time with their children, and fathers began working in locations physically distant from the home. As a result of these structural changes, the mother-child dyad apparently became stronger, while fathers moved to a peripheral position in children's lives.

More recently, studies confirm that middle-class families in Japan provide different kinds of experiences to their children from those in the working class; these experiences appear related to the children's academic progress and achievement. For example, a comparison of the ways in which parents prepare children for school in Japan and the United States found particularly strong social-class effects in Japan. The most powerful predictor of Japanese children's school performance at the age of 11 or 12 was the mother's expectations (when the child was aged 3) as to how far her child would go in school, a variable highly associated with social class (Azuma, 1994a). In a retrospective account of the research project, Azuma (1996) describes the surprise that attended these results: ". . . we had predicted there would be little social-class variation in Japan, which has been viewed as a single-class, middle-class society. But in our results there was as much social-class variation in the Japanese as in the American data. . . . And surprisingly, when we looked at our follow-up data on the children in upper elementary school, there was actually greater social-class variation in Japan than in America" (p. 237).

Kondo's ethnography (1990) also portrays the powerful ways in which social class affects the educational aspirations of families in urban Japanese settings. She contrasts the down-to-earth customs of the working-class Shitamachi area of Tokyo with the supposedly more refined tastes of the elite Yamanote dwellers. According to Kondo, many residents of Shitamachi had little desire for their children to be upwardly mobile, and freely expressed their acceptance of—or resignation concerning—low school achievement.

Those Japanese parents who wish their children to attain (or maintain) a higher level of social status try to help them do well on the examinations determining admission to a good high school and subsequently to a well-regarded university. While there is a meritocratic side to the examination process, wealthy families can help children succeed on examinations in ways that poorer families cannot. In relatively wealthy families, mothers are more educated and do not have to work, ensuring that they can help children with their studies. They can hire tutors and send the children to expensive "cram schools" (*juku*). Children in high-status families are more likely to have their own rooms for studying and have fewer siblings to compete with for resources. Even if a child does not do particularly well on the examinations, he or she can attend a (costly) university that accepts less-qualified students but maintains good relationships with prestigious corporations (Rohlen, 1983).

Another form of evidence concerning the link between family background and schooling comes from examining data on school financing and the supply of preschools in various regions of Japan. Per capita spending for middle and elementary school varies dramatically by prefecture, with urban areas like Tokyo outspending rural areas by a two-to-one margin (Smith, 1994). National data also suggest that preschool attendance is not equally distributed across the country; it is higher in areas that are characterized by generally greater educational opportunity (for example, number of elite high schools) and where parents are more educated (Smith, 1994).[10]

This chapter examines social stratification among preschools by comparing two schools that are quite disparate in terms of the social-class backgrounds of the families they serve. Takenoko Preschool serves very wealthy families. The fathers of students attending Takenoko are mostly executives in large corporations. Most of the mothers whose children attend Takenoko are not employed (with the exception of several who are high-level professionals). Nada Preschool, on the other hand, is located in a run-down, semi-industrial section of the city. The fathers whose children attend Nada work in small, local manufacturing plants or in the service sector. Many of the mothers of Nada students are self-employed, doing piecework at home or running small businesses. Both schools are private, and therefore their survival depends largely on income from tuition. Because the families whose children attend Nada pay far less than those sending their children to Takenoko, Nada faces many more budgetary constraints than does Takenoko.

I begin with a case study of Takenoko, examining the physical site and educational materials available, the curriculum, and the director's ideas about the goals of the preschool experience. The nature of teacher-child relations, as well as relations among peers, are also described. A detailed description of Nada is then provided, followed by a general discussion of the way social class is manifested in other schools in the sample.

A DAY IN THE LIFE OF KAZUKO AT
TAKENOKO PRESCHOOL

Every morning, Kazuko and her mother face a steep climb on their way to Takenoko Preschool. As Kazuko and Mrs. Nishikawa approach the school, luxury apartment buildings give way to an expanse of trees and shrubbery. A long driveway curves through the greenery toward the entrance to the preschool. By 9 A.M. the street is filled with a long row of BMWs and small Mercedes station wagons that are well designed for the narrow, crowded streets of the city. Kazuko and her mother approach the school building as children in expensive play clothes emerge from the cars and run into the building.

The long rectangular foyer of the preschool is bright and cheerful. Large murals of mosaic tile depict pandas, giraffes, swans, and other animals. As they enter the building, mothers and children step onto the gray tile floor of the entryway and approach cubbyholes for storing the children's indoor shoes. Six feet in front of the cubbyholes, gray tile gives way to elevated red flooring, a symbolic boundary that demarcates the terrain accessible only to insiders, who are, in this case, the children. Mrs. Nishikawa hovers at this boundary, as Kazuko drops to the floor and exchanges her street shoes for white gym shoes. Kazuko joins the line of children waiting to greet the director. When it is her turn, she bows carefully in synchrony with Ms. Sato, and exchanges polite greetings: "*Go kigen yō.*"

The entry ritual at Takenoko—particularly the greeting and formal bow to the director—is distinctive, and serves as a clear indication of the elevated social status of the children and their families. The term "*Go kigen yō*" is a somewhat old-fashioned phrase used to convey a wish that the other person fares well. It is considered to be elegant and very polite, and its use would typically not be expected of preschool-aged children— nor directed toward them. Throughout the day, teachers at Takenoko Preschool speak to their students using formal language rather than the informal form typically used in conversing with young children. The teachers' formal language appears to reflect a sense that the children are particularly worthy of regard—different from and somehow more special than the average child. It is one of many symbolic indications to children of their "entitlement"—the notion that they can expect attention, material resources, and respect (Lareau, 1989).

Material Conditions at Takenoko

Kazuko's classroom is large enough to accommodate all her classmates comfortably. Like most Japanese preschools, Takenoko devotes more floor space to tables and chairs than to activity centers. This classroom for four-year-olds does feature a housekeeping area, however, complete with a real tatami mat floor. The classroom has a number of built-in shelves for books and blocks as well as for displaying artwork. The children have created large self-portraits, which they cut out and posted on the bulletin board. Each figure is labeled with the child's name and birth date. The children have also colored flags from countries around the world; these are suspended from a cord strung across the classroom.

Kazuko and her classmates have access to a play yard that occupies a space the size of half a football field—extraordinary to find in a city where the price of land is among the highest in the world. At one end of the yard are two large sandboxes, as well as several swing sets, slides, and a variety of climbing equipment. When bad weather prevents them from going out, the children at Takenoko can play in an auditorium large enough to accommodate activities like tag or soccer. The children also have a wide variety of materials for both indoor and outdoor play. In the outdoor play area, for example, they have an extensive collection of sand and water toys in addition to balls, hoops, stilts, and stationary play equipment. Their classroom contains fewer materials than would be found in many centers in the U.S., but far more than those available in most Japanese preschools. In addition to regular classroom materials, the school purchases extra materials and props for special occasions such as sports day.

In most preschools, children are required to come to school wearing blazers and hats that they exchange for a smock upon arrival. Sometimes

A boy receives help with Montessori materials from a parent volunteer in a preschool serving high-income families.

a full change of clothes is required—out of traveling clothes and into "at school" clothes. Most schools also require all children in a certain classroom to wear hats of a particular color. Thus a child is readily identified as a member of a certain school and, within the school, as a member of a certain class. Takenoko students, however, wear no school uniform. They are distinguished only by the small straw baskets they use to carry their lunch and other supplies; these baskets are quite different from the plastic satchels required by most schools. Takenoko has chosen to deviate from the norm in order to give children an opportunity to express themselves, according to the director. This policy may also signal that there is no need to protect children's clothing from the wear and tear of school life, since their parents can easily afford to replace play clothes that have become soiled or damaged.

Social Relations, School Readiness, and Self-Expression in the Context of Play

Ms. Sato, director of Takenoko, identified the following as the central objective of her program: helping children learn to form human relationships. She directly connects children's ability to express their own thoughts and feelings with their ability to relate well to others:

> We want children to develop an ability to understand others' feelings and to be honest enough to say: "I like you." Our overall objective is to help each child express himself well and also to be a helpful person and very compassionate.

Her strategy for fostering these social competencies is to allow as much free play as possible, with invisible but carefully planned guidance from the teachers. On three mornings each week, Kazuko attends a brief schoolwide meeting in which the children do morning exercises, sing, and listen to a brief message from the director about safety or upcoming events. The rest of the morning is spent playing, both indoors and outdoors. Ms. Sato is wary of introducing academic work in preschool. Many of the children at Takenoko Preschool attend lessons or enrichment classes after school, and Ms. Sato is concerned about putting too much pressure on her students:

> No matter how much we talk to mothers [about not signing their children up for after-school classes] they do it anyway. So we changed the *yōchien* to be a place where children can just play. The *yōchien* has always been a happy place, but when my parents ran it they not only allowed play but also did some teaching.

At Takenoko, even though there was no explicit emphasis on academic preparation, the children receive cognitive stimulation and academic readiness experiences in many of the everyday classroom activities. The teachers of four-year-olds design numerous literacy-based activities, encouraging the children to make Mother's Day cards, write down their wishes for the future, and read their lines when practicing for dramatic performances. The staff also embeds experiences with numbers into daily activities. Children were encouraged to count and use pretend money in the housekeeping area, for example, or to count items as they are being distributed by the teacher. The teachers felt that these enrichment experiences were acceptable as long as they remained fun for the children.

A graduate of a two-year junior college, Ms. Takahashi had been employed at Takenoko Preschool for five years. Most of the teachers had been at Takenoko for longer than the average tenure of a Japanese preschool teacher. Additionally, teachers at Takenoko stayed with their class for two years in order to build up a strong relationship with the children. The teachers at Takenoko had ample opportunity to interact with individual children because class size was small and because their time was less occupied with peripheral duties like cleaning or preparing materials than was the case for teachers in less affluent communities.

Strong Measures to Encourage Thoughtfulness and Independence

Kazuko, who is four years old, watches as a class of three-year-olds finishes relay race practice. There are seven classes at Takenoko, and next week each will be running in a relay race as well as performing musical numbers for their parents. Kazuko's class moves onto the yard to practice their performance. They arrange themselves in four long lines. Each child holds a brightly colored flag. A medley of Disney tunes blares from speakers positioned at the side of the yard, and the children run through a routine involving synchronized movement of the flags. The children perform the routine twice with few mistakes, prompting applause and praise from the classroom teacher, the head teacher, and the director. Kazuko stands quietly until the teacher announces that practice is over, and the children run to the sand area for a period of free play.[11]

After lunch, it is time for another practice session. This time, Kazuko's class is practicing for the relay race. A large oval race track has been marked out on the yard, with four lanes to accommodate the runners. The children line up and prepare to race. At a signal from the teacher, the first set of children takes off while their classmates cheer loudly. Several minutes later, the runners complete the circle and tag the next set, who take off to loud encouragement. But one boy breaks out of his lane and cuts across the inner portion of the oval, arriving at the track on the other side well ahead of his competitors. As he heads for the finish, the head teacher runs over to him, grabs him by the wrist, and yanks him to the sidelines. Then, as the other children run by, she joins them, taking the boy's place and leaving him behind. He stands there by himself for the remainder of the race.

Later, when asked about the boy's misbehavior, the head teacher gave the following account:

> He is a relatively capable child so he could see that the class was just rehearsing the relay race. He concluded that he did not have to take it seriously, unlike the other children who concluded that because the teachers are serious, they should be serious also. His actions made the other children uncertain about their positions. I decided that since he did it on purpose and it bothered others, I would have him watch and I would run the race in his place. Afterward I told him to tell his classroom teacher what had happened, but he did not. He finally realized that I had already spoken to his teacher, so he decided to give up and apologize. After school, his teacher brought him to me and said to him: "You have something to say." He said: "I will behave in a proper manner and will do my best tomorrow."

This example illustrates how seriously the teachers at Takenoko treated misbehavior involving intentional disruption of a class activity. This boy's misbehavior resulted in a variety of repercussions: being segregated from the others while the teacher finished for him, as well as being required to apologize to his classroom teacher and to the head teacher. These punishments were publicly administered and involved direct assertion of power by the staff. Other examples where teachers insisted upon firm adherence to established routines emerged throughout my observations at Takenoko. For example, at the end of the day, each child was required to present him or herself individually to the school director, bow, and bid her a formal goodbye. Children who bowed in a hurried, slipshod manner were required to keep trying until they performed it correctly. Like many of their colleagues in other preschools, the teachers at Takenoko felt that they had a special responsibility to provide this type of instruction in correct social comportment (*shitsuke*) because mothers seemed unwilling or unable to do so themselves.

Day's End

> When the race is over, the children return to their classroom and pre-pare to go home. They stand briefly around the piano and sing a few songs, concluding with a bow to the teacher and to the rest of the class. Forming a line at the door, they then march out to the foyer, where they again bow to the director and bid her farewell. The mothers are waiting on the gray tile floor. Kazuko changes her shoes and places them neatly in her cubbyhole. She greets her mother with a smile and the two set off down the hill toward home.

In summary, it is apparent that children at Takenoko received consistent, daily messages about their personal importance and uniqueness. Their individuality was accentuated by being allowed to wear their own clothes instead of uniforms. They were one of few—not one of many—by virtue of small class sizes. They were given much autonomy and had a wide range of choices when it came to selecting materials for play. Their teachers conversed with each of them at length, and praised their accomplishments. A sense of privilege and special status was conferred by the use of refined expressions and polite grammatical conventions.

However, the teachers were conscious of ensuring that their students do not become overly individualistic. Lest these experiences of choice and personal attention result in a self-centered or spoiled child, the teachers were painstaking in their efforts to teach children to think of others' feelings, to cooperate, and to follow along in group activities. Periods of free play and choice were punctuated by group activities in which they were expected to fall in with the rhythms of their classmates. Children who purposefully ignored the goals and processes of the group were dealt with forcefully. Overall, I would characterize this as a child-oriented program, with the exception of the more power assertive discipline style, which can perhaps be viewed as designed to offset the ill effects of children's receiving so much personal attention and material benefits.

A DAY IN THE LIFE OF AIKO AT
NADA PRESCHOOL

Aiko jumps back and forth over a small puddle in front of her mother's small beauty salon as she waits for her teacher to pick her up for preschool. She is dressed in the school uniform—a polyester navy-blue skirt and blazer. A few minutes later she spots Ms. Watanabe and several of her classmates moving slowly up the narrow winding street. She turns to wave goodbye to her mother, who is already shampooing her first client. Aiko's teacher greets her with a smile and motions for her to fall into line behind the other children. The little band of children continues past the restaurants, food stalls, and small shops that line this street in downtown Osaka. There are no sidewalks and the street is only one lane wide, so the children are careful to stay close to the buildings when a car passes by.

Within ten minutes they arrive at school. They pass through a gate into the play yard, which is separated from the street by a tall wall made of concrete and decorated with whimsical cartoon paintings of animals. The past several days of rain have created a small lake and many smaller puddles in the yard. The teacher walks carefully around the edge of the yard to avoid the water, and delivers the children to the door of the main school building, a two-story concrete structure built in the 1950s.

Aiko runs to her classroom, where she removes her blazer and dons a powder-blue smock. She puts away her bright yellow plastic satchel emblazoned with the school name. On a typical day, Aiko plays in her classroom or outside for an hour or so after her arrival. Two thirds of the children at Nada walk to school, either with their mothers or teachers, and the remaining third are brought in by bus. Because the bus makes several trips, the children arrive in waves between 9 and 10 A.M. Today, the bus has broken down, causing the teachers to delay the morning meeting until the last group arrives.

It is too wet to play outside, so Aiko remains in the classroom, which is crowded and noisy. Half of Aiko's classmates have arrived and are talking and playing in small groups. Ms. Watanabe is sewing costumes for the school play and occasionally raises her head from her work to quiet the children. Most of the classroom space is occupied by scuffed wooden tables arranged in three long lines. The walls are dirty; long jagged cracks in the drably painted concrete walls run from floor to ceiling. A smell of sewage wafts in from the bathroom down the hall. At one end of the room is the teacher's desk and an organ. There is a bookshelf and two crates, one filled with large plastic blocks and a second containing stuffed animals. There is no children's artwork on display in the classroom.

Aiko pauses briefly, deciding what to do. She runs to her cubby and removes a box with crayons, colored pencils, and clay. She brings the clay to her table, where five of her classmates are already occupied with clay or coloring. She spends the next 20 minutes working with the clay. Around her, the noise level rises. Several boys have made guns out of blocks and run around the room pretending to shoot each other. Other children watch them or stare into space.

Material Conditions at Nada

Overall, Nada Preschool is run-down and poorly maintained. The play yard is inaccessible during the rainy season, and there is no large indoor space for active play as there is at Takenoko. The classrooms are small and crowded and because there is no other indoor space available, children must spend most of their time sitting at their seats when the weather is bad. There is little in the way of play materials; aside from a few building blocks and stuffed animals, the children rely mainly upon pencils, paper, and clay for amusement. Instead of purchasing special materials for performances, the teachers are responsible for creating them by hand, which takes up much of their time. The bus service, although convenient for parents, extends the unstructured arrival and departure periods, and creates problems on the rare occasions when the

Free-play time at a school in a working-class neighborhood.

bus breaks down. While Nada appeared to be among the most impoverished schools that I visited, others also extended the arrival period over an hour or more to accommodate multiple bus trips to collect children in the morning. At Suma Preschool, for example, teachers did not come to school until the last wave of children had arrived. When some mothers expressed concern that their children were unsupervised at school for as long as one hour, the teachers began leaving written work for the early arrivers to complete while waiting for the others.

Teachers' Role in Guiding Social and Cognitive Development

At 10:30, the teacher of the other four-year-olds' class comes in and tells Ms. Watanabe that the teacher of the three-year-olds is sick and will not be coming to work. The four-year-olds' teachers will be responsible for supervising her class. Several minutes later half of the class of three-year-olds crowds into the room, each child carrying a wooden chair. Ms. Watanabe instructs them to place the chairs in pairs, and then tells them to get their art materials. The children return quickly with clay or crayons. Each child kneels in front of a chair and gets out something to do. For the next half an hour they remain kneeling in this fashion, drawing or playing with clay while talking with their partner at the adjoining chair.

It is after 11 when Ms. Watanabe puts aside her sewing and announces that it is time to practice their musical numbers for the upcoming *happiōkai* performance. *Happiōkai*, like sports day, is a common fixture of Japanese preschools; it offers an opportunity for children to perform a musical or other theatrical performance, or to display their artwork. Aiko's class will be performing two musical pieces. Ms. Watanabe retrieves a box of instruments—xylophones, triangles, and bells—from behind her desk and passes them out. Aiko takes the triangle she is handed and begins hitting it. When the teacher runs to the organ and plays a chord, the children quickly quiet down and, at a second chord, begin playing and singing. When they have finished, the teacher tells them they did well, and then plays a chord to begin the second song, this one unaccompanied by instruments. Aiko seems to remember her teacher's encouragement to sing the song in a lively manner, and competes with her classmates to see who can scream the loudest.

After lunch, which the children eat at their seats, it is still too wet to play outside. They again take out the blocks and stuffed animals, or their art materials. Ms. Watanabe sits at her desk with a tall stack of daily attendance books. As the noise level mounts, she methodically moves through the stack, stamping each child's book to document his or her attendance.

At 2 P.M., Ms. Watanabe finishes her paperwork. She announces to the class that it is time to prepare to go home. The children take off their smocks and put on their hats and coats. They sing three songs and end the school day with a group bow to the teacher and to each other. They rush down the stairs to the wet yard, where a cluster of mothers is waiting, some with bicycles. Aiko and the other children who walk home with their teacher line up behind Ms. Watanabe and they head out of the gate and down the street.

Children at Nada spent the majority of the day in free play with little supervision by adults. Their play was more free than that of the children at Takenoko because the teachers made little attempt to guide their social interactions; however, the limited space and materials available for free play constrained their activities. During my observations, teachers at Nada rarely spoke to individual children, and when they did, it was usually to reprimand a child who was seriously misbehaving. Rowdy behavior and aggression were usually ignored or quelled with a quick comment or directive. Most of the children at Nada appeared to go for the whole day without having a personal conversation with any of the teachers. Compared to the children at Takenoko, they received little explicit guidance or encouragement from the teachers in relation to their social interactions.

Although given a lot of time for free play, the children at Nada had few choices in terms of materials, and rarely seemed to engage in object- or teacher-mediated activities that offered cognitive challenges. During the time they spent drawing and involved in pretend play, there was no attempt by the teacher to extend their skills beyond the current level of functioning. In general, children at Nada were expected to get along without a lot of special attention.

The limited space and materials available at Nada clearly set limits on the types of activities that could occur there, but it could be a mistake to assume that the curriculum as described was solely a function of material constraints. The nature of daily activities at Nada appeared somewhat—but not entirely—congruent with the ideas of its director. In our conversations, Mr. Kumamoto emphasized the importance he placed on the development of social relationships. He argued that "developing children's human relationships" was the most crucial goal of preschool, and one that was particularly important for most Japanese. He focused on the importance of helping children develop a capacity for deep feelings as well as the ability to express them, and wanted them to develop "a mind filled with empathy." He expected that children would derive these skills from membership in the preschool community. He noted that, unlike other directors, he limited enrollment at his school to 150 students so that he could come to know each child personally. He expressed a feeling of deep connection to the neighborhood where he had spent his personal and professional life, and he expressed his pride in the long-standing relationships he had formed with resident families.

What distinguished his philosophy from the views of the staff at Takenoko was not the goals themselves, but the manner and intensity with which he approached them. When asked about the ministry's emphasis on individualized instruction, Mr. Kumamoto shrugged somewhat dismissively and responded: "I ask the teacher to try to promote individualism. To achieve this end . . . teachers should try to find each individual child's strengths as well as weaknesses, and they provide suggestions appropriate for each individual child." This type of encouragement was far from evident during my observation, and, although his words were supportive of individualization, the lack of enthusiasm in his response suggested to me that this was not a strongly held priority. Faced with large classes and little materials, it would in any case be very difficult for the teachers to carry out these general guidelines.[12]

Another clear difference between Takenoko and Nada concerned the role of the school in promoting children's cognitive development and future school achievement. In our conversation, Mr. Kumamoto expressed disagreement with the practice of cognitive stimulation, which he found prominent among the preschools he has visited in the United States and Europe. Although familiar with the ideas of famous early childhood educator Friedrich Wilhelm Froebel, whose portrait hung in his office, he preferred not to introduce young children to "intellectual matters," predicting that young children who were pushed into cognitive activities would rebel against the teachers or lose confidence in themselves. As he put it, "I should not pick the loquat before it is ripe." Mr. Kumamoto drew a firm distinction between the interests and capabilities of adults and those of children. He believed it best for children to be *kodomo-rashii* ("childlike"), and felt it was unrealistic to expect them to engage in serious conversations or be interested in adult matters. At Takenoko, the staff also took a developmental stance but believed that activities could be developed, in the area of literacy for example, that were appropriate for children of preschool age.

CONCLUSION

These two case studies are suggestive of the socialization that occurs in preschools serving wealthy children and working-class children. Observations in two other preschools (Fukui and Okayama) serving elite families revealed similar characteristics to those noted at Takenoko. Each of the two preschools is private and located in an exclusive suburban area. Like Takenoko, they feature extensive landscaped grounds, spacious buildings, low student-teacher ratios, and abundant materials. Both schools focus the curriculum on social and emotional development, partly in recognition of the fact that the children are exposed to music lessons and sports during private lessons in the afternoon. Staff at both schools discussed at length the ways in which they attempted to give children opportunities for personal expression and free choice while helping them develop sensitivity to others and an ability to get along smoothly in groups. And when children misbehaved in a way that seemed to stem from being self-centered, the staff at these schools acted forcefully to counteract the misbehavior.

I classified Takenoko and Fukui as child-oriented. They had the resources necessary to provide extensive materials for free play and they could limit the number of children in each classroom, thus making it possible for each child to receive individual attention from the teacher. They offered relatively high salaries, which enticed teachers to stay longer, enabling the children to form long-lasting relationships with their teachers.

However, not all the exclusive schools were child-centered. In particular, I noticed variation in the amount of pressure children in exclusive schools received to conform to group norms. At Okayama, the director spoke forcefully about the importance of teaching children not to be a bother to others (*meiwaku*), and his wife mentioned mild corporal punishment as an occasionally needed tactic. As detailed earlier, a child at Okayama who demanded more milk than his share was scolded and forced to apologize for his selfishness. Additionally, while the physical site was relatively spacious and materials were abundant at Okayama, they were not set up for free play; instead, the day was structured around group experiences such as completing art projects in which everyone was expected to construct a product based on a model provided by the teacher. I classified Okayama as a relationship-oriented school.

Preschools that I visited in lower-income neighborhoods experienced some of the same problems as did Nada. In one facility in central Osaka, children spent their days in small, dark rooms that were virtually devoid of any materials. Staff did their best to keep the children occupied, but expressed frustration at their inability to address the many psychological problems they perceived among their students, problems that they believed to stem from living in cramped apartments with mothers who often felt isolated, depressed, anxious, or angry.

The relatively low level of cognitive stimulation found at Nada was also characteristic of another small private preschool in a working-class neighborhood, where many children spent the larger part of a day watching others practice for an upcoming performance. The teachers at that school expressed concern about the long periods of relative inactivity, but felt that unless the school was able to reduce class size they would never be able to provide a program that afforded consistent, ongoing stimulation.

These low-income schools illustrate how closely resource issues are intertwined with philosophical matters. At Takenoko, the abundant space and low teacher-student ratio made it possible to elaborate and deepen the child-oriented philosophy, whereas at Nada, the crowded conditions and deteriorating school were surely major obstacles that discouraged staff from moving toward the stated goal of giving children individual attention and encouraging self expression. I would say that Nada was relationship-oriented, although the program was so minimal that it appeared unlikely to fulfill its goals of helping children deepen their social relationships. The role-oriented schools served some working-class families as well; as I mentioned in Chapter 4, parents who are on the borderline of the middle class may have viewed these schools as a way to boost their children's later school achievement and hence their subsequent employment opportunities. Thus a family's social-class position may have served to limit the range of programs available but did not definitively determine the nature of the program attended.

These data also illustrate the way in which collective values such as cooperation and mutual obligation have persisted in Japan subsequent to its becoming a wealthy, highly industrialized, urban country. Some theories predict that if a society sheds its rural, agricultural structure, it will begin to devalue collective responsibilities and emphasize individual freedom. At preschools like Takenoko, however, staff sought a precarious balance—hoping to foster self-fulfillment while also strengthening feelings of collective obligation. Psychologist Çiğdem Kağitçibaşi (1990) finds that this is a characteristic pattern among modern urban elites in societies that have traditionally held strong collective values. According to Kağitçibaşi, families adhering to this pattern are less embedded in strong community or kin networks than are those in traditional societies, and assume that children will eventually live independent lives rather than dedicate themselves to the financial and emotional support of their parents. However, parents in this pattern do not adopt the individualistic orientation of Western industrial nations. Rather, they attempt to strike a balance between family loyalties and individual loyalties, blending acceptance of children's autonomy with firm control over their behavior. The staff at Takenoko and other schools in wealthy areas appeared to be expressing similar goals to the elite families described by Kağitçibaşi.

Takenoko and Nada can serve—to an extent—as examples of how schools can help reproduce class structure through the types of competencies that they encourage children to obtain (see also discussion in

Joffe, 1977). At Takenoko, the teachers (who themselves tended to be from privileged backgrounds) provided children with abundant opportunities for self-direction by interacting extensively with them and letting them determine their own involvement in activities. Children who have these experiences can be expected to develop skills that are needed in fulfilling the requirements of middle-class and professional occupations. At Nada, the opportunities for self-direction are limited by the small space and meager assortment of materials. Children learn to tolerate and adapt to an imposed structure rather than express their personal views and desires; these competencies may prove helpful for survival in working-class jobs that afford little opportunity for personal direction and little cognitive stimulation, but may limit a person's ability to gain access to the middle class, a goal for many families.

7

SHINTO, BUDDHIST, AND CHRISTIAN PRESCHOOLS

Shinto, Buddhism, and Christianity have been intertwined for over a century in Japan, creating a rich tapestry of spiritual and philosophical thought that has had a profound impact on the nature of preschools.[13] For a sense of how these distinct ideologies are intermingled, imagine Tokyo in 1870, the year William Elliot Griffis, fresh from the Rutgers Theological Seminary in Philadelphia, arrived by ship to effect the spiritual salvation of the Japanese people. Only two years earlier, Japan had ended 250 years of isolation and was in the throes of appreciation for the "civilization and enlightenment" (*bunmei kaika*) that Japanese then associated with the West. At that time, Shinto, with its focus on the multitude of divine spirits that inhabit both living and inanimate objects, had been practiced alongside Buddhism for over a thousand years.

As he settled into his new life in Tokyo, Griffis became enthralled with the people he encountered. Unlike many of his American counterparts, he reacted with interest to the rituals of Shinto, and within a year of arriving in Japan he also found himself thanking the Lord for creating Buddhism, with "its humane creed of brotherly kindness and charity and its solid foundation of immutable morals" (quoted in Rosenstone, 1988, p. 107). As time passed, Griffis became increasingly uncertain about the benefits that Christianity might confer

137

upon the Japanese, writing: "It gives one solemn pause to think that along with the many luxuries and unnecessary extravagances that attend the solid blessings of the Christian civilization, there must also come fearful evils and sorrows that these simple people never before knew" (p. 103).

During the years subsequent to the forced opening of Japan by Commodore Matthew Perry, Christian missionaries like Griffis attempted to gain a foothold in the country. Protestant missionaries were allowed to reside in the four ports open to foreign commerce, but faced hostility from the government, which had prohibited Christianity among its own citizens throughout most of the preceding Tokugawa period. During the 1890s, an antiforeigner, anti-Christian resurgence resulted in new restrictions in travel and residency, and foreign missionaries found few Christian converts. Christianity also lost favor due to divisiveness among the denominations; this plurality was inconsistent with the dominant push of the times, which was for establishing national unity via centralized religion.

PRESCHOOLS AND RELIGION IN HISTORICAL PERSPECTIVE

The first few preschools in Japan were established by the Ministry of Education subsequent to the introduction of the modern national education system in 1872. The Fundamental Code of Education of the time reflected the liberal orientation of the early Meiji government, stressing the individualistic nature and the personal benefits of learning (Wollons, 1993). Both private and public preschools were based upon the German kindergarten idea, which also espoused the principle of individual development. Christian missionaries were involved in the preschool movement from its earliest days, having learned that Japanese citizens perceived value in educational institutions established by Westerners (Reischauer, 1981). Several Christian preschools were established in the 1890s; the best-known is Glory (*Shoei*) Kindergarten, which was founded by Annie Howe along with a teacher training school (Wollons, 1993). Howe's preschool followed the philosophy of Froebel, a German educator who is generally credited as the "father of the kindergarten." His philosophy was a synthesis of the ideas of other early philosophers and educators such as Rousseau, Pestalozzi, and Comenius, along with his own experiences and religious views (Beatty, 1995; Spodek et al., 1991). The basic emphasis was on the fundamental unity of all living things, including humans, nature, and God. The curriculum Froebel developed was intended to aid children in their play activities as well as to teach the concept of unity among nature.

Howe gradually adapted Froebel's ideas to fit the Japanese context (Shirakawa, 1996; Wollons, 1993). She translated his primary text into Japanese, commissioning an artist to redraw the illustrations so as to depict Japanese people in familiar settings. While initially holding firm to the views and practices of the Congregational Church, she eventually agreed to acknowledge Japanese national holidays and permit a picture of the emperor in the classroom. Her influence was magnified as many of the Japanese teachers who had attended her teacher training program went on to establish their own preschools.

However, the conservatives in power during the 1890s began to resist the wholesale adoption of Howe's ideas, favoring instead moral education emphasizing filial piety, loyalty, physical training, and patriotism. In 1899, religious instruction by Christians and Buddhists was formally banned in the schools, an action designed to increase the influence of the state-sponsored form of Shinto. Although severely disadvantaged, many religious schools managed to remain in business.

The political tide shifted again during the progressive Taisho era, which began in 1912, and with it came a growing diversity in the preschool curriculum. In 1926, an imperial ordinance gave each preschool the freedom to determine its own curriculum (Shwalb et al., 1992). Many took the opportunity to introduce the newly developed Montessori method as well as the ideas of John Dewey. Religious organizations were able to move more openly into the market, and in 1929, the Japanese Buddhist Nursery and Kindergarten Association (Nihon Bukkyo Hoiku Kyōkai) was founded to support "the improvement and development of preschool education for infants and children" (Japan Buddhist Nursery and Kindergarten Association, 1998).

With the end of the Taisho era, nationalistic sentiment again picked up, resulting in another swing toward a national curriculum emphasizing patriotism and moral education. Preschools and child-care centers were converted into "war time day nurseries" which operated year-round to care for the children whose mothers were involved in industrial production (Shwalb et al., 1992). Following Japan's defeat in World War II, preschools were again placed under the Ministry of Education, which published guidelines "reflecting U.S. rather than Japanese values and philosophy (e.g., to foster individuality through free play)" (Shwalb et al., 1992, p. 335). Subsequent revisions of the guidelines will be be discussed in Chapter 8 in the context of comparing public and private preschools.

In contemporary times, it is rather difficult to know how many preschools are deeply religious. Many preschools that are housed on the grounds of religious organizations do not themselves espouse religious views (Tobin et al., 1989); in these cases, the motivation for running a preschool is primarily financial. Fully 40 percent of Buddhist temples raise funds through nonreligious activities, and running a preschool is one of the most common of these activities. Some Buddhist directors are members of the Buddhist Nursery and Kindergarten Association; this association reports membership of 598 child-care centers and 763 preschools (Japan Buddhist Nursery and Kindergarten Association, 1998). Many Buddhist temples with preschools are not members of this organization, however. The total number of Christian preschools is easier to determine; figures from 1990 show that there were 1,636 Christian preschools in Japan, of which two thirds were Protestant and one third Catholic; this represents slightly more than 10 percent of preschools, which numbered 14,988 in 1990 (Christianity Almanac, 1990).[14]

This chapter is built upon the comments of directors and teachers from four Buddhist preschools, four Christian preschools (Catholic and Presbyterian), and two Shinto preschools. In all of the religion-affiliated preschools I visited, the directors professed an explicit link between their faith and the curriculum of the preschool.[15] My observations confirmed that the children in all these preschools engaged in overtly religious practices, although there was quite a bit of variation in the depth and breadth of these activities. The Christian preschools, for example, included a daily morning prayer and a prayer before and after meals. Attending a church service of some kind once a week was common. At Christmas, they engaged in a number of religious activities, including a reenactment of the Nativity.

While they may represent a minority, preschools affiliated with religious organizations are very interesting because they set in relief certain cultural models that are represented—often in diluted form—in nonreligious preschools as well. It is simply inevitable that religious beliefs that have existed in a society for well over a thousand years—in the case of Shinto and Buddhism—will have permeated people's thinking about the nature of children and their care, and are thus manifest in nonreligious as well as religious organizations. The director of a public preschool director in downtown Osaka may not have attributed the presence of the school's aviary, rabbit hutch, and goat pen to Shinto views of nature, but her ideas about what the children learned from caring for these animals was quite similar to the views of a Shinto priest who referred explicitly to the divine nature of living creatures.

A PRESBYTERIAN PRESCHOOL IN KOBE

Arima Preschool is located in an old neighborhood of downtown Kobe. Along the narrow streets, traditional wooden houses with tile roofs are interspersed with new structures made of concrete. At the street level many small shops jostle for space—fishmongers, tofu stands, and fruit-and-vegetable sellers are crammed together on tiny lots. As I arrive at the school, the director is standing in front of the Presbyterian church of which he is the minister. He leads my colleague and I through the front yard of the small church and into the preschool playground. On one side of the yard stands the simple, one-story, 1950s-era building that houses three classrooms. Since the weather is warm, the large sliding doors that form one wall of each classroom are open, and each of the three teachers is standing in front of her classroom, smiling broadly, awaiting our arrival. We are then ushered into a classroom, where we begin the visit with tea and conversation with the director.

In our conversation, Mr. Kobayashi explained that his preschool was very small—only 55 children in three classrooms. The school could accommodate more students, but there is not a lot of demand because the number of young children in central Kobe is declining as more and more families move to the suburbs. While Mr. Kobayashi would welcome the opportunity to serve more students, he also acknowledged that small class sizes were compatible with the objectives of his school.

Children of God: Balancing Individual Expression and Social Commitments

Mr. Kobayashi built his preschool program around the view that God's love is the primary message of Christianity. According to him and other Christian administrators, because children are a gift from God, each one should be deeply appreciated (*hitori hitori o taisetsu ni*). For example, Ms. Watanabe, director of Hikari Preschool, expressed the following sentiment:

> Jesus Christ delivered God's message of love. The love of God means that God loves each individual child. Each individual child is precious because he or she is a gift sent by God. Through his or her parents, each individual child is delivered by God. We sincerely appreciate God's production of children.

For these directors, one way of respecting the individual was to allow children considerable freedom to decide what they wanted to do and when they wanted to do it. Accordingly, free play formed the basis of the curriculum. Mr. Kobayashi reported that, as he came to realize the fundamental importance of self-determination in Western religious thought, he became more and more convinced that it was essential to avoid teacher-centered activities:

> We respect children's spontaneous activity (*jihatsuteki kōdō*). In the past, the children went to the chapel once a week to pray. They had to walk with their hands folded. It was teacher centered, and the adults ordered the children around. The children tried to respond properly. I decided to change that atmosphere. I didn't like it because . . . the teacher's desire was different from the desires of the children. If the children aren't paying attention during a story it means it is not interesting to them—and the teacher shouldn't just tell them to be quiet.

Mr. Kobayashi's cautious rebellion against a regimented, authoritarian approach was echoed in the animus other Christian directors expressed toward certain elements of Japanese society. In particular, some found fault with what they perceived as an overemphasis on accommodating to the group. For example, Ms. Watanabe expressed her concern about Japanese people who seem to lack a personal moral compass:

> After all, Japanese society is group-oriented as a background to the culture. If you are the same as others, you feel secure. But you might lose something important. In reality this happened in the course of history. Children should grow in a way that enables them to judge what is right.

Christians have had a long history of struggle in Japan. While they no longer experience active discrimination, as they did in the nineteenth century, they remain somewhat marginalized in Japanese society. In light of their experiences as "outsiders," as well as the moral lessons embodied in Christian doctrine, it is not surprising that Christian educators are attuned to such notions as respect for the individual rights of each child (Reischauer, 1981). In Japanese Christian preschools, the staff who were oriented toward individualism did not reject the importance of learning how to be a group member but felt that, in the context of Japan, sensitivity to the individual child tends to be overlooked. Not surprisingly, therefore, all the Christian preschools that I visited were child-centered (as described in Chapter 5).

In addition to providing children with opportunities for self-directed activities, teachers arranged group experiences to help them develop a sense of shared community. On the day I visited Arima, Ms. Nagatomi facilitated a class meeting for the purpose of discussing each child's "junk art" project. This carefully conducted discussion is consistent with the Arima philosophy of paying attention to the individual child in order to help him or her develop an awareness of others and obtain skills in interacting with them:

Each child had spent an hour or more working with tape, glue, scissors, and a large array of discarded household objects to construct some sort of project. After a break for active, outdoor play, the children returned to the classroom and sat in a circle as Ms. Nagatomi moved around the room, picking up each project and engaging the children in a discussion about it. The projects were imaginative and intricate: a peacock whose tail could stand up when pulled with an attached string; a cardboard jewelry box with tissue paper cut into small squares and pasted to resemble stained glass; a serving of assorted sushi, complete with rosette of ginger and a wedge of plastic grass. Ms. Nagatomi asked each child to describe his or her creation. Then she explored the properties and features of each project. Picking up a box containing a seated clay figure, she learned from Junko, its creator, that it was a man taking a bath. She commented on how skillfully Junko had painted the outside of the box to look like wood, adding to the class: "I was surprised to see that the inside was a different color, weren't you?" She then asked whether Junko had thought about adding anything else to signify the presence of water in the bath. Junko said she hadn't been able to think of anything. Ms. Nagatomi asked: "Anyone have any ideas for Junko?" Several children gave some ideas, including cutting up plastic straws into small pieces, or using strips of blue paper. She asked the class to think about which of these options would be better. They preferred the idea of strips of paper, and Junko nodded in agreement.

This use of group time to discuss children's projects resembles the practices described by Kotloff (1993) in her ethnography of a Japanese Christian preschool, where staff "designed an innovative curriculum that uses group and individual activities to build a supportive classroom group fostering the growth and creativity of each child" (p. 19). As in the child-oriented schools in my sample, the teachers observed by Kotloff "moved about the room playing with the children, answering their questions, helping them select an activity, listening to their explanations and plans, and providing them with materials and supplies." Then, in a class meeting after the projects were completed, the teacher asked certain children to describe their creations, how they were made, and any difficulties they had encountered. Kotloff conveys clearly the teachers' skill in drawing the other children into the discussion. Her description aptly characterizes the techniques used by Ms. Nagatomi as well:

> The teacher tried to ensure that each child received positive feedback from his or her classmates. She modeled appropriate behaviors by listening intently to each child's presentation. . . . Through her enthusiastic tone of voice and obvious interest, she conveyed respect for the child's work. She tried to sustain the listening children's attention and involvement by asking for their questions and comments. In addition, rather than directing her praise to the presenting child, she praised the child's work to the group and tried to elicit their agreement by saying, for example, "This is great, isn't it !" "This was done so prettily, wasn't it, with black crayon, then yellow crayon. . . ." This practice not only focused the children's attention on the positive aspects of their classmate's work but gave the impression that the teacher was acting as the group spokesperson, expressing *their* positive appraisal, not merely her own. (p. 22)

Ms. Nagatomi and the other teachers at Arima were interested in nurturing the children's imagination and self-expression, both artistic and verbal, but were careful to balance this focus on the individual with attention to how the children interacted in the group context. As Ms. Nagatomi expressed it:

> Three-year-olds just tend to put a couple of boxes side by side and say, "That's it." . . . But only they themselves know what they are making. Then they realize that others may see their creations differently. They realize the importance of how the other party sees their productions. Through the creation of a work [of art] they learn to develop a common understanding (*kyōtsū rikai*). This is my goal. . . . Instead of one child learning a particular subject, we try to involve all the children in the shared learning.

In their attempts to identify opportunities for developing children's empathy and skill in working harmoniously with others, teachers at Christian schools were particularly welcoming of children with disabilities because they felt it was valuable for the nondisabled children to encounter someone who had characteristics that differed quite saliently from their own. As a teacher at Arima said:

> As you may have noticed, we have a handicapped child in the class. I pay particular attention to that child, but I also ask other children, "Please help him while I am working with these other children." At first his learning or working speed was very different from the others. Because of that he had difficulty in getting along with them. Gradually, however, he became involved with other children. In that process, the children came to understand each individual's differences and started to acknowledge each individual's characteristics. I think this process applies to children's mutual interactions in general.

LEARNING ABOUT WESTERN THEORIES OF EARLY-CHILDHOOD EDUCATION

Perhaps because of their understanding of Western religious beliefs, the directors of Christian preschools appeared more interested in learning about and adapting Western theories of early-childhood education than were directors in other preschools I visited. For example, a number of Catholic preschools in Japan use the Montessori method, as do many American Catholic preschools. I visited one Catholic preschool where all the teachers were Montessori-certified. The school boasted a very complete set of Montessori materials. The teachers interacted with children in the approved Montessori manner, offering short lessons to individuals or small groups who appeared ready to engage in new types of "work." Because the Montessori curriculum provides for instruction in literacy and mathematics, the children were exposed to these topics much earlier than children at Arima, where teachers preferred to leave these subjects to the elementary schools.

At Aizawa, another Christian preschool, the staff was in the midst of implementing a constructivist curriculum focused on emergent literacy. Ms. Ishida, the director at Aizawa, had sought wide exposure to Western theories of early childhood education. Although the major emphasis of her training at a local Christian college had been on the methods of Froebel, she had also pursued coursework on the Montessori method and had attended workshops on how to support emergent literacy by infusing the environment with print and by creating opportunities to experiment with writing.

The classrooms at Aizawa reflected Ms. Ishida's insights concerning emergent literacy. In each room, children's artwork was displayed along with written narratives describing the artist's vision. Activities on the day I visited were imbued with opportunities to build literacy skills. The four-year-old children were making vegetable soup using a recipe that featured written directions accompanied by pictures. The five-year-old children were recreating their experience at a summer fair. They constructed food stalls and activity booths from large cardboard boxes. Their writing skills came into play as they created signs, menus, price lists, and other artifacts.

Although these practices for encouraging early literacy are fairly common in the United States, they are not at all widespread in Japan. Ms. Ishida reported that at first she had a "guilty conscience" about implementing these new ideas:

A student preparing vegetable soup at a Christian preschool. The recipe on the wall gives instructions using pictures and simple language.

> What I was instructed to do [in college] is different from what chil-
> dren are actually doing and want to do. If children have a desire to
> learn literacy, I think we should teach them, even three-year-olds, if
> we do it in a good way. These things can be incorporated into
> play. . . . We hesitated very much initially. We did not find this
> answer soon. We were gradually convinced that we were not wrong.

My primary purpose in conducting this research was to obtain a
descriptive account of the views motivating directors rather than to
evaluate them. However, I would certainly say that Japanese Christian
schools provide many instances of good practice for those American
educators who also endorse this particular constellation of social,
personal, and cognitive goals.[16] It is not surprising that the more positive accounts of Japanese preschools in the academic literature have
often focused partly or exclusively on Christian schools (e.g., Kotloff,
1993). If I had to select one type of Japanese school that would best
exemplify excellence to "mainstream" American early-childhood edu-

cators, it would be these Christian preschools. The strategies the teachers use to implement Christian views concerning the importance of the individual along with Japanese cultural models pertaining to harmonious social relations are very powerful. In the Japanese Christian schools—as in American child-centered facilities—social development and personal development are seen as intertwined. Children who come to respect others are believed to be learning something about themselves as well, and at the same time, children who demonstrate a sense of confidence and security are thought to be better prepared to engage in social relations.

As American preschool teachers experience increasing pressure to focus on cognitive objectives, they receive less encouragement to work with children on the social and emotional skills deemed so important in the past. The Japanese Christian preschools may help remind Americans of the benefits of a holistic approach, even as preparation for later schooling becomes the salient purpose of early childhood education.

SHINTO PRESCHOOLS

History of Shintoism and Buddhism in Japan

The first signs of Shinto practice in Japan date from the Yayoi period, which began in 250 B.C. During this time, there appeared to be a coalescence of diverse religious elements within the various groups inhabiting Japan. Prominent among their views was the belief in divine spirits, or *kami*. The term *kami* is often translated as "gods," but a more thorough definition of this complex term is provided by Tsuda (1966, in Kitagawa, 1987, p. 44): "[*Kami*] may be interpreted as a material thing or an embodied spirit possessing some kind of divine potency, or as a non-corporeal spirit, in either case believed to possess an intrinsic magic power, or established as an object of worship." The corporeal objects viewed as *kami* are certain physical elements such as fire and stone, certain animals, the sun and moon, and man-made objects such as swords and mirrors. The noncorporeal *kami* include any element with strong power over nature or humans. From this early period, particular *kami* were singled out for veneration—Mount Fuji is one salient example.

Shinto has always had a strong association with the Japanese state and is generally considered a belief system rather than a religion per se. Sacred texts dating from the subsequent Kofun period, which lasted until 550 A.D., describe the role of the *kami* in the creation of the Japanese nation (Kitagawa, 1987). The political structure during the Kofun period consisted of a confederation of clans (*uji*) which performed social, economic, political, military, and religious functions. Each clan was identified with a particular *kami,* whose needs were attended to by the clan leader. The basic rituals developed during the Kofun era are still associated with Shinto practice, including purification, presenting offerings, petitioning the *kami* with prayers, and participating in sacred movements (Nelson, 1996).

During the fifth century A.D., increased contact with China and Korea brought Buddhism to Japan. Although Buddhism was flexible enough to intermingle with indigenous belief systems, there was tension between the universalistic orientation of Buddhism and those Shinto beliefs that pertained directly to the Japanese nation. One function of Shinto was to uphold the imperial family's right to rule Japan by virtue of its direct connection to the *kami* who created the universe. Rulers during that period attempted to balance the two belief systems (as well as Confucianism), but ultimately Shinto emerged as the more powerful force. While the more subtle nuances of Buddhism were lost on average Japanese citizens, who rarely had access to Buddhist writings in Japanese, they appreciated the emphasis on providing them with spiritual and material benefits in the here and now, as well as in their lives to come. Shinto and Buddhism continued to influence each other through the sixteenth century, resulting in several new schools of Buddhism in which the notion of *kami* was fused with their divine Buddhist counterparts.

Throughout the ensuring Edo period, the relative power of Buddhist and Shinto groups waxed and waned with the shifting of political alliances. By the 1600s Buddhist clerics had gained significant power by allying with the Tokugawa leaders. All households were required to register with a Buddhist temple, effectively putting the Buddhist priests in charge of "thought control" (Kitagawa, 1987, p. 161). This system was used to combat the influence of Catholic missionaries, particularly the Jesuits who had begun arriving in the 1500s. The Shinto notion of the emperor's divine ancestry was also used by the Tokugawa shoguns, who maintained national peace for 250 years by tightly controlling the numerous feudal overlords. Eventually, the National Learning Movement (*kokugaku*) attempted to create a "pure" Shinto that emphasized Japanese history and language, and expunged Confucian and Buddhist thinking. These increasingly nationalistic allies collaborated in the overthrow of the Tokugawa government in the late 1800s, replacing it with Meiji leaders who swore their allegiance to the emperor rather than the shogun.

The Meiji government acted to weaken Buddhism further, removing all Buddhist priests to secular life or reinstalling them as Shinto priests and destroying many Buddhist temples. To bolster the power of the emperor, the government established State Shinto, a nonreligious cult that featured ethnocentric patriotism, emperor worship, and inculcation of a moral code based loosely upon Confucian values. State Shinto continued to serve the purposes of the imperialist, nationalistic government throughout the early part of the twentieth century, culminating in World War II. In the mandatory reforms subsequent to Japan's defeat, Shinto was deprived of its privileged association with the government. The principle of religious freedom was upheld, and the emperor was declared to be mortal rather than divine. While initially shunned in the postwar years because of its connection to the government, Shinto has largely regained its reputation and remains the largest single (quasi-) religious institution in Japan, with more than 90,000 registered shrines (Nelson, 1996). Many people who are not officially associated with Shinto participate in Shinto rituals, whether it is the blessing of a new car or visiting a shrine to pray for good luck on school examinations (Nelson, 1996).

A Visit to the Shrine

The children in the Wisteria class of Bunka Preschool stand quietly under the big trees that shade the entry to a Shinto shrine in downtown Osaka. They stare solemnly at a large statue of a ferocious guard dog and a painting of the twelve animals of the zodiac. The overhang of the tile roof creates deep shade, making it difficult to see through the small passageway into the building. Moments pass and nothing happens. The yard, filled with over a hundred preschoolers, is completely silent. Then a solitary drum begins to beat, followed by the quavering trill of a Japanese flute. Out of the shrine bursts a tall figure clothed in a bright gold brocade robe and purple silk pants. On his feet are black patent leather shoes with a platform heel, and on his head is an elaborate black hat secured under his chin with a gold cord. He carries a long stick, from the end of which dangle white streamers. He waves the stick back and forth and, turning abruptly, strides back inside the shrine. The sound of chanting filters out of the shrine, filling the cool November air. No one moves; no one speaks.

After a few minutes the chanting ceases, and the berobed figure once more appears. This time, he walks softly and his face is composed in a gentle, relaxed smile. The children now recognize the familiar face of the mild-mannered director of their preschool. He explains to the children: "I dress this way in order to talk to the gods. I am asking them to be sure you are healthy and grow up nicely. Now, you will each get a souvenir gift from one of the room mothers. Please do not open them until you get home." The children chatter excitedly, and line up in front of two women who hand out plastic bags containing several carefully wrapped gifts for each child.

The Christian and Buddhist preschool directors articulated many clear connections between their respective religious orientations and their preschool programs. In the case of Shinto, on the other hand, the implications for preschool education seemed more nebulous.

At a local shrine, children receive a blessing from the director of their preschool, who is also a Shinto priest. This activity is part of the 7–5–3 celebration.

Shinto is not a complex religion with an elaborate philosophical base. Furthermore, in the years subsequent to World War II, it has undergone significant transformations in the process of detaching itself from the political authority of the state. However, aspects of Shinto are woven throughout the fabric of Japanese society and many common preschool practices can be traced to Shinto beliefs. By looking carefully at Shinto preschools, where these elements are present in their most conscious form, we can get a better sense of how these elements operate in their implicit guise in non-Shinto preschools as well.

In the preschools I visited, two aspects of Shinto were identified by the directors as affecting their programs: appreciation for nature, and observance of traditional Japanese festivals and ceremonies. In addition to these two factors, a third element appeared to me to characterize the directors of Shinto preschools: a desire to strengthen the children's feeling of connection to their local community.

Appreciation for Nature

In Japanese art and literature, nature is a common theme. Japanese appreciation for nature extends not only to sacred sites such as Mount Fuji but also to ordinary animals such as insects. This sensitivity is rooted in the Shinto belief that divine spirits, or *kami*, reside in these elements of nature. The Buddhist appreciation for living creatures is consistent with this orientation as well.

In the Shinto preschools I visited, directors emphasized the importance of exposing children to plants and animals. They believed that by caring for living things, children develop a sensitivity to plants and animals and, by extension, to human beings as well. Bunka Preschool, located in the center of urban Osaka, is home to an extensive menagerie. A large aviary on the playground houses more than ten different kinds of birds, as well as several rabbits and guinea pigs. On the school grounds there is also a variety of fruit trees, a vegetable plot, and a flower garden. The importance accorded these living things is best illustrated in the booklet describing the preschool, of which a full 25 pages are devoted to captioned photos of the school's animals and plants. Each page features four or five photos of a particular bird, animal, or plant. Even the string bean plant merits close-up photos of the beans in different stages of development as well as a drawing of the outside and inside of a bean pod.

Many of the special activities that I observed at Bunka revolved around nature. One day I watched the children pick over a thousand persimmons from the school's trees. The teachers and office staff spent all afternoon and much of the night peeling the persimmons and tying them to strings which were then suspended from the roof all along the edge of the veranda. The effect was dramatic when the children entered the yard the next day and saw bright orange curtains of persimmons transforming the familiar building. Following tradition, the persimmons were left to dry naturally in the open air. When they had become sweet and were ready to be eaten, the dried persimmons were sent home with the children. The children at Bunka also went on many seasonal forays into the countryside for picnics, sweet-potato digging, tangerine picking, leaf and acorn collecting, and grape picking. A highlight of the year for the five-year-olds was an overnight excursion to the school's cabin in the mountains.

Observance of Traditional Festivals and Rituals

As Nelson (1996) notes, the marking of special occasions is an important feature of Japanese society: "Of all the aspects of Japan that are stereotyped in the West . . . one of the cultural traits actually deserving a certain fame is the Japanese love for formal recognition of events. Whether it is starting kindergarten, buying a new car, joining a company, or getting married, a formalized acknowledgment of significant moments and transitions is deeply a part of what it means to be Japanese" (p. 34). The Shinto priest plays a large role in all of these special ceremonies, and in Shinto preschools, the children and staff more fully celebrate the traditional festivals and ceremonies than do the secular schools. On *Shichi-Go-San* Day, for example, when Japanese children who are three, five, or seven years old dress up in traditional clothing and visit a shrine with their families, the Shinto preschools may further mark this day by taking the three- and five-year-old students to participate in additional special ceremonies at the shrine. Other cultural events emphasized by the Shinto schools include the creation of an elaborately decorated portable shrine (*mikoshi*) that is traditionally carried through the streets during festivals. In the Bunka literature for parents of prospective students, a picture shows the children, clad in shorts and vividly patterned *happi* coats, bearing a child-sized *mikoshi*. The caption reads, "Even though it rained, we persevered!"

A special feature of the Bunka preschool is that the affiliated shrine is the home base for a school of *sumo* wrestlers. The training facility includes housing for the wrestlers, a practice ring, a kitchen for preparing the rich stew that is the staple of their diet, and a specially designed bath that can accommodate four of the large fellows at a time. The school sponsors a special day when the wrestlers pit themselves against the children in tug-of-war and other games. The wrestlers also appear again at graduation day, when a *sumo-san* helps the director distribute diplomas.

It is interesting to consider how Shinto beliefs, as reflected in ceremonies and rituals, also permeate the staff's views about children and how they should be treated. The shrine visit by the Wisteria class, described earlier, contained all the classic elements of a Shinto ritual: purification, presentation of offerings, petitions to the *kami* for protection and assistance, and participation by the worshipers. The notion of purification, symbolized in this ceremony by the waving of the *harai-gushi*, a stick to which paper or cloth streamers are attached, is particularly interesting. Basically, by conducting a purification ritual, Mr. Tamiko was eliminating any *tsumi* (defilements, evil, or impurities) that the children may have accumulated and that threaten the renewal of life energy emanating from the *kami*. These defilements are not antithetical to virtue or harmony: "They are simply a fact of existence afflicting all of us, Kami included, but they can be completely obliterated, with no lingering guilt complexes either, by rituals such as [these] . . ." (Nelson, 1996, p. 104).

These two powerful notions—that impurities can arise through no fault of one's own, and that they can be removed by following the correct procedure—stand in stark contrast to Calvinist views about original sin that have been so influential in Western societies. The Shinto belief in the random and transitory nature of "defilement" no doubt contributes to the common Japanese view that children are basically good at heart (White & LeVine, 1987) and need only be gently instructed in the details of how to behave in society. Such a view reinforces the tendency of many Japanese teachers to focus discipline techniques on getting the child to understand the reason for correct behavior, rather than blaming the child or attributing misbehavior to fundamental character flaws.

Existing within a Community

According to Mr. Tamiko, director of Bunka, one of the important functions of the many ceremonies and rituals held at his preschool was not only to deepen children's ties with the past and with Japanese culture, but also to create a feeling of connection to the immediate community. Mr. Tamiko sought to extend his own relations with community members beyond the usual duties of a Shinto priest. He felt a moral obligation to support families through his work as a cleric, a preschool director, and a counselor. His view was that "the role of the preschool is to provide not only the children but also their mothers and fathers with a place for study. The preschool serves the role of counseling center for both children and adults." Like many of the other directors, he believed that Japanese families are experiencing severe problems as a result of urbanization, dissolution of the extended family, and lack of paternal involvement in child rearing. He feared that contemporary Japanese parents no longer believed they played a crucial role in the rearing of their own children:

> When I was a child 30 years or so ago, children used to walk down the street hanging on to their mothers' kimono sleeve. When the mother walked fast, the child was dragged by his mother. When the mother took a turn, the child was swung off his feet by centrifugal force. Children knew that unless they hung on tightly to their parents they would not survive. . . . Now people think that even if the child is separated he can survive. No children hang tightly onto their mothers. This means that from the child's point of view his guardian is no longer limited to his mother. Unless the mother is educated properly she will not raise her child in the right way.

Mr. Tamiko wanted the teachers in his program to become more familiar with the community so that they could better understand the families and children at the school. He set up a number of situations so that the teachers could become acquainted with the community that he already knew so well:

> The teachers commute to work from other communities. They are not necessarily familiar with the details of this community. They need to be more exposed to the local community. That is why they

take the children back to their homes on foot [at the end of the day].
While doing this, the teachers can learn more about the vicinity.
Shop owners say hello to the teachers when they are taking the children home. Unless the teachers themselves become members of this
community, they are not able to understand the children's life here. I
am the only staff person in this preschool who is a member of this
community. When I walk on the street I have to bow and greet people all the time.

Mr. Tamiko also encouraged teachers to take the children on outings
as a way of deepening the children's knowledge of the activities that
occur in their local community:

> The children in one class had decided they wanted to run a [pretend]
> dumpling shop. They took a field trip to a store in front of the train
> station. The shop owner is a good person. Even though the children
> were bothering him, he generously showed them how he made
> dumplings. The children enjoyed the good smells and asked him how
> to be successful at selling dumplings. He answered: "If you make
> dumplings with all your might and if you say thank you to your cus-
> tomers, you will sell plenty of dumplings." They then visited a police
> station. . . . The policemen jokingly handcuffed the children in the
> car and drove around the town. . . . The objective of the field trip was
> to let children experience real shops. By observing them, children
> were able to understand . . . basic ideas about the community. They
> realized that the police must guard the dumpling shop. . . . They
> were then able to incorporate these ideas into their play.

In summary, various aspects of Shinto thought appear to be embedded in the practices of the preschools run under Shinto auspices. The
Shinto view that even the most humble of objects is a manifestation of
a divine spirit surfaced in the particular attention given to plants and
animals in these preschools. Additionally, a respect for the unique traditions and characteristics of Japanese life was evident in the full celebration of traditional holidays and the incorporation of traditional

activities such as *sumo* in the curriculum. It was also apparent that the Shinto priest continues to play a role in defining and supporting the immediate community served by his shrine. Creative individuals like Mr. Tamiko are adapting this traditional role to current problems and opportunities experienced by Japanese families.

The Shinto directors I spoke with held some child-centered beliefs; they seemed to have a benign view of children, as did staff in the relationship and child-oriented programs, and, like them, were more interested in social development than in cognitive stimulation and academic learning. But they were not as prepared as were the child-oriented directors to downplay participation in group structures nor to emphasize creativity and individual expression highly. I believe that their emphasis on respecting tradition and fostering the connections among members of a community constituted a relationship-based approach.

BUDDHIST PRESCHOOLS

From the front, the Tennoji Preschool looks like an insurance company. The imposing modern structure is three stories high, with many windows whose darkened glass prevents outsiders from seeing in. Yet, as one moves through the entryway and into the play yard, the traditional peaked roof of a Buddhist temple looms into view. The old temple and the corporate-style preschool building share the same campus but evoke different periods in Japanese society. A close examination of the school philosophy reveals how traditional elements of Buddhist thought have been artfully synthesized with modern preoccupations about preparation for elementary school. And this strategy has paid off. Even with the number of preschool children dwindling, this school is flourishing, with an enrollment of 600 students in 21 classrooms.

We begin with a glimpse of the weekly prayer service that I observed at Tennoji:

> Jun stands in line, waiting to walk over to the temple. He fidgets
> with one of the suspenders attached to his navy-blue shorts, and

jumps up and down a couple of times, a little restless from spending the morning sitting at his desk. On a signal from the teacher, the class moves out into the corridor and down the stairway. They cross the sunny play yard, with its giant climbing structure fashioned to look like a European castle, and move into the darkness of the temple. With a wave of her hand, a staff member silently motions the children to fill in a new row behind the three-year-olds, who have already entered.

Jun kneels on the floor next to his classmates in the grand hall. The ceiling soars 25 feet overhead, supported by sturdy beams of cedar that run the length of the room and by highly polished wooden columns so thick that it would take two or three children with outstretched arms to encircle their diameter. The warm colors of the cedar and the tatami platform in front of the altar form a beautiful setting for the golden statue of Buddha within the sanctuary.

When all the children have filed in, the assistant director begins her brief sermon. She talks in general about the importance of being kind and considerate toward all living creatures. Moving to a more concrete level, she asserts that it is important not to throw rocks at small animals, and encourages the children to give water to flowers, which are also living things. She points to a screen painting that occupies the wall to one side of the sanctuary; it portrays a fanciful bird with a large, multicolored tail, surrounded by rocks, trees, and reeds. She explains that birds can move and talk to other birds but, since they cannot speak human languages, they cannot tell us their problems. She acknowledges that people eat fish and plants in order to live, but stresses that we owe thanks to the rice and the fish we eat. She encourages them all to remember to have a mind of appreciation, and ends with the observation that the teacher cannot see everything, but that Buddha can, so all children should remember to give thanks to him.

There is a moment of silence, then the sound of chanting filled the temple. Jun begins to repeat the phrases that are familiar after months of practice but still seem strange because the words are in archaic Japanese. For ten minutes, the sound of children chanting fills the temple. From time to time, Jun stumbles over the words, but tries to keep up with the others. In less than a month's time, he and his classmates will participate in a special ceremony along with the adult members of the congregation.

As the chanting concludes, the assistant director smiles broadly at the children, commenting that little by little they are becoming very skillful, and motions for them to rise. Jun stands up, his legs stiff from kneeling on the wooden floor for close to 30 minutes. It is time for the final element of the service, singing the school song. Hands behind his back, he sings loudly, his voice rising to the highest beams in the ceiling like the smoke curling up from the cones of incense burning on the altar.

Compassion for Others: The Primary Element of Virtue

Buddhists emphasize that compassion is necessary to help relieve the pain and suffering of the human condition. Buddhist ethics advocate "a deep sensitivity to the life of the cosmos, an ecological consciousness which combines esthetic refinement with a sense of responsibility" (Dumoulin, 1994, p. 65). Japanese Buddhism is particularly explicit in its strong emphasis on compassion. One of the strongest and oldest schools of Japanese Buddhism, the Shingon sect, urges its followers to practice Four Embracing Acts: charity, kind speech, beneficial acts, and adapting oneself to others.

The Tennoji Preschool's emphasis on showing consideration for others is consistent with Buddhist teachings on compassion. The essence of becoming a virtuous person, according to the staff at Tennoji, lies in developing one's consideration for others (*itawari no kokoro*). They felt that kindness and consideration should be extended to all living things, including animals and plant life as well as other human beings. They emphasized this message in the weekly prayer service at the temple, as revealed in the passage cited earlier.[17] They also provided relevant practical experiences such as caring for the preschool's plants and animals.

For the director at Suma Buddhist Preschool, informal daily prayer was a particularly important vehicle for teaching about compassion:

> Through a variety of activities we would like children to appreciate the spirit of Buddha. Putting one's hands together in prayer is the most important activity, particularly in today's society. . . . We teach the children Buddhist songs and show them how to offer flowers to the altar celebrating Buddha's birth. . . . Obviously young children do not understand a deep philosophy like this, but I want teachers to convey gentle feelings to the children. Through activities we would like the children to appreciate gentle feelings . . . . Japanese put their hands together in prayer before eating a meal. They take doing so for granted. In Christianity, people say "Amen," which corresponds to the Buddhist chant of "*Namuamidabutsu*." A sense of gratitude is what we should consider most important. But today's Japanese people tend to forget the importance of this activity, which is the foundation of life. . . . Children should extend their gratitude and then have a meal. Also they should extend their gratitude to their parents. They acquire this as a habit, and this is most important.[18]

Determination as a Component of Virtue

The Buddhist directors emphasized being gentle and kind, but the director at Suma was quick to point out that Buddhism called for strength and determination as well:

> Raising cheerful, gentle, and healthy children (*akaruku sunao genki na kodomo*) is our overall philosophy. This is from the Buddhist belief in which being strong, happy, and gentle is emphasized. You might think that in Buddhism you are generous to everything. This is not necessarily true. Living in a strong way is important in Buddhism. By being strong I mean that one should do everything with confidence and determination.

One of great impediments to becoming a compassionate person, according to the Buddhist directors, was the natural human tendency to act in a selfish, egocentric manner. They viewed children as wild animals who needed to be tamed in preschool. At Tennoji, three-year-old children were considered to be a particular challenge because they typically do not understand the school rules, resulting in a situation that is "chaotic" and leaves teachers feeling as if they are "fighting a war." As one teacher put it:

> I try to tame one child after another every day. I first try to tame those children who seem to adapt easily. I may tame one child today but may not be able to do so tomorrow. . . . By July [four months into the school year] all the children have become calm and quiet except for a couple of children who are still naughty. . . . By now [November], they are calm and quiet.

This view was echoed by the director of Suma Preschool:

> When it comes to developing children's individual character (*kosei*) I think it is important to allow them to play freely and at the same time to discipline them. But children tend to do only what they want. They tend to seek self-centered individualism. They tend to ignore the notion of love or empathy (*omoiyari*). Thus we tend to feel that we need to control children. This is a very important aspect of Japanese education.

This view about children's fundamental nature contrasts sharply with the opinions of the Japanese Christians, who emphasized the idea that children are "precious gifts" from God. It is interesting that the Buddhists' views are close to the position held by many conservative Christian educators in the United States—namely, that adults must be vigilant to prevent children from succumbing to the wickedness that is an inherent part of human nature (Cleverley & Phillips, 1986).

The emphasis the Buddhist directors place on firm control suggests that they may employ more strict modes of discipline than do other types of schools, particularly those that are Christian. In the Zen Buddhist tradition, masters are particularly known for treating disciples harshly, rebuffing questions, scolding them, and subjecting them to physical punishment (Hori, 1996). In my observations of Buddhist preschools, I saw no criticism, scolding, or physical punishment; however, other data support the hypothesis that Buddhist teachers are particularly strict, even in the preschools. Allison (1996) interviewed mothers whose children attended a Buddhist preschool, and found that they were concerned about scolding and public criticism of children by teachers seeking to perfect the sports day performance. A number of mothers also reported receiving very critical evaluations from teachers at conferences:

> One mother was told that her daughter was effectively incompetent in every task, skill, and behavior expected of children her age. An example was given that she failed to draw triangles the "correct" way. When this woman . . . pointed out that Sachiko drew triangles at home all the time, she was told that her drawing order was incorrect. Privately my friend laughed, telling me that she found the teacher's world view too rigid and her assessment of the girl ridiculous. (p. 150)

A strategy used by staff at Tennoji to overcome children's weakness and individualism was to feature large group activities as much as possible. In a pamphlet for parents, the director made the following argument in favor of large class sizes:

> I suspect that most of you [mothers] think that small class sizes, such as five or ten children per teacher, are better for your children. I do not think so. Among 20 or 30 peers in a class, the children are more motivated to learn by competing with each other. Therefore, class sizes of five or ten students are not good at all. Of course, parental overprotectiveness (*kahogo*) is not good. Children aged four to five need a group [translation from original Japanese].

Another strategy in the Buddhist preschools was to develop the child's "weak points" rather than allowing him or her to focus exclusively on strengths and areas of interest. This view was also discussed in a parent brochure put out by staff at Tennoji: "Young children need balanced care that focuses on various aspects of development such as music, intelligence, creativity, and health (physical ability). In a preschool there are future artists and future scholars. There are also future athletes, and yet it is not a good idea to develop only their athletic abilities. If you improve only the musical ability of a child who is good at music, this child will have unbalanced overall ability" [translation from original Japanese]. This emphasis on helping each child obtain the same wide range of basic skills as his or her peers was also discussed in Chapter 4, in describing the role-oriented preschools.

Chi: The Goal of Obtaining Knowledge

Buddhism holds that ignorance, in combination with desire, is the force that prevents people from moving beyond the pain of life on earth. Wisdom and faith are important keys to salvation, and a primary strategy for obtaining knowledge is to study sacred texts. The texts themselves are considered authoritative, so the believer is a "hearer of the word." Expression of Buddhist faith has traditionally focused on "pious copying out of scripture," a practice that is still considered meritorious (Dumoulin, 1994, p. 55).

During the eighteenth and nineteenth centuries, Japanese schools featured intensive study of classical texts. There were two kinds of schools: *hanko* for samurai, and *terakoya* for commoners. *Hanko* students memorized and recited selected passages from classical texts of China, whereas in *terakoya,* established by Buddhist monks, students were required to copy textbooks containing passages from classical works (Sato, 1998). This Buddhist approach to learning—what Hori (1996) calls "ritual formalism"—is also used in Japanese Zen monasteries: "By ritual formalism, I am stretching one term to cover several kinds of behavior: repetition, rote memorization, behaving according to traditional prescription. In ritual formalism, students imitate form without necessarily understanding content or rationale. They are instructed in 'what' to do but given very little instruction in 'why' and 'how' to do it" (Hori, 1996, p. 21).

In the Buddhist preschools I visited, students were strongly encouraged to orient themselves toward external sources of knowledge, including both texts and the teacher. At Tennoji, as illustrated in the description of a visit to the temple, children were required to memorize long passages in archaic Japanese. In addition, they spent much of their day sitting at desks receiving instruction from the teacher. Literacy was a major focus of the curriculum, including instruction in reading *kanji* (Chinese characters) and writing *hiragana* (the simplified syllabary). Children also engaged in poetry reading and writing, and learned the basics of grammar. For example, they learned the use of the honorific prefix "o" in terms such as *otōban* (class monitor). The children also participated in activities designed to "develop their intelligence" (*chinō kaihatsu*), in which a wide range of materials were used to stimulate basic cognitive skills like visual perception and memory, as well as to teach such Piagetian principles as seriation and class inclusion. In addition, children attended classes in art, ballet, English, instrumental music, and choral singing.

At Sannomiya preschool, a more radical curriculum had been implemented that featured decontextualized cognitive stimulation. Children were exposed to complex visual and auditory patterns, which they

Children in a large Buddhist preschool learn to play Japanese drums.

memorized, with no exploration of the meaning of the stimuli. For example, in one auditory memory exercise, teachers clapped out a variety of complicated rhythms for children to repeat. The students also memorized the flags of nations around the world. They learned to recognize the *kanji* for, among other things, train stations throughout Japan. They memorized poetry in archaic Japanese. The purpose of all these activities, according to the director, was not to learn facts per se, but rather to receive brain stimulation in a rhythmic, fast-paced tempo:

> Cramming children's heads with knowledge is wrong. What children need is intellectual stimulation, as can be seen in what we do with children's language development. Visual stimulus represented by literacy is important so that children absorb many things from the environment. Children's brain functioning is strengthened by absorbing a lot of things from their environment. We are not teaching literacy. We are strengthening children's brain functioning by teaching literacy. . . . As you saw today, giving stimuli is good for children. The rhythm [of the activities] is so quick. Without a quick rhythm, children would not concentrate on anything. Rhythm and tempo are important. . . . Children are equipped from birth with the rhythm of their mother's heart beat, and so can easily accommodate to that fast rhythm later on. . . . Children who have difficulty catching up with the quick rhythm need this stimulus. They will change amazingly. Children who are slow will become quick. This can be attained only during the early-childhood period.

The director at Sannomiya emphasized that this philosophy had been adopted by 180 affiliated preschools across Japan. A brochure (in English) put out by the association representing these preschools states that they "don't limit child education to the usual knowledge, moral and physical training. Rather, we modify them into a three-in-one process composed of knowledge, sentiments and body-based process. The execution of the process is based on actions, words and rhythms which abound in the child's environment, thus providing a natural and interesting way of training the child."

What unites the Buddhist preschools, then, is an emphasis on the ultimate authority of text and teacher as sources of knowledge. This view contrasts with the Christian emphasis that knowledge results from children's individual exploration in combination with teacher-guided social interaction among peers. All the Buddhist preschools provided teacher-structured lessons, but they differed as to the content of those lessons. One school embraced a radical view of learning based upon cognitive stimulation by decontextualized visual and auditory stimuli. The others were more conventional in their approach, preferring to use practices commonly found in upper elementary school. It is probably the intensely academic approach that makes these schools appealing to many parents, even though such didactic methods directly contradict the guidelines put out by the Ministry of Education.

Tai: The Significance of the Body

In the Zen tradition, composing one's body for meditation—sitting and breathing correctly—is a crucial practice for attaining higher consciousness. By emptying oneself of physical discomfort, emotions, and thoughts, one achieves unity of mind and body, and detachment from the self. Analysis of the moral implications of a person's physical state is commonplace in Japan, in Buddhist as well as secular contexts. In many of the preschools, not just those that were Buddhist, the children were constantly reminded to sit up straight and keep their feet together. The writing teacher at Wakaba Preschool, for example, argued for a link between posture and intelligence, and suggested that children who had good posture were more likely to do well later in school.

In Buddhist preschools, developing good posture was one of many objectives related to the physical development of the children. At Sannomiya Preschool, for example, the children sat on benches rather than chairs in order to strengthen their back muscles and prevent them from lounging. They received constant reminders about how to position and move their bodies. When the teacher called attendance, each child was required to raise his hand upon hearing his name. The teacher watched to be sure the child's arm was pitched at the proper angle, with fingers together and straight. The Tennoji Preschool's pamphlet explicitly links posture and spirituality: "Going to the temple makes one's spine straighten. One feels renewed, formal, and serious. One grows in appreciation for Buddha who protects us all" [translation from original Japanese].

Because much of the day was occupied with academic classes and music instruction, the children at strict Buddhist preschools had little opportunity to engage in physical activity. When it did occur, physical exertion was routinized and teacher structured. For example, children at Sannomiya Preschool received direct instruction in how to shinny up a pole. Six children at a time approached their respective poles and waited at the bottom. Upon a signal from the teacher, they shinnied up and held their position until she blew her whistle, at which time they slid down and yielded their poles to the next group.

Physical activities at Buddhist preschools were sometimes designed to provide a challenge that would help toughen up the children. This was especially true at Sannomiya Preschool, where, as described in Chapter 4, the director purposely designed field trips to provide experiences that would be physically challenging for the children. Here is another example of the type of physical and emotional challenge he devised for his students, this time involving a trip to a castle with steep narrow stairs and no handrail:

> The staircase [at the castle] is very steep. The people at the castle told me that preschool children were not allowed to use the staircase. They insisted: "This is the rule." We said: "After all, we are here." They said: "We are concerned about possible injury." We finally convinced them and entered the castle. [A staff member at the castle] was amazed at the children's proper attitude and said, "I have never seen preschool children behave in such an orderly manner." I think our children are fortunate to have had such an experience.

The directors in the Buddhist preschools were also concerned about the spiritual and physical effects of receiving proper nutrition and exercise. The director at Sannomiya was concerned that Japanese children were overweight, out of shape, and "mentally sloppy" due to inactivity and poor diet. He deplored mothers who wished their children to be excused from strenuous exercise because of being "too weak":

> My response [to those mothers] is: "If you insist on [exempting your child from physical activity] you must be sure that you can take full responsibility for your child's entire life." I would say: "Your child is not intrinsically weak. Instead, you have made him weak because you did not give him opportunities or experiences." Therefore we provide children with a lot of opportunities and experiences, although we do not force them to do anything. . . . As you see, we do not have any overweight children at this school. This is because they are trained physically as well as intellectually. They become mentally tense in a good sense. Children become overweight not only because of eating too much food but also because of mental sloppiness.

A notation on the brochure for Tennoji Preschool sums up the connection between nutrition, group orientation, and spiritual awareness. In a list of the five best attributes of the preschool, number two was the following: "The perfect lunch system!! Everyone eats the same thing and everyone eats everything that is served because we are showing our appreciation to the living things whose lives we are taking."

Rejection of the West and Search for Traditional Japan

The Buddhist directors were not sanguine about extended contact between Japan and the West. They tended to attribute many of Japan's problems to Western influence. While cautioning me that his remarks may be reminiscent "of the imperial army," the outspoken director of Sannomiya Preschool did not hesitate to state his critique of Western influences on Japanese children:

> Nowadays because of Westernization we have fewer children and nuclear families. Mothers do not have to do anything. Everything is instant. Japanese children will be bad. Or they have already become bad. Therefore correcting that predicament is our goal. I admit that Japan's rapid growth is due to copying Western societies. But we

should not copy Western culture. The worst things are television and Nintendo computer games. Children do not read books or write anything. And automobiles are bad. Everywhere you go you drive. People lose the chance to move their bodies. They eat too much meat and too much sugar. Copying the Western lifestyle is bad.

Buddhism is considered by Japanese feminists to be one of the most influential social forces shaping the status of Japanese women as subordinate to men (Okano, 1995). Indeed, the directors in the Buddhist preschools felt that one of the worst legacies of Western influence was the growing equality between men and women. The director at Suma was preoccupied with what he saw as women's usurpation of men's role of authority in the family: "In many ways, males feel that unless they are gentle, females will not consider them attractive. . . . But I believe that we have to provide measures to make boys strong. . . . We would like to work hard to keep traditional values." The increasing individualism and, as he saw it, selfishness, of contemporary Japanese mothers, led them to depart from traditional childrearing models: "They want to educate their children in the way that they believe works best. Their way may not fit well with Japanese traditional customs. Since they have their own way, there is no clear consensus among them either."

All the Buddhist schools I visited could be classified as role-oriented. This analysis of the key elements of Buddhist preschools—from the goals (academic learning, moral development, and physical strength) to the methods (large group instruction, exposure to physical challenges, and firm discipline)—makes it clear that Buddhism is a key macrolevel influence on role-oriented schools, even those like Wakaba (featured in Chapter 4) that are not directly under the auspices of a Buddhist temple.

The elements of the role-oriented program are also compatible with Confucianism, which includes an emphasis on the heirarchical structuring of relationships and the belief that "social order is ensured by each party's honouring the requirements in the role relationship" (Bond & Hwang, 1986, p. 216). I have chosen not to conduct a more detailed analysis of the role of Confucian thought in these preschools because, in contrast to their explicit mention of Buddhism as a source of inspiration, no director made direct reference to Confucianism. While Confucianism may indeed be a powerful influence, analogous to the legacy of Calvinism on American child-rearing practices, it is a comparatively diffuse and indirect one. In my analyses I have tried to stay closer to the elements of religion that affect the directors' "near-experience" (Wikan, 1991).

I would also argue that the role-oriented schools are heavily influenced by market conditions as well as cultural models related to Buddhism. The danger for schools that espouse a conservative political philosophy and adherence to traditional values is that Japanese parents may reject these demands for obedience and conformity, which are at odds with modernizing trends as well as a powerful cultural model that views children under seven as little treasures who should be treated indulgently (Allison, 1996; Boocock, 1989; Vogel, 1996).[19] What may save these schools is that, by offering a downward extension of elementary programs, they are perceived as valuable by education-oriented parents. As we noted in the case of the secular, role-oriented schools, for parents living on the margins of middle-class life, these schools will likely continue to be a very appealing method for giving their children a head start in school.[20] So for the role-oriented schools, the curriculum may represent a blending of traditional Buddhist views with a very up-to-date consideration of market factors. As we will see in Chapter 8, market factors play a much larger role in dictating the curriculum in private schools than they do in those receiving financial support from the state.

In this chapter, we have seen concrete ways in which the ideology of Christianity, Shintoism, and Buddhism continue to influence Japanese preschools. The Japanese are sometimes described in Western writing as a nonreligious people. But it is more accurate to say that Japanese religiosity is expressed in a way that differs from that of America. Japanese appear more willing to mix and match religions, invoking Shintoism at birth and marriage, and Buddhism when faced when death. The cultural models that are rooted within these ideologies have migrated into many corners of social life, including the preschool.

8

THE SLOW DEMISE
OF PUBLIC PRESCHOOLS

Since the 1950s, the proportion of preschools that are public has grown, but the share of children enrolled in public preschools has declined steadily—from 38 percent in 1955 to just 20 percent in 1998 (Morigami, 1993, 1999). What has contributed to this movement from public to private preschools? What are the likely outcomes of a move to a system operated by individuals with a profit motive as well as educational objectives? These questions—as crucial to American educators as to those in Japan—are explored in this chapter.

To illustrate some of the key differences between public and private preschools, I will contrast Taisho, a well-established private school in central Osaka, with Nikko, a suburban public preschool in Tokyo. The focus will be the extent to which public and private preschools are modeled on the guidelines for preschool education developed by the Ministry of Education, particularly the call for a more individualized approach to instruction. The case of Umeda, a public school attempting somewhat unsuccessfully to implement the ministry guidelines, is also discussed to illustrate the difficulty some educators have experienced as they attempt to interpret these new cultural models and incorporate them into their programs. Additionally, I will discuss the results of a survey conducted among preschool directors in the Kansai region to provide additional insight into the differences between public and private schools as well as distinctions associated with religious auspice.

A HISTORY OF OVERSIGHT BY THE
MINISTRY OF EDUCATION

Over the last century the Japanese government has played a key role in the operation of both public and private preschools. The first preschool was public; established by the government in 1876, it served 75 children from wealthy Tokyo families. In spite of this early initiative, the national government did not move aggressively to develop the preschool system as it did with elementary schools and beyond. Preschools were seen as a service for the wealthier citizens, unlike day care, which served the national development agenda by freeing parents to work and build up the country's economy (Uno, 1987). Early schooling would not, in fact, become widespread for half a century, and private initiative has played a role in its development throughout the century (Shwalb et al., 1992). National control over preschool education was established in 1899, with the publication of the "Act of Content and Facilities of Kindergarten Education" (Boocock, 1989). The number of preschools did not rise substantially until the 1950s, however, as the effects of the postwar reorganization of the education system began to take hold. The number of preschools rose from just over 5,000 in 1955 to over 15,000 in the 1990s (Morigami, 1993, 1999).

Looking over the 90-year period from the first set of guidelines published in 1899 to the current version published in 1989, it is clear that the role of the Ministry of Education has changed, sometimes exerting strict control over the content of preschools and at other times specifying virtually no oversight. The earliest guidelines specified four educational areas: play, song, speech, and handicrafts; although detailed descriptions of appropriate activities were provided for each area, preschool directors had considerable latitude in what they actually offered in their programs (Ishigaki, 1992). These guidelines were discontinued in 1911, and each preschool was permitted to develop its own curriculum. In 1926, the government passed an ordinance reviving these guidelines in the form of suggested activities rather than proscribed areas. During the war years (1937 to 1947), preschools were expected to emphasize patriotic activities and wartime readiness. Following the war, a new set of guidelines was published which was then revised in 1956 and again in 1989. As we will see in this chapter, many preschool directors pay little attention to these guidelines, while others, particularly in public schools, take them seriously and try to implement them in some form.

It is interesting to compare the content of the three sets of postwar guidelines, because they reflect cultural changes in the competencies that are considered important for young children to acquire (see Ishigaki, 1992, for a translation of these various versions). Certain general areas have been included in all three versions: health and physical development, social relations, and appreciation of nature. However, a shift has occurred from emphasizing educational activities such as arts and crafts, field trips, drama, and music to a focus on developmental processes. There is now far more emphasis on developing one's individual skills in addition to social competencies. For example, while the 1947 guidelines emphasize such objectives as having "the right attitude towards the surrounding social life and happenings" (Ishigaki, 1992, p. 127), the new guidelines place substantial emphasis on developing and expressing personal thoughts and feelings. In the 1989 guidelines, language and expression are key areas, along with health, human relationships, and the environment. Individualistic goals are emphasized throughout the five areas in the 1989 guidelines. In the section on human relations, for example, one of the three goals is "Listening to what others say carefully, and telling experiences and thoughts" (p. 134). The section on expression encourages the development of creativity and aesthetic sensitivity as well as emotional expression (that is, "expression of feelings and ideas in various ways" [p. 134]) and imagination. The guidelines stipulate that the way to attain these objectives is through play and warm social interactions with teachers, who are asked to acknowledge that "each child has its own experience in life" and to offer "appropriate guidance for a child's individual needs and . . . development[al] tasks" (p. 131). This individualistic focus is very different from the early guidelines, where teachers are held responsible for teaching children certain skills and helping them become attuned to social relationships.

In my interviews it became clear that the public school directors did not always totally agree with the 1989 guidelines, but they had apparently considered them seriously, discussed them with their teachers, and attempted to implement them in some fashion. Many of the private school directors, on the other hand, expressed little interest or knowledge about the guidelines and emphasized their dislike for the Ministry of Education. Whereas many public school directors described sweeping changes they had made as a result of the 1989 revisions, few private school directors reported any such alterations to their programs.

Taisho, whose program I describe next, is typical of the private programs I visited in its relatively negative attitude toward the Ministry of Education. The staff at Taisho had carefully crafted the identity of the school based on their own ideas and their sense of parents' needs, interests, and desires.

TAISHO PRESCHOOL: FAMOUS FOR ITS OLYMPIC-SIZED POOL

Hiro shivers slightly as he runs across the yard toward the building that houses the pool. It is time for his weekly swimming lesson. This January a cold, wet blanket of air has settled over Osaka, but a blast of warmth greets him and his classmates as they enter the locker room. Hiro moves quickly through the now-familiar routine of changing into his bathing trunks, making sure to fold his school uniform carefully and stow it away properly in a small plastic basket. He finishes ahead of some children, and squats patiently, unfazed by the hubbub created by 75 children crammed into one large room. When everyone is ready, the teacher signals for them to line up, and they walk out to the pool area. The air in the large room is heated to 80 degrees, and the flat, smooth surface of the pool looks inviting. Hiro's class of 38 children takes one end of the pool; another class of four-year-olds is on the other end. Each class is accompanied by the classroom teacher and a swimming instructor. The children do warm-up exercises, then the two teachers jump in the water. Hiro and his classmates sit on the edge, kicking and splashing themselves. At a signal from the teacher, they turn over on their stomachs and dangle their legs in the water. They begin kicking vigorously, and the teacher wades down the line, splashing anyone who is not yet thoroughly wet. A short swimming lesson follows. The routines are well organized and thoroughly established; the teachers spend no time admonishing children for misbehavior. The atmosphere is fun and light; teachers smile and encourage those who are timid. There is a lot of chatter and laughing. For the last 15 minutes, the children are allowed to play with inner tubes and kickboards. In a school of 585 children, the tight schedule permits little time for free play, but Hiro and his classmates respond enthusiastically to their carefully planned, smoothly executed lessons.

Children attending their weekly swimming lesson in the school pool.

Taisho is located in the middle of Osaka. The large, modern building is sited on a spacious lot. Inside, there are not only ample numbers of classrooms, but also meeting rooms, teacher offices, and a large auditorium. The pool and locker rooms are housed in a separate facility across the street. In a country that is renowned for housing its populace in "rabbit hutches" and "capsule hotels," it is striking to walk down spacious halls past large, airy classrooms, light-filled meeting rooms, and an atrium with a carefully tended garden—all in the middle of a large city.

The school's curriculum is anchored by three objectives: improving physical strength and stamina (*tairyoku*); teaching polite behavior (*shitsuke*); and fostering social relations (*shakaisei*). Physical strength is achieved through weekly swimming and gymnastics lessons. To build up their resistance to the cold, children wear only shorts and a shirt year-round, and go barefoot indoors. On the cold, rainy, winter day I visited, the building was minimally heated. The second objective, polite behavior, is encouraged, according to the director, "by scolding children immediately if they have misbehaved." And social relations are fostered by teaching children to make correct assessments of what behavior is called for in certain situations (*kejime o tsukeru*). As the director, Mrs. Shimokaji, explained:

> When the children go on a field trip, we encourage them to realize the situation calls for public (*soto*) behavior. We hope they can recognize the difference between public (*soto*) and private (*uchi*) behavior. Within the preschool, it is part *soto* and part *uchi* behavior. There are certain things you can do at certain times and not others.

According to Mrs. Shimokaji, the curriculum at Taisho has remained relatively stable since it was founded in the late 1940s. When I asked her about the changes in the Ministry of Education guidelines, she remarked:

> The Ministry of Education has decided that there should be five areas of education. We are teaching in these five areas. We haven't

changed anything as a result of the guidelines; we've always taught in those five areas. When it comes to individualization, I have never thought about it particularly. Our goals are to help children adjust to group life, follow the rules, and learn appropriate greetings. These goals have not changed in 30 years. Individualization is not a special focus.

The Taisho orientation toward honing the skills needed to participate in group life was echoed by the head teacher. She thought that the children particularly learned a lot from participating in school performances. At the time of the interview, they were in the final weeks of rehearsing for an elaborate *happiokai* performance. Each class was performing a play, singing several songs, and performing a couple of numbers with musical instruments. With 18 classes, this event was expected to take two full days, with morning and evening sessions. The head teacher mentioned how time-consuming the practices for this performance had been, and commented that the public schools would not devote so much time to a teacher-directed group activity. With a smile, she remarked:

> I have to admit that it is very important to me that the children put on a very beautiful *happiokai* performance. The teachers feel the same way, and they are very nervous about it. Maybe it's a bad thing, but I can't do anything about it.

Among the private schools, most were either relationship-oriented, like Taisho, or role-oriented. Takenoko (the school for wealthy children featured in Chapter 6) and the Christian schools were the only private schools to implement a child-centered curriculum. Many private preschool directors shared Mrs. Shimokaji's lack of interest in the Ministry of Education's views on the topic of individualized instruction. A few were substantively in agreement with the ministry on most issues, but felt it was financially impossible for them to implement fully a more individualized approach because they needed to keep the number of children per classroom as high as possible.

NIKKO PUBLIC PRESCHOOL

Mrs. Fujita, director of Nikko, wanted to create a calm, peaceful (*nodoka*) environment where children could feel relaxed and free. This goal was reflected in the design of the playground, which was located behind the school away from the street noise. The usual bare yard had been replaced by a lush garden. Butterflies hovered among the flowers and dragonflies dipped in and out of the splashing water of a small fountain. During my visit, children wandered in and out of the two classrooms; a small group was running relay races with a teacher, while another couple of children helped a staff member remove the stems from the sweet potatoes collected during the previous day's field trip. The 41 children enrolled at Nikko appeared to experience little of the intensity found in the larger private preschools like Taisho.

According to Mrs. Fujita, the school day at Nikko had once been devoted mostly to teacher-structured group activities. However, subsequent to the release of the 1989 guidelines, the staff had worked toward eliminating most of these activities and was giving children more time for free play. Initially, the teachers had felt very uncertain about their role in a free-play environment, but they were gradually feeling more comfortable. As the following dialogue reveals, they were critical of the notion of individualized instruction (*koseika*), but were trying to think carefully about the ways in which it could be used productively in their classrooms:

> *Interviewer:* In the new guidelines, the Ministry of Education has emphasized the notion of respecting the individual character (*kosei*) of the child. I'm curious what this phrase means to you.
>
> *Teacher 1:* *Kosei* means the power that the child has intrinsically. People have started to emphasize *kosei*. The idea that you can do whatever you like—that is not individualized instruction (*koseika*). Instead, from our viewpoint, individualization means to develop the good points

that each individual child has, developing and cultivating the good aspects of the child.

Teacher 2: There is an idea that if you do the same thing as others, you will not feel isolated. Some children feel comfortable expressing their feelings, but others don't want to feel isolated and thus simply follow others. Even if you think differently you are not necessarily wrong, or that is not something to feel ashamed of.

Teacher 3: Some children think one way, while others think differently. The more diverse ideas we have, the better ways of thinking we may be able to identify. Expressing your idea is a plus, not only for you but for others. By expressing your own idea, you realize that people have different opinions.

Teacher 1: I don't understand the meaning of "*ka*" in "*koseika.*" "*Ka*" means to change something by external force. Thus "*ka*" and "*kosei*" do not go together. It seems me that "*ka*" and "*kosei*" are a mismatch.

Teacher 4: Even if a child's behavior or ideas are not acceptable in society in general, his or her behavior should be regarded as his or her *kosei*. It is natural for everyone to have something different. If teachers can accept children and respect children's individual differences, this will lead to the child's *koseika*. I cannot express my ideas well because of my weak understanding of *koseika*. [This speaker is preparing to become a teacher by working in an administrative capacity in the school.]

Teacher 1: *Koseika* involves problems. The previous guidelines emphasized the power of the group experience. But in the current guidelines this idea has totally disappeared, except for the idea of doing something toward a common goal. We no longer have the idea that children get together and complete something toward a common goal. This time, the ministry has emphasized *koseika*. . . . But the problem is that we can help those who are smart become even smarter, while it is difficult to support those who are not so smart. In physical education classes [in later schooling], the teacher used to teach all students to do a forward circle on the horizontal bar, for example. But now the teacher does not teach techniques or skills but just shows how to enjoy playing on the bar. Obviously, this is very important because Japanese people did not used to know how to enjoy sports. These two opposing ways have both merits and demerits.

This dialogue reveals that the teachers at Nikko viewed individualized instruction as different from providing unfettered freedom, a distinction that seemed to elude the teachers in Umeda, as we will see presently. The teachers at Nikko were committed to providing a more individualized approach, but did not wish to lose sight of the children's need to learn how to work and play together. And they did not want to give up the idea that certain skills can and should be taught at particular ages, as opposed to simply allowing children to engage in familiar activities.

At Nikko, the teachers used many of the strategies we saw exemplified in the child-oriented preschools described in Chapter 5. They helped to develop social skills by providing many opportunities for free play and by scaffolding the more challenging social interactions, such as when there was a dispute. They tried to foster creativity and self-expression through designing art projects that included frequent opportunities for one-to-one conversations between teacher and individual children. For example, one teacher described how she used an individualized approach during a puppet-making activity:

We had children make the puppets in a free-play situation so that we could interact with each individual child quite extensively. If the puppet has two heads or no clothes, we accept it anyway. We do not have a standard of what things should be like. For example, people used to think that carp-shaped streamers had to be a certain color. Now we do not have such a "paint-by-the-numbers" mentality where there is little room for creativity. In today's schooling, children can create what they want.

The teachers at Nikko were aware that the benefits of their program may not be understood by parents. As one teacher commented:

We think that even if children continue to play in the sandbox most of the year, they will learn many things, such as feeling the sand and interacting with others. Children spend these two years in an easy, comfortable environment, and they fully enjoy their early-childhood period. But parents want tangible results that would result from teachers teaching their children *hiragana* and musical instruments. Since elementary school crams many things into children and the pace is very fast, parents are afraid that the easy, comfortable environment here may not be a good way to prepare their children

In this public school classroom, materials are arranged on low shelves so that children can select them during free play.

to keep up with the fast pace of elementary school. So parents have a strong desire for the teacher to teach letters and mathematics. This leads them to choose private preschools rather than public ones.

Although Nikko's enrollment is down 30 percent from previous years, the teachers are not willing to change the preschool program in order to attract more students. Like Higashimachi, the public school described in Chapter 5, if Nikko's enrollment drops much lower, it will be closed or consolidated with another preschool. I did not have an opportunity to talk to the parents of children enrolled at Nikko, but found myself wondering whether they were aware of the thought and skill that the teachers had devoted to the program.

SCHOOLS IN TRANSITION

Some of the directors who had made changes in response to the 1989 guidelines were less confident that the quality of the program had indeed improved as a result. One example of such a program was Umeda, a public preschool serving suburban Osaka. Mrs. Ito, the director, seemed to be interested in the notion of individualization, but was groping for a way to apply it in her school. She had eliminated virtually all the group activities. There were no morning exercises and no instruction in music. Aside from a brief period for singing or art, virtually the whole day was devoted to free play. The children had free reign to go wherever they wanted, indoors or out. They had access to some outdoor equipment, but little was available indoors. The rooms were not divided into curriculum areas, or "corners," as they often were in child-centered classrooms. The teachers had little presence in the classroom; they appeared to busy themselves with cleaning and paperwork, as well as responding to the occasional accident or serious dispute among children.

The program at Umeda was not constrained by limited space or funding for materials. The school grounds were spacious, particularly since the school was serving far fewer children than originally envisioned. The school seemed well funded by the government and owned quite a bit of expensive technology, including a wide-screen television.

Rather, it seemed that the staff did not perceive the need for a more structured, rich classroom environment.

The rather limited scope of available activities and the absence of teacher direction manifested itself in the children's daily experience. During my observations, some children engaged in prolonged periods of pretend play. Others seemed to have difficulty focusing on any particular activity. Groups of boys chased each other in and out of classrooms. A number of isolated children wandered around by themselves without settling into any play pattern.

When I asked Mrs. Ito about her educational philosophy, she replied that:

> In preschool education, I think it is very important that we do not spoil the child's individuality. I think this is the most important thing, but not all the teachers would agree with me.

When I asked her how she implements this philosophy, she replied that:

> Every day I try to watch them carefully, but sometimes we have discussion with their parents, and I can find out about their life at home. Mainly, in everyday life, I see what they are like. . . . This school's way is freedom, first of all. Especially for five-year-olds. They are free to say whatever they want. . . . I hope with no pressure or forcing I can create a program where they can play freely and safely. . . . I think that playing and friendship raises sensitivity, and I do want them to play freely. . . . Today, children can play only in preschool because after school they have so many things to do, like swimming and piano. So, we have to give them a good opportunity to play, especially in a group.

Mrs. Ito articulated the importance of freedom from all constraints. She did not describe any skills that children might need to take advantage of a curriculum based on free play, nor—unlike the directors in child-oriented schools—did she articulate how teachers could work within such a program to extend children's interactions with each other, improve their ability to communicate their thoughts and feelings, or learn to channel their personal competencies into the dynamics of a group. This left the school without a clear mission or set of guiding principles.

Not surprisingly, the teachers at Umeda seemed somewhat uncertain about what they should be doing. When I asked a teacher in charge of five-year-olds to describe her role, she paused from her task of mopping the floor and replied:

> Before, teachers had to teach many things, but now we don't have to teach or give any direction. So now children have self-direction (*shutaisei*). We used to teach them exactly how to use the musical instruments. Now I just leave the instruments for them, and they can play them freely. I just put on the cassette tape recorder and they play what they want. We don't teach a method or a skill. Then I ask each one how he or she played, and I summarize what happened during that group activity.

The teachers' perplexity did not go unnoticed by the director, who remarked to us:

> Actually, I doubt that every teacher can understand the guidelines fully. It is very difficult. Teachers also have their own individuality or personality. So, I hope they will have the opportunity to watch the style of teaching that I prefer. But I believe individuality is important, so I can't force them.

Perhaps over time the staff at Umeda will find their way, adapting the concept of individualization in a way that makes sense for them. But with such a pervasive sense of bewilderment emanating from the staff, it seems unlikely that the school will attract many new families. The danger is that a downward spiral has begun; as fewer new children enroll, the school gains a reputation as unpopular, and the teachers become more discouraged, leading to less motivation to energize and revamp the curriculum.

PUBLIC OR PRIVATE?
HOW DOES A PARENT DECIDE?

The programs at Umeda, Nikko, and Taisho help to illustrate the factors that have moved many parents to select private schools for their children. It is worth mentioning at the outset that tuition is considerably higher in private schools. Generally, public school tuition is roughly one quarter that of private schools (Morigami, 1999).

Which factors make private preschools attractive to parents? Two important factors are captured in the following comments by Mr. Tamiko, director of a private preschool. One, private schools work hard to offer distinctive, interesting programs; and two, they are more likely to cater to parents:

> The public preschools have made a big contribution. After World War II, Japanese society had to start from scratch. Public schools did a very good job of providing a minimum level of service for everyone in the country. . . . The public preschools follow Ministry of Education guidelines, with some additions of their own. The private preschools also follow Ministry of Education guidelines, but have a lot more to add. They can get color from their local neighborhood and from the individual characteristics of the teachers. They can be more creative.

> About 70 percent of private preschools are free-play oriented, while 30 percent are skill oriented. I learned these figures from a publishing company that publishes books for preschool children. The company sells difficult books to 30 percent of the preschools. Among this 30 percent of schools that emphasize "brilliance" (*eisai kyōiku*), some teach Chinese characters because that's what parents request.

The problem with catering to parents, according to Mr. Tamiko, is that what parents want may not be what children actually need. Private preschools can be established by people with no particular training or background in education; schools are run by religious organizations, private social service corporations, employers such as hospitals and department stores, labor unions, and a number of other groups (Boocock, 1989). To be licensed, private preschools are supposed to abide by the Ministry of Education guidelines pertaining to class size, qualification of personnel, days and hours of operation, physical space, and equipment. However, in their quest for financial solvency, schools do not always follow these and other guidelines. Taisho is one of many schools that accept far more students than the recommended maximum of 400, for example.

My impression was that, while the teaching of academic material was one way some private preschools attracted students, a more common approach was to offer special lessons and activities, such as the swimming program at Taisho. Private programs were also likely to offer services that benefited parents directly, including a lunch service, bus pickup and delivery, and extended day programs. Furthermore, private programs typically mounted a more extensive, sophisticated marketing effort to recruit and retain students. The brochure describing Taisho, for example, is a glossy, full-color, ten-page booklet featuring an artist's rendering of the school, more than 15 professional photographs of the adminstrators, school grounds, classrooms, auditorium, bus fleet (four vehicles) and pool, and maps of the whole facility accompanied by a chart indicating the area of each classroom in square meters. One photograph is an aerial shot of the entire campus; the children are arranged in formation on the playground to spell out the school name. In general, the private school materials convey a clear sense of the distinctive character of the school and a concrete idea of what facilities and activities are available.

The brochure for Nikko, in contrast, was a single sheet of pink paper folded in half. Reproduced on the school copier, the flyer featured pen-and-ink drawings of children and cartoon animals engaged in seasonal play activities, such as swimming in the summer or digging up sweet potatoes in the fall. The accompanying text includes two paragraphs summarizing the school philosophy, an overview of the school calendar, and the words to the school song. Most of the public schools had designed a similar flyer; the same activities appeared on most of them, and even the cartoon animals begin to look familiar. The public school pamphlets may appeal to those who don't like a slick, corporate image and want a simple, easygoing approach, but the Nikko flyer simply did not convey the school's ethos as I heard it eloquently expressed by the staff and director.

A SURVEY OF PRIVATE AND PUBLIC SCHOOLS

In order to find out whether the differences I noticed in my interviews were characteristic of the region as a whole, I conducted an auxiliary survey of preschool directors in the Kansai region. The survey was intended to tap into their basic program goals as well as curriculum issues. Based upon my interview data, I developed a number of hypotheses. I expected both public and private schools to emphasize social relationships, although my qualitative data made me aware of important differences among the schools in how these relationships were conceptualized and fostered. I suspected that the goals of the private preschool directors would be oriented more toward elementary school preparation and less toward self-expression than their public school counterparts. I expected that the private schools would be more likely to offer enrichment lessons such as English or gymnastics, instruction in academic skills such as reading and writing, and performances for parents. Also, because my qualitative data clearly pointed out differences among the preschools affiliated with religious organizations, I was interested in comparing the views of Buddhist and Christian educators with those operating private nonsectarian programs.

Names and addresses of 300 directors were selected randomly within auspice (that is, private or public) from a published list of all preschools in the Kansai region. I stratified the sample (30 percent public and 70 percent private) to oversample on the more common and heterogeneous private schools. Complete responses were obtained from 141 directors (77 percent private and 23 percent public). Among the private schools, 11 were affiliated with a Buddhist temple, three

TABLE 8.1

COMPARISON OF PRESCHOOLS BY AUSPICE

	Buddhist & Shinto	Christian	Private	Public	Public versus Private	Buddhist and Private versus Christian and Public	Buddhist versus All
Curriculum							
# children enrolled	184.92	124.97	238.51	73.23	***	***	ns
% time free play	28.50	52.11	39.86	50.04	*	***	***
# performances/year	5.86	3.41	3.86	5.45	ns	ns	ns
# enrichment classes	4.22	3.72	3.79	3.18	***	**	*
# academic classes [a]	1.86	1.58	1.73	1.52	***	**	*
Goals for Children (Rated on 4-point scale from "not important" to "very important")							
Become accustomed to school life	2.78	2.57	2.71	2.58	ns	ns	ns
Discover own likes, dislikes	2.17	2.75	2.41	2.85	**	**	ns
Learn to read and write	1.00	.40	.75	.62	ns	*	ns
Get along with others	2.78	2.74	2.85	2.84	ns	ns	ns
Learn musical instrument	1.50	1.20	1.27	1.14	ns	ns	ns
Learn physical skills	2.50	1.92	2.24	1.95	ns	**	*
Relax and have fun	2.64	2.97	2.88	2.92	ns	†	ns

[a] Could include reading kana, reading kanji, math with abacus, other math.

NOTE. Test of contrasts conducted when overall F for equation was significant at .05, except "learning to read and write"
$F_{(3,129)}=1.30$, $p = .09$.   † $p < .10$;   * $p < .05$;   ** $p < .01$;   *** $p < .001$.

with a Shinto shrine, 12 with a Catholic church, and 20 with a Protestant church. The Buddhist and Shinto responses were combined for these analyses, as were the Catholic and Protestant responses.

Table 8.1 provides the findings of a series of analyses of variance (ANOVAs) to examine the differences in activities and director goals across three groups of private schools (Buddhist/Shinto, Christian, and nondenominational) and the public schools. The analyses examined contrasts along three dimensions. While significant differences emerged between the public preschools and the private preschools (contrast 1), the Christian schools were often more similar to the public schools than to the other private schools (contrast 2). Furthermore, the Buddhist schools were sometimes significantly different from all the other schools (contrast 3).

The public schools had an average of only 73 students, as opposed to the nonsectarian private schools, which had 238 on average. The public schools also offered a less structured curriculum. Both the Christian and public school directors reported allocating roughly half the school day to free play, whereas free play averaged roughly 40 percent of the time in the nonsectarian private schools and only 28 percent of the time in Buddhist/Shinto schools. The number of performances per year did not follow the expected pattern. The Christian schools and nonsectarian private schools averaged between three and four per year, but Buddhist/Shinto and public schools each averaged more than five per year. The number of classes, both academic and enrichment, followed predicted patterns, with public schools offering the fewest, followed closely by Christian schools, then the private nonsectarian, and finally the Buddhist/Shinto schools. I was surprised to see that public schools reported any provision of academic training, since it is contrary to ministry recommendations. Many public school directors reported teaching children to recognize the Japanese syllabary (*hiragana*), and some reported instruction in a second area as well. A more detailed survey would be needed to provide a sense of how often instruction occurs, whether it is offered to all students or only the five-year-olds, as well as what is covered and which methods are used.

Understanding the directors' stated goals helps to shed some light on these program characteristics. The goals of becoming accustomed to school life and getting along with others received high ratings from all groups. Becoming accustomed to school life is a catchall phrase used to encompass such things as learning proper greetings, inhibiting or controlling one's behavior during group times, improving academic skills such as handling scissors, listening to the teacher, and so on. It is worth noting that the trend—although not statistically significant—was for the private and Buddhist schools to place more emphasis on this than the Christian and public schools. I view this set of skills as highly compatible with the role- and relationship-oriented approaches, both of which emphasize the acquisition of daily routines.

The importance placed on learning to get along with others, as well as the lack of emphasis on acquiring skills in reading and writing, suggests why Japanese is consistently described as "group-oriented" and "collectivistic." This simple survey item does not do justice, however, to the richly varied interpretations of what it means to get along with others and how one goes about helping children attain competence in this area.

The strongest group differences were found in response to the goal of helping a child discover his or her own likes and dislikes. Public school and Christian school directors were most likely to emphasize this goal, and the Buddhist/Shinto directors were least likely to do so, giving it an average rating of 2.17 on the four-point scale. In my qualitative data, this focus on personal exploration and self-expression is a major characteristic differentiating the child-oriented programs—all of which were either public or Christian—from the role- and relationship-oriented schools. The Buddhist and nonsectarian private schools were more likely to value learning to read and write as well as learning physical skills. The endorsement of learning specific skills is characteristic of the role-oriented schools, half of which were Buddhist and none of which were public. There was also a marginally significant trend in the survey for the Buddhist and private nonsectarian schools to place less emphasis on relaxing and having fun. Again, this fits well with the qualitative findings, which showed that the role-oriented schools tended to focus on enduring hardship and persevering during challenging conditions.

Overall, the survey findings suggest that private and public schools do differ in significant ways from each other, both in terms of the directors' stated goals and in particular features of the curriculum and activities. However, the private schools are a heterogeneous category that needs to be considered in connection with religious auspice. Christian preschools were often more similar to the public schools than to the other types of private school. Taken together, these two forms of institutional affiliation are helpful in explaining the variation across the sample.

CONCLUDING COMMENTS

These qualitative and quantitative data revealed that public preschools may be more likely than private preschools (except for Christian preschools) to adhere to the principles of good practice articulated by the Ministry of Education. Yet the number of parents selecting public preschools is diminishing relative to those opting for private schools. Parents are apparently willing to pay more for their children to attend a school that offers admission to three-year-olds, extended hours, conveniences such as a hot lunch and bus service, enrichment classes, and, in some cases, instruction in reading and writing.

Public school directors find themselves in a difficult situation as they compete for the dwindling number of preschool children. They may feel that parents' demands are unjustified or not in children's best interests, and thus are unwilling to give in just for the sake of boosting enrollment. Some, for example, expressed grave concerns about the dangers of exposing children to academic material as early as the age of three and feared that market-oriented directors were unwisely ignoring basic realities about how young children learn.

Some of the reasons they gave for their refusal to accommodate parents—although based upon firmly held principles—seemed to me a bit myopic. Some directors, for example, declined to add classes for three-year-olds because they felt children at that age are not yet ready for a group experience. When I asked the principal of Higashimachi Preschool and Elementary School why enrollment at the preschool had diminished to one quarter of its original size over the last decade, he remarked: "I tell myself that our enrollment is down due to the low birthrate in Japan, but I myself can see the large numbers of mothers and children walking past our school to go to the Kokoro Private Preschool. I know the mothers send their children there because the school offers admission to three-year-olds. But I personally think three-year-olds should be at home with their mothers, not in preschool." While his concerns may be sincere, I found myself wondering how sensitive he was to the social isolation experienced by many young children and mothers spending long days together in small apartments (e.g., S. Vogel, 1996).

While public schools may never have the funding for such attractions as Olympic-sized swimming pools, there might be other ways to address parental concerns and desires without compromising their basic values and professional commitments. Some of the Christian schools appeared to be successfully maintaining their educational integrity while trying to understand and respond to parental needs. For example, one of the Catholic preschools used a Montessori curriculum to address the desire of parents that their children be prepared for the literacy and numeracy challenges of elementary school.

Concerned about the declining birthrate as well as stress experienced by young families, the Japanese government is encouraging schools to develop policies that are more cognizant of parental needs. In 1994, the Ministry of Education conducted a survey of parents to assess their views of the problems and opportunities facing children. Parents reported concerns about the lack of opportunities for children to have contact with nature, read, socialize with friends, and engage in volunteer and community activities. A vast majority indicated that adults other than parents should be actively involved in their children's lives, and acknowledge that they cannot succeed without support from the schools. They also expressed uncertainty as to what sort of educational experience would best suit preschool children. I would argue that both public and private schools need to move more aggressively to understand and assist parents in making these important choices.

9

"FINDING OUR WAY"

I can pinpoint the occasion when I truly realized how deeply cultural values are embedded in the ways we rear and educate our children. It happened during a lecture I was giving for a course on the role of the family in children's social development. It was my first semester as a visiting professor at the Harvard Graduate School of Education, which enrolls a substantial number of foreign students. The topic for the day was discipline. I briefly ran through an introduction to the literature, citing studies that showed the relationship between authoritative (that is, firm, democratic) discipline by parents and a variety of outcome measures, including school performance, self-confidence, verbal assertiveness, and the like. At some point, I paused for questions. One student, a middle-aged man from India spoke up: "What research has been done to discover what makes children show respect for their parents?" My snappy response was basically, "Uhhhh. . . ." The student had exposed the Achilles' heel of developmental psychology: the choice of outcome measures—the "gold standard" by which parenting and educational practices are evaluated—is heavily influenced by culturally based values. In selecting certain outcome measures, we set up a system that identifies "good parents" as those who utilize the practices that support those culturally desirable outcomes and "bad parents" as those who do not. Respecting one's elders has not made it onto the list of child competencies favored by American researchers.

Once the dam had been breeched by this student from India, the flood of questioning did not cease for the entire semester. A student from Zimbabwe challenged the attachment literature with her descriptions of how children in her community were often raised by relatives other than their parents. A Native-American student from Minnesota questioned the premium developmental psychologists place on verbal stimulation of infants, describing her community where adults expect children to learn through quiet observation. A student from an aboriginal group in Australia challenged the premium currently placed on androgyny in the sex-role socialization literature—and so on until May. We spent the rest of the semester exploring the literature not from the perspective of "what are the attributes of an effective parent" but, rather, what are the constructs through which the American research literature proposes to capture the important aspects of parenting? How do these constructs operate in white, middle-class, American families—the population from which over 90 percent of the research samples in American journals are drawn (New, 1994)? And what questions does this research pose for the development of children from other societies?

Of course, I am not the first person—or even the first developmental psychologist—to discover that there are cultural norms for child rearing. Having studied Japanese child rearing myself for some ten years prior to the day of my epiphany, I had read the work of anthropologists who were making this point as early as the 1960s and seventies (e.g., LeVine, 1974; Whiting and Whiting, 1975). But sometimes it takes a while for an intellectual notion to sink in so deeply that everything is colored differently from how it had been before.

I subsequently became much more interested in exploring how parents in different communities within the United States were raising their children, including how they made choices about the types of nonparental care they desired for their children. I also found myself becoming increasingly uncomfortable with researchers' attempts to create a single "yardstick" to measure preschool quality. To evaluate the effects of children's preschool experiences on their development, it was becoming increasingly common for researchers to evaluate programs along a single global dimension, with end points defined as "high quality" and "low quality." I found myself wanting to revive the debates of the 1960s and seventies about different models of preschooling, no matter how inconclusive and frustrating it had proven to evaluate their efficacy!

My investigation of Japanese preschools presented a welcome opportunity to explore diverse models of early-childhood education. In Japan, the basic value of early-childhood education has never been questioned as it has in the United States. For one thing, the role of mothers has been defined quite differently in Japan and America over the last century. In the nineteenth century, Japanese mothers were the junior members of their husband's *ie*, or extended household; due to the combination of their youthful vigor and low status, they were expected to undertake the most physically demanding household chores, leaving the comparatively light job of child rearing to older relatives, servants, or siblings (Uno, 1987). In the early part of the twentieth century, mothers were expected to participate in building the modern nation; while the Confucian dictum, "good wife, wise mother" was frequently invoked, the government seemed to prioritize the "good wife" element of the injunction, and interpreted it as meaning a productive member of the household economy. So it has been rather more recently that the role of mother has been conceptualized as the sole important aspect of a married woman's responsibilities. The notion of communal child rearing has been so integral to Japanese family life that the prospect of putting young children into group care has never raised a public outcry as it has in the United States during the past 40 years (see Fuller & Holloway, 1996, for a review).

And, as the directors in my sample pointed out over and over again, there is cultural consensus in Japan on the need for young children to learn how to get along with others. This lesson is not learned just in the home; it also results from experiences in a real group, a category that does not include the family (Peak, 1991). While there are many different views about what skills are necessary for children to learn and disagreements as to how those skills can be inculcated, people are viewed

as inherently social creatures that need some sort of support to actual-
ize their social competencies. Given this basic societal mandate and
reasonable financial support, Japanese early-childhood educators do
not have to be defensive about taking children out of the home and
away from their mothers. In the United States, where this is still an
issue, educators and advocates feel more pressure to present a unified
front to politicians and policy-makers. They seek to quell debate about
how best to educate young children, because the ensuing messy quib-
bling detracts from their image as professionals who may have something to add beyond the intuitive wisdom of grandma or the lady down
the street. In Japan, early-childhood educators have the luxury of
engaging in open reflection about their own practices and can participate in a debate about the relative merits of different approaches without imperiling the entire institution.

This lively debate is what drew me to this investigation and sustained me throughout the life of the project. As we have seen throughout this book, a number of circumstances have conspired to give a wide
range of players a voice in the discussion. First, the Ministry of Education helps pay the bills but does not force its vision on the preschools
as strongly as in other centralized systems such as France's. Second, the
sheer number of privately operated institutions—including diverse
religious organizations—also ensures that the government voice does
not dominate the discourse. Third, the Japanese academic community
is not engaged in research on the efficacy of preschooling in Japan and
has not advocated a particular model of excellence to the same extent
found in the American literature. While there are certainly drawbacks
to this lack of a research base, its absence has kept the spotlight on the
practitioners themselves.

As I have tried to illustrate in the pages of this book, the Japanese
debate about preschools focuses explicitly on visions about the future
and culturally based models about how to raise a child to be a good person. Scientifically based knowledge about children and their development was represented in their thinking as well; Western thinkers like
Froebel and Montessori came up in conversation, as did Japanese writ-

ers like Kurahashi and Suzuki. But most of the directors I spoke with did not have the faith in "one best system" that ethnocentrism can often engender. Rather, the Japanese educators I interviewed were attuned to developments abroad. They kept an eye on the dominant players and were thus constantly nudged into relativism. Hence their preoccupation with "finding their way," a way that fit their visions and values, but that involved neither simple appropriation of Western cultural models nor unquestioning acceptance of traditional Japanese models.

DIVERSE CONCEPTIONS OF SOCIAL RELATIONS IN A "COLLECTIVISTIC" SOCIETY

As we saw, the paths taken by the directors and teachers in these schools were circumscribed by the available cultural models. At a very general level, all directors were explicitly concerned with fostering children's ability to participate effectively in social relations, both dyadically and as members of a larger group. But beneath this overall shared purpose lay quite different approaches to what skills were necessary and how they should be instilled in young children. To me, these differences were profound and suggested that the dichotomous designation of "collectivisitic" or "individualistic" was essentially useless in understanding the dynamics of socialization in this society.

One path, represented by the role-oriented schools, involved reinvigorating the notions of role commitment, self-sacrifice, and self-discipline. The fierce words of the Buddhist director of Suma Preschool sum up this determined search:

Nowadays [Japanese] mothers are similar to Western mothers in many respects, such as their lifestyle, values, and educational points of view. They grew up emulating the Western type of education. Their outside appearance is yellow racially, but they are not so inside. We are now interested in Asia. We want to find our identity in Asia. This might sound rude to you, but westernization or copying systems from Western countries has proven to be wrong. Our goal is old but new. We advocate being Asians. Our confidence comes from inner motivation. We have lost many things in the process of democratic education. People might think that our goal is reactionary. You might be stunned by my reactionary remarks. Our way of disciplining children might remind you of the imperial army. However, such criticisms are very superficial. People who criticize us do not understand our theories, and they tend to judge only partial aspects of our education. It might sound self-flattering, but at least what we are doing here in this preschool is based on different ideas. It is imperative that you understand why we need Asian education once again.

In the role-oriented preschools, individual opinions were seldom solicited and behavioral choices were rarely made available. Whole-group instruction was the preferred medium. Children learned to read and write, play instruments, and do backward rolls. They also learned to sit for long periods of time, listen to the teacher, and move quickly and efficiently during transitions between classes. But the goal of these directors was not just obedience to rules dictated by authority figures. The role-oriented directors wanted children to be receptive to adult guidance, but also gradually to take the responsibility for proactively detecting which behaviors were required, monitoring whether they were fulfilling those behaviors, and making adjustments to their actions when needed. A sense of agency and the ability to make choices are required for fulfilling one's role. Kim's (1994) view—that the subordination of individual desires to the group mandate characterizes this "coexistence" mode of social relations—captures part but not all of the dynamics at role-oriented schools. Suppression of the self was certainly expected of teachers and children at Wakaba and other role-oriented schools. But directors such as Mr. Waseda, with his goal of increasing harmony, not just conformity, had a more complex view that involved nurturing a particular sense of individualism within the overall mandate of contributing to the group welfare.

The cultural models that dominated the role-oriented schools were drawn in part from elements of Buddhism and can be identified in educational settings serving older children as well. It is their use with children as young as three or four that makes them new and controversial even within Japan. My sense is that their viability depends largely on the fact that they serve the modern goal of preparing children to enter elementary school a step ahead of their peers. It is ironic that these ancient models have been given new life by virtue of their utility in a system that is thoroughly modern (and heavily influenced by the West).

Directors in the relationship-oriented schools had a different image of what is "truly" Japanese, and advocates of this path questioned the legitimacy of the claims made by the role-oriented directors. The relationship-oriented directors looked into Japan's past and found cultural models that contradict the authoritarian images preferred by the role-oriented directors. They emphasized the view that children are innately wonderful and deserve to enjoy their early years. They recognized a social impulse in young children and felt that it could be honed and perfected with appropriate guidance. At the heart of their philosophy lay the notion that forging human relationships was the most important task for young children. They hoped that these relationship skills—particularly empathy and cooperation—would blossom during free play with other children. They also used lighthearted group activities as a way of helping children become more skilled in understanding and cooperating with others.

The relationship-oriented schools had developed strategies for fulfilling their goals within the economically mandated context of large class sizes. By admitting as many as 40 children per class (or more in earlier times) they are able to keep costs down and are therefore available to families from all social classes. But both elements of this synchronous arrangement are changing. With the falling birthrate, the sheer number of students has also plummeted. Without the subsidies enjoyed by public schools, it is difficult for private schools to survive with smaller classes. Their response so far has been to add special features such as English and swimming lessons, as well as to engage in aggressive recruitment campaigns. The adequacy of their approach to instilling social competence has also been challenged, as the Ministry of Education advocates an individualized approach and parents clamor for a more explicit cognitive component.

The schools serving wealthy families are moving away from the relationship-oriented model. They have the funds to operate with lower class sizes. As Kağitçibaşi (1990) has argued, elite, urban families in non-Western societies can develop a hybrid approach, retaining a focus on social relations but simultaneously emphasizing their children's individuality and means of self-expression. For these families, the child-oriented approach is attractive. In the child-oriented preschools I visited, the staff placed a great deal of emphasis on social relations. The twist that they added was a substantial focus on bolstering the child's interests, helping him or her identify his own desires and feelings, and nurturing the ability to express those interests, desires, and feelings to others. The ultimate goal was to realize one's human potential—one's potential to engage in social relations, that is. The staff in these schools had ready access to cultural models developed within societies that traditionally emphasize individualism; the Christian schools called directly upon religious ideology, and the public schools grappled with the Ministry of Education guidelines, which build upon ideas originating in the West. These models were blended with other elements that are more traditional to Japan, resulting in a distinctive approach. Furthermore, these schools had the financial capability to ensure a low teacher-child ratio, without which a child focus is essentially impossible.

These different paths illustrate the variation that results from the artful appropriation and synthesis of diverse cultural models, as well as the ways in which institutions shape the perceived utility of different models and the opportunities and barriers to using them. Contestation and change are inevitable results of this process. Shore (1996) recaps this valuable insight, describing his experiences conducing field work in Samoa: "I have found myself insisting that Samoans value community over the individual . . . because of a value system that placed emphasis on diffuse family ties rather than on exclusive attachments. While statements like these contain some truth, they also squeeze the life out of the reality of a people by treating human action as if it proceeded from a simple activation of unilateral models. *Instead . . . real life often involves the problematical and always partial resolution of dilemmas proposed by the existence of competing models, or models that are incompatible with key experiences*" (p. 302, emphasis added). And, I would add, the expression and relative strength of those models are highly affected by political and economic realities.

WHO CONTROLS ACCESS TO CULTURAL MODELS?

The directors I spoke with often described themselves as "finding their way" as they worked continually to develop a program that neither replicated beliefs and practices from the imagined Japanese past nor mimicked strategies developed by educators from Western countries.

If the metaphor of "finding our way" has a conceptual weakness, it lies in the implication that one's "way" may be chosen freely, depending on personal inclination and propensity for soul-searching. This ignores the role of powerful institutions and individuals who try to shape the paths that are taken by others, making their own preferred paths salient and obscuring those that pose a threat. While anthropologists have long been aware of how power determines who has control over the cultural "messages," the point is less commonly acknowledged among psychologists, who are relative newcomers to the study of culture (see Shore, 1996; Turiel, 1999). The effects of differential power can be observed at many levels and in a variety of guises in the preschool world.

Role of Government in Regulating Quality. As we have noted, the central government exerts some authority over the makeup of programs as well as over the features of the physical school site. Many of the private preschool directors bridled over the restrictions imposed by the Ministry of Education. Some of the regulations seemed overly bureaucratic and out of touch with the reality of preschool life. For example, Mr. Tamiko learned that he could not write the instructions on fire extinguishers in *hiragana*, the more simplified alphabet; they had to be in *kanji* and thus were guaranteed to be indecipherable to anyone under the age of ten. While frustrated, Mr. Tamiko and others were slowly removing red tape that hampered their efforts to offer a program that made sense for their communities. For other directors, the concerns were related to fundamental disagreement with the values embedded in the guidelines issued by the ministry. For role-oriented directors like Mr. Waseda, the ministry was merely parroting a quasi-Western philosophy that was ill fitted to the challenges facing Japan. While they expressed annoyance, these directors did not appear to let the ministry guidelines stand in the way of providing a program that reflected their own views.[21]

A full analysis of the role of the Japanese government—and particularly the Minstry of Education—in stimulating educational reform is beyond the scope of this book (see Horio, 1988). But the interviews I conducted suggest that the ministry is not acting efficaciously in its attempts to transform the preschool curriculum. The ministry appears to have little credibility with those on the right, who deplore its embrace of Western values and structures, or those on the left, who see it as a despotic agency out of touch with the realities of modern Japan. When it comes to preschools, the ministry has little actual power over the majority of institutions because they are private. Its role as occupant of the "bully pulpit" may be having some impact over the public schools but not with the ultimate consumer—the parent. The public schools that follow ministry guidelines are being beaten out by the private schools, which make a more energetic attempt to connect with parents.

The ministry has also overlooked its role in evaluating programs and stimulating the development of new knowledge. The agency has not been aggressive in funding research to examine the nature of Japanese preschools or their efficacy in preparing children for elementary school. What few studies have been done are not publicized by the ministry; it has been virtually impossible for me to find out what research has been commissioned and whether any documentation exists concerning the research. At one point, following up on a rumor that several years ago a study had been commissioned to examine the use of different curriculum models in preschools, I asked two graduate students to visit the Ministry of Education in search of relevant documents. After many difficulties, they succeeded in locating a report describing the study, but were told that the report was not available for distribution; they were allowed to look at it in the ministry library but could not copy any portion of it using the public copy machine located in the building!

Distribution of Power between Mothers and Preschool Directors. Regarding their relations with mothers, staff members were quite consistent in expressing concerns about their parenting skills. Some expressed annoyance with mothers' expectations of the school and exasperation at their perceived selfishness.[22] The expectation of role perfection—which I have discussed in relation to the role-oriented schools—was applied quite thoroughly by most of the directors to the role of mother. The involvement required of Japanese mothers exceeds anything I have seen in the United States. Mothers were expected by most preschool staff to engage in most or all of the following: purchase or make by hand a great many items such as smocks, hand towels, and seat covers; label every item according to exacting specifications; prepare a gourmet box lunch six days a week; participate in the PTA but seek little influence over the curriculum or activities; attend performances and ceremonies; and regulate the child's behavior at home and on holidays according to school guidelines (see also Allison, 1996).

The staff I spoke with generally argued that the things they expected a mother to do were important to helping the child have a good school experience, but sometimes I wondered what the real point was of requiring the mothers to spend so much time on certain things that seemed of marginal importance to the child. Were the child's interests really the main point? Or, I often wondered somewhat cynically, were these attempts to remind the mothers that their own inferior knowledge had to be constantly augmented and structured by the staff at school? In some cases, the child's best interests seemed to get lost amid the rhetoric and assertions of power. For example, one source of tension between staff and mothers at some schools was the contents of the box lunch brought from home. The schools under-lined the importance of mothers packing special lunches containing a wide variety of ingredients deemed necessary to the child's nutrition, and there were exacting norms regarding their arrangement and deco-ration, which were said to convey the mother's love for the child. Yet those preschools that contracted with a food service often served sub-standard fare. In more than one site that I visited, the school lunch consisted of a hot dog on a white-bread bun, a carton of milk, and nothing else. A cynic might argue that, having failed to win the power struggle with mothers over school lunches, directors who desired to hold down expenses quickly jettisoned the goal of ensuring that chil-dren receive nutritious lunches.

Many of the directors in my study felt that parents had adequate opportunity to express their views about education, give teachers infor-mation about their children, and voice their complaints about the pro-gram. They felt that they tried to accommodate reasonable suggestions and deal with complaints. It would be interesting to learn more about the perspectives of the mothers. Allison's study (1996) is one of the few that examine these issues from the mothers' point of view. She found that mothers felt powerless to resist the practices that they felt were inconvenient or even harmful to their children; the only avenue they felt open to them was changing schools, but this was not common because they felt it would be difficult for their children to adjust to a new setting. For the most part, the mothers' feelings were represented by the words of one woman, who said: "We have no choice (*shigatta ga nai*). All mothers in Japan need to 'hang in there' (*ganbaru*) and make their children do the same" (p. 150).

Essentially, Japanese mothers' greatest source of power lies in the ini-tial act of selecting a school. Conditions are in their favor in this respect: there are more openings than students, there is a diversity of programs to choose from, and tuition is reasonable. All preschool directors have to be somewhat mindful of the market situation, and attempts are made to varying degrees to satisfy parents' desires. But once a child has been enrolled, the balance of power seems to shift over to the side of the directors, where it remains until the child graduates.

Diversity in the Balance of Power between Teachers and Directors. The internal dynamics of the director-teacher relationship bears further investigation. I could ascertain only a general sense of the patterns in the various types of schools. In the child-oriented schools, teachers appeared to have substantial autonomy in developing their programs. This was actually essential to operating a classroom in the way these directors envisioned—the whole point was to be able to observe each child's needs and interests, and change the environment accordingly, and clearly, this would be impossible if the teachers had to stick with a director-mandated curriculum.

In the role-oriented and relationship-oriented schools, the curriculum was decided far in advance, and techniques for delivering instruction were more routinized. These teachers appeared to be closely following the instructions of the directors. In the role-oriented schools, the teachers seemed to come in for some of the same treatment as the children; they were expected to work very hard and were subject to close surveillance and strong public criticism. It would be very interesting to know more about their perceptions of their work. I was very curious about whether they felt that their seemingly arduous socialization to the ways of the preschool contributed to the "polishing of their hearts." However, as I have noted, I had a hard time getting a sense of how they evaluated the program and how they conceptualized their own role as professionals.

Future research should consider the issue of gender and how it plays a part in structuring teacher-director relationships. The directors of the public schools in my sample were almost all women who had been trained as teachers and had spent much of their careers in the classroom. The private schools were, in this dimension as in many others, more heterogeneous. A number of directors were men who had no formal training in education. The Buddhist schools, for example, were usually run by men with a religious background. One fairly common pattern was for the nonsectarian private schools to be run by a married couple, with the husband in charge of the business side while the wife was responsible for day-to-day operations. In other cases, the male director hired an experienced female teacher to be the assistant director. My sense is that this combination of gender, training, and experience was quite influential in determining the nature of the programs.

Overall, the role of power in shaping the practices in preschools deserves additional scrutiny. As Rosenberger (1996) has argued: "People's reactions to symbolic forms should not be assumed but should be studied on the ground, in relation to contradictions among powerful institutions" (p. 13); in Japan, and particularly among women, resistance may be "fragile and momentary, . . . intended to increase options rather than to change the status quo decisively" (p. 37). Missing the signals of this fragile resistance, the outsider may assume that general external compliance by mothers, teachers, and directors signals agreement with the dominant cultural models. Sometimes, however, these tensions are thrown into relief when the balance of power shifts, as is the case with the role-oriented directors, who sense the Ministry of Education moving farther and farther from the cultural models that used to hold sway in many more schools. Indeed, Lebra and others have argued that it is precisely in situations where harmony is valued and cooperation is expected that conflicts become all-the-more pointed (Krauss et al., 1984; Lebra, 1984). It just takes more patience, focus, and skill for the researcher to elicit and understand the quieter voices.

MULTIPLE CONCEPTIONS OF EXCELLENCE

Academic rhetoric about how to raise the quality of preschools across the United States currently resembles the two-headed pushmi-pullyu found in the story of Doctor Doolittle. Pulling in one direction are those who advocate developing a set of standard guidelines for good practice that can be applied in any community across the country. This trajectory is reflected in the dichotomous concept of "appropriate" versus "inappropriate" practice; the elements of appropriate practice have been articulated by the National Association for the Education of Young Children (NAEYC) and are based upon the organization's reading of the research literature on child development and presumed consistency with "democratic values" (see Lubeck, 1994, for a review). But pulling in the opposite direction are those who advocate moving toward "partnerships" and "dialogues" between early-childhood educators and parents, with each contributing their perspectives and knowledge to the conversation. According to this view, multiple conceptions of excellence are bound to result from a process that puts as much emphasis on parent goals and community values as it does on the experiential base of professional teachers (Holloway & Fuller, 1999).

In my view, the data obtained in these 32 Japanese schools can provide insight to American educators frustrated with the current impasse. Having developed a shorthand way of discussing quality that bundles distinct elements together, we also make a lot of unexamined assumptions about what is good or bad for children, based on a few global indicators. Recently, for example, I attended a conference on culture and early-childhood education where the topic of developmentally appropriate practices was being discussed. One participant introduced her remarks about the need for guidelines such as those developed by the NAEYC by saying we had to be concerned about programs with names like "Jellybeans and Jesus." I began wondering what lay beneath this shorthand criticism; why does naming a program "Jellybeans and Jesus" automatically telegraph low quality to many professional educators? Is it because some would reject a preschool where religious beliefs are in the foreground? Are there underlying assumptions about the cognitive stimulation or discipline strategies that would be used in a program that is religiously oriented? Are there class-based issues lurking below the surface, making us wary of a name that opts for kitsch over dignity? These questions have to be addressed more carefully as we discuss the choices parents make for their preschool children. I think this examination of Japanese preschool begins to illustrate how these various strands can be unpacked and understood.

One reason for Americans to study Japanese education is to identify practices that seem to produce benefits that are desired in the United States as well. I can mull over my experiences in Japanese classrooms and select examples of particular practices that would probably be appealing to American educators. As I have mentioned earlier, the Christian preschools are probably the most likely model to appeal to mainstream American educators, with their dual emphasis on individual capacity-building as well as strengthening the community. But I can identify elements of the other types of schools that might be consonant with "American values" but which are perhaps underdeveloped in American institutions. For example, the emphasis in relationship-oriented schools on explicitly teaching routines and practicing them until they are smooth may be worth implementing in our schools. As a society, we tend to favor spontaneity and reject routine; we may think of routines as regrettable but necessary for crowd control. But experienced teachers are aware that children gain a feeling of control when the people and events in their lives are somewhat predictable. In American preschools, this sensitivity takes the form of setting a daily schedule, for example, or taking care to warn children if the room is going to be rearranged. Japanese teachers may simply take this emphasis a bit farther, taking more time in the day to work on routines, being more systematic in instructing children about how to do certain things, and establishing routines to cover more domains of daily life. It seems to me that Japanese children derive a sense of pride in concrete accomplishments like folding their clothes before putting them in their backpacks, for example, or donning aprons and a chef toque when it is their turn to serve the school lunch.

The role-oriented schools obviously departed radically from practices deemed acceptable by mainstream American early-childhood educators. Yet they too engaged in certain practices that piqued my interest. In particular, I remember sitting in an auditorium watching a large group of three year olds perform a song on the *pianica*. After they finished and marched off the risers, a group of staff and teachers swarmed the stage, quickly and silently removing the *pianicas* and replacing them with the instruments to be used by the four-year-olds in the next performance. Serious and intense, they communicated to me the sense that the quality of this performance really mattered to them. What is the message that the children take away from participating in these carefully orchestrated events? On one hand, as I documented in my discussion of the music classes at Wakaba Preschool, this highly structured, high pressure performance situation must produce a certain amount of anxiety. On the other hand, I sensed that children must get the message that they are considered to be very important and worth fussing over. And by watching their teachers work so hard to put on a good show, they could see how everyone's effort is needed to obtain desired results.

While it is interesting to identify these intriguing elements of practice, this is not the only lesson or even the main lesson that American educators can take away from this study of Japanese preschools. If we take seriously the goal of understanding the values that form the underpinnings of a curriculum, then a discussion and clarification of these values must precede decisions about whether a practice is desirable or appropriate. Overall, I agree with the Japanese approach, which relies on the national government to set basic guidelines to ensure children's basic needs will be met, but which also gives considerable latitude to directors. I think there is an important function for professional organizations as well, but I would argue that their efforts should not be directed at mandating certain program models but rather at strengthening the capacity to identify the cultural models that are synchronous with staff and community objectives. In other words, they should concern themselves less with whether a particular practice is appropriate or not, and more with helping staff develop a thoughtful process for identifying, implementing, and evaluating what they are trying to accomplish. They should be less concerned about schools that are based on the "wrong" theory and more about schools that have no theory at all or are too overwhelmed or uncommitted to implement one.

Thinking about the various preschools I visited that seemed successful in their attempts to create a distinct philosophy and uphold a standard of excellence, I identified the following four principles. These are related to the organizational functioning of the school rather than to particular pedagogical or socialization content.

Principle 1. Good Programs Have a Clearly Formulated Set of Goals and the Values Embedded in Their Practices Are Explicitly Declared and Articulated.

As I have tried to show throughout this book, I felt that most of the directors were very thoughtful about the identity of their programs. For the most part this identity was centered on core beliefs about the experiences that make someone a good person. The role of values was particularly clear in the case of the religious schools, probably because the religious ideology provided a detailed framework for exploring these values and their educational implications. In the literature on American preschools, the role of values is rarely made explicit. The topic of religious affiliation and preschool programs is virtually unexplored. In conferences and casual conversation, I have heard researchers and policy-makers express concerns about, for example, programs run by fundamentalist Christian churches, but I know of little research that has tried to find out more about the goals and operations of those programs. (In contrast, the K-12 literature on Catholic schools, for example, is quite extensive and there is an emerging focus on the effects of religious beliefs on socialization within the family.)

Principle 2. In Good Programs There Is Synchrony between Valued Cultural Models and Actual Practices.

Building on the first principle, this corollary states that if a school's philosophy is clearly articulated, then the practices can and should follow along. If the values underlying a program are explicit, staff can engage in more meaningful conversations about their practices. During my observations, on rare occasions I had the experience of hearing one thing from a director and seeing another when I actually went in the classroom. For example, in one small private school, the director talked about the importance of children learning to work together when putting together performances for parents. But during the rehearsals that I observed, the children had no opportunity to talk with each other or to influence the staging of the performance. The teacher rushed the children through the performance, literally pushing and pulling them into the proper position as they read their lines from a script she had prepared.

When philosophy and practices are in synchrony, the evaluation process is also much clearer. Conversations and creative investigations can ensue about whether program practices actually promote desired values. For example, I always wanted to know whether the children in role-oriented school actually developed a sense of pride in their work, as did their purported role models, the traditional artisans. I also wondered whether they were aware of the contributions of others to their welfare, since the sentiment of gratitude was a major focus of the directors, and I was curious about their sense of self-reliance, which the directors were trying to develop more fully. It would also have been interesting to assess the skills that critics of these programs felt were being neglected, such as the nurturing of an intrinsic motivation to learn.

Principle 3. In Good Programs, Staff Engage in Continual Reflection on Goals and Practices, Relying on Self-Examination, Dialogue with Relevant Actors (Including Parents), and Interactions with Sources of Professional Knowledge.

In Japan, the practice of self-reflection (*hansei*) is common in many institutions, from schools to corporations (e.g., Hersh & Peak, 1998). The capacity for reflecting on educational practices is seen in the use of "research classes" (*kenkyū jugyō*), for example, in which a teacher's lesson is observed by other teachers from area schools, and the strengths and weaknesses are analyzed in a subsequent meeting. When I sat in on a *kenkyū jugyō*, I was amazed that the focal teacher was able to remain calm and analytical while her practices were being openly criticized by a group of 20 colleagues; her ability to profit from this group reflection had no doubt been honed over countless *hansei* sessions beginning perhaps as early as preschool.

Indeed, in most of the schools that I visited, the directors tried to get me to criticize their programs. I could feel myself being drawn into the very process that I was studying, as directors attempted to extract my cultural models of early education and toss them into the pool, where they would be examined from all angles and eventually appropriated (or rejected). At one point, I noticed that my translator was even writing down my off-the-cuff comments to her about the things we were observing; she ultimately revealed that she was intending to write an article about these reactions for publication in an academic journal!

While the reactions of Western academics like myself appeared to be of major interest to the directors, they seemed to vary quite a bit in their interest in engaging in professional dialogues with Japanese colleagues. Some of the directors had little contact with the Ministry of Education: others had quite a bit. A few belonged to networks of schools with similar philosophies, such as the association for Buddhist preschools. The teachers may have provided a source of information on new thinking in the field, but I had the impression that they did not challenge the views of the directors, especially when they were new to the job. As a result, some of the directors seemed rather immune from pressure to change. This isolation made me uncomfortable, because it could potentially lead to extremist positions that might result in child mistreatment. The sense that power was concentrated in the hands of the director was increased by the relatively subdued role of parents in monitoring or challenging the school's practices. Without a system of checks and balances—provided by active oversight by parents or community members with some sense of power—the possibility for abusive or otherwise undesirable practices remains a concern.

Principle 4. Staff in Good Programs Are Energized and Committed to Children's Welfare.

From my first observations on stifling August days when I saw teachers routinely don bathing suits and jump into swimming pools crammed with screaming four-year-olds, I was impressed with the dedication of most of the teachers that I observed. Overall, their degree of engagement seemed more intense and less variable than the engagement of teachers I have observed in the United States. My field notes from Japan contain literally no mention of a teacher merely sitting and watching children play, either inside or outside, or engaged in activities not related to the job. Even in schools where free play occupied most of the time, teachers were usually either actively playing with the children or helping someone with materials. Since few schools employed more than one teacher per classroom, they had little opportunity for socializing with other teachers while the children were present. Even in those class-rooms with two teachers, I never saw them exchange more than a few, brief, job-related comments. In general, while their concept of the role of teacher certainly varied from site to site, they remained "on task" throughout the day. This is likely one reason why the gap between phi-losophy and practice seemed negligible in the sites I visited.

The engagement of Japanese teachers may be connected to the structure of the teaching profession in that country. Uniform standards for teacher preparation ensure that all preschool teachers have the equivalent of an associates degree in early childhood education. They are paid well by American standards and are given a measure of respect that is less evident in the United States. Since the preschool system is overseen by the Ministry of Education, teachers are viewed as educa-tors rather than "baby-sitters." In the United States, the professional identity of child-care providers is more diffuse. Many center-based providers are working for minimum wages. While the average level of education of center-based providers is high relative to the general pop-ulation, it is quite varied. Many children are cared for by family day-care providers and relatives, reflecting a belief on the part of many parents that providers should be parent surrogates, not teachers. And recently the child-care field has been increasingly viewed as an option for the least employable women being forced off welfare, further dilut-ing the sense that caring for young children is a profession that requires skills and knowledge obtained from sources other than personal experi-ence. Until these factors are addressed in a more satisfactory manner, it is unlikely that American children will experience the same intensity on the part of their caregivers that their Japanese counterparts encounter in preschool.

CONCEPTUALIZING CHANGE AND VARIATION IN JAPANESE PRESCHOOLS

As I worked on this book, I sought a metaphor to illustrate the dynamic process by which preschool teachers and directors select from diverse beliefs and practices in order to weave together a coherent program. One representation of this process could be found in the *shimenawa*, a rope ornament created by twisting rice stalks into intricate patterns. *Shimenawa* are used to distinguish the sacred space within Shinto shrines from the profane area outside. During one of my visits to Japan, I came across a spectacular *shimenawa* hanging across the entry to the Izumo Shrine, one of the oldest and most sacred in Japan. This huge festoon is of monumental proportions; it appears to be a plaything left behind by a giant. It extends for some 40 feet across the entrance of the shrine, and its circumference must measure nearly 15 feet. Surprisingly, the *shimenawa* at Izumo conveys a feeling of movement as well as profound stasis. Composed of three large ropes twisted together, it entices the eye to follow each strand as it weaves in and out of the others. The end of each rope emerges dramatically and unexpectedly from a different spot along the bottom edge of the *shimenawa*, plunging toward the ground but stopping abruptly some three feet from the head of the viewer below.

Like the *shimenawa*, Japan conveys an impression of unity and stasis when viewed from afar. Yet a close inspection reveals perpetual metamorphosis as the society continually reinvents itself, a process that is fueled by constant introspection as well as a propensity to seek and appropriate ideas and practices from outside Japan. Each preschool also resembles a *shimenawa* in the sense of having an identity that is ongoing yet constantly changing. Many of the preschools I visited had served the same family for two or three generations. Yet they also respond to trends in early-childhood education, to macrolevel societal changes such as the declining birthrate and increasing employment rates of women, and to changing views of parents about socialization and education.

And, like the individual rice stalks that make up each strand of the rope in a *shimenawa,* multiplicity is evident at several levels of the preschool world. Japanese preschools are combined into a system that has substantially more coherence than the widely diverse patchwork of arrangements available in the United States. However, the unique identity of each preschool must also be acknowledged. Additionally, it is important to identify the components that come together and constitute the program in any single preschool. Varied cultural models from diverse sources are woven together by the director to form a particular program. Symbols, beliefs, and practices from Buddhism, Shinto, and Christianity represent important influences on the curriculum in many schools. Another strand derives from contact with the Ministry of Education. Ministry officials give directors of public preschools access to theories about pedagogy and child development culled from Western early-childhood educators. Folk theories about the nature of childhood are another important component of preschool programs.

There is a tradition among visitors to the Izumo Shrine: to gain the attention and favor of the *kami* or gods of the shrine, they stand beneath the giant *shimenawa* and throw coins up into the dangling bushy ends of the big ropes. It is not easy to penetrate this sacred object. Most of the time the coins bounce off the sharp ends of the tightly bunched rice stalks and rain back down on the heads of the visitors. But occasionally, if the visitor persists, a coin will become lodged in between the stalks and stay high overhead. In writing about Japanese preschools, I have sometimes felt like a supplicant determined to penetrate the apparent integrity of the *shimenawa.* In the end, I will have accomplished my goal if, to paraphrase Shore (1996), Japanese preschool directors are no longer viewed as "hypothetical or average natives" but as real people whose specific experiences, interests, and social position have led them to develop diverse and contested approaches to educating young children.

NOTES

1. Extreme physical violence is found in the Japanese family as well. A survey of 1,500 women conducted by the Tokyo metropolitan government found that one third reported being physically abused at least once by their partners, with one quarter reporting repeated abuse ("One-third of women," 1998). A recent survey of families in Tokyo found that 9 percent of mothers rearing preschool children "repeatedly abuse them by beating or denying them necessary care" ("Nine percent of moms abuse kids," 1999, p. 4). Another source of concern to many Japanese is the upsurge in violence by adolescents toward family members (Kumagi, 1986).

2. The term *yōchien* is often translated as "kindergarten," particularly by the Japanese. However, I have chosen to translate it as "preschool" because *yōchien* are not part of the elementary school, as are most American kindergartens. Also, like American preschools, *yōchien* often serve three-, four-, and five-year-olds. Japanese children begin elementary school at the age of six, and enter the first grade. In describing the programs under the auspice of the Ministry of Health and Welfare, I have used the term *hoikuen* which I translate as "child-care centers." The term *hoikujo* is also correct, but most of the people I interviewed did not use it.

3. In this book, I focus primarily upon the preschools rather than the child-care centers. Given the differences I saw between the two types of institution, I feel they must be described and analyzed separately. My decision to

focus the analysis on preschools was based upon the fact that the majority of the research literature has focused on preschools, and the fact that I had much more data on preschools than on child-care centers (but see Fujita & Sano, 1988, for more on Japanese child-care centers).

4. Rohlen's comment is as follows: "Compared to prewar practices of governance, the postwar system is less assertive of central authority and prerogatives. This would be a reflection of two basic considerations: the discrediting of autocratic style by defeat and the Occupation, and the increasing social integration permitted by economic success. In thus leaving the center more open, so to speak, the opportunity for dynamic interchange among the participating entities has been very great. Considered as a space, the center's openness is a source of creative potential, just as it is in a preschool classroom, as long as routines are well laid down and the level of attachment is high" (Rohlen, 1989, p. 39).

5. Autobiographies by Haase (1998) and Philip (1989), Americans who served as apprentices to Japanese potters, provides insight into the cultural models pertaining to this type of master craftsman.

6. A 1952 survey by Lanham of child-rearing strategies found use of physical punishment reported by 72 percent of mothers, whose own childhood memories were of receiving comparable treatment (Lanham & Garrick, 1966).

7. The director of Bunka Preschool, Mr. Tamiko, was an exception because he did actively work with parents and other members of the community, providing counseling, education, and opportunities for involvement (see Chapter 7 for a description of these efforts).

8. As will be described in chapter 7, American and European missionaries were involved in founding some of the first preschools in Japan in the latter half of the nineteenth century (Wollons, 1993). The number of preschools that profess a Christian orientation is still large relative to the number of practicing Christians in the country. In the U.S., the term "Christian preschools" has come to characterize those under the auspice of evangelical groups associated with the political right. This is not the case with Japanese preschools, where "mainline" forms of Christianity are espoused.

9. Uno (1991b) points out that the features typically assigned to the *ie* are particularly characteristic of samurai households: "no one has yet demonstrated conclusively that *ie* ideals had diffused widely among rural and urban commoners during the Tokugawa period" (pp. 22–23).

10. Schools also develop reputations linked to their position in the social-class hierarchy. Shimizu (1992) found that children in a school identified by his informants as a

shindoi gakkō (a tough, difficult school) had very different experiences from their counterparts in a school serving middle-class children.

11. The director and assistant director emphasized repeatedly that this particular day was more structured than usual because the performance date was looming.

12. The program at Nada, while not rigid and authoritarian, did not aim to promote autonomy or encourage self-expression. The traditional goals of empathy and attachment to the group (in this case, the school and the community) were approached in a manner that was difficult for me to perceive and appreciate. Mr. Kumamoto did not offer a detailed account of his philosophy, and this may have made me more prone to view the program in terms of its deficits rather than its strong points. It is possible that I have misunderstood his philosphy, and that the program is indeed a faithful instantiation of that philosophy. Perhaps the socialization that occurred can best be described using Azuma's concept of "osmosis" (Azuma, 1994b; Hess & Azuma, 1991). In contrast to a direct verbal style of teaching, osmosis is "a less intentional influence of the social environment, the effect of which is based primarily on modeling on the side of the teacher and incidental learning on the side of the learner" (p. 279).

13. Helpful overviews of Japanese religion can be found in Dumoulin (1994), Hunter (1989), Kitagawa (1987), and Nelson (1996). The diary of a young wife living in Kyoto at the turn of the century provides an interesting glimpse of the Shinto and Buddhist practices prevalent in middle-class households (Nakano, 1995). Sugimoto's charming memoir (1929) of life in a samurai family in the late nineteenth century contains a fascinating description of her education by a Buddhist priest and her subsequent conversion to Christianity.

14. I was unable to find any report of the number of preschools affiliated with Shinto shrines.

15. Shinto is not regarded as a religion by scholars, but I use the term "religious" to refer to schools—including Shinto, Catholic, and Buddhist—whose programs take a spiritual approach to pedagogy.

16. Ironically, while Japanese Christian preschools represent a relatively permissive approach within their national context, American Christian preschools are typically quite conservative. American Christian preschool staff often find themselves deploring what they perceive to be the overly individualistic orientation of American culture and frequently take pains to emphasize the child's duty to conform to the authority of God, teachers, and parents. Both groups appropriate certain elements of Christian doctrine, but they apply them in the context of the cultural models in their

own settings—and end up with quite different ideas about how to construe preschool education.

17. Tennoji's emphasis on special services to convey the importance of having "a mind of thanks" is not unique. Another example is provided by the literature available from a Buddhist preschool that I did not visit which mentions that it holds ceremonies to acknowledge Buddha's birth, the birth of Kōhō taishi (a Bodhisattva), the day Buddha received enlightenment, and Buddha's death. Additionally, every month a Buddhist term is selected for special recognition and emphasis—including the terms *gasshō* (putting one's hands together in prayer) and *jihi* (showing mercy for the value of life).

18. A pamphlet put out by Tennoji Preschool echoed the view of the director at Suma that Japanese parents may not offer much spiritual guidance to their children: "Children don't have many opportunities to press their hands together in prayer at home these days. It must be precious for them to have such quiet moments [at preschool]. . . . The act of pressing one's hands together in prayer has a beneficial effect."

19. Throughout the history of Japan, Shinto has been used by the federal government to bolster its credibility and has been associated with ethnocentrism and extreme nationalism. This association was particularly intense in the years preceding World War II. In the Shinto preschools I visited, however, the directors did not express the same sorts of nationalistic sentiments that I heard in the Buddhist preschools.

20. I am indebted to professor Hiroshi Azuma for this comment.

21. In fact, one Japanese colleague suggested the following title for this book: "Ministry of Education? Who Cares!"

22. As someone who has criticized the early-childhood education establishment in the United States for a tendency to view parents as incompetent and uninformed (e.g., Holloway & Fuller, 1999), I found these disparaging attitudes somewhat frustrating. I tried to keep an open mind and understand the perspectives of my informants, but sometimes I had to stifle feelings of indignation.

REFERENCES

Allison, A. (1996). Producing mothers. In A. E. Imamura (Ed.), *Re-imaging Japanese women* (pp. 135–55). Berkeley, CA: University of California Press.

Azuma, H. (1994a). *Nihonjin no shitsuke to kyōiku: Hattatsu no nichibei hikaku ni motozuite* [*Education and socialization in Japan: A comparison between Japan and the United States*]. Tokyo: University of Tokyo Press.

————. (1994b). Two modes of cognitive socialization in Japan and the United States. In P. M. Greenfield & R. R. Cocking (Eds.), *Cross-cultural roots of minority child development* (pp. 275–85). Hillsdale, NJ: Erlbaum.

————. (1996). Cross-national research on child development: The Hess-Azuma collaboration in retrospect. In D. W. Shwalb and B. J. Shwalb (Eds.), *Japanese childrearing: Two generations of scholarship* (pp. 220–40). New York: Guilford Press.

Barth, F. (1989). The analysis of culture in complex societies. *Ethnos, 3–4*, 120–42.

Baumrind, D. (1989). Rearing competent children. In W. Damon (Ed.), *Child development today and tomorrow* (pp. 349–78). San Francisco: Jossey Bass.

Beatty, B. (1995). *Preschool education in America: The culture of young children from the colonial era to the present.* New Haven, CT: Yale University Press.

225

Benjamin, G. (1997). *Japanese lessons: A year in a Japanese school through the eyes of an American anthropologist and her children.* New York: New York University Press.

Bond, M. H., & Hwang, K. (1986). The social psychology of Chinese people. In M. H. Bond (Ed.), *The psychology of the Chinese people* (pp. 213–66). Oxford, England: Oxford University Press.

Boocock, S. S. (1989). Controlled diversity: An overview of the Japanese preschool system. *Journal of Japanese Studies, 15* (1), 41–65.

———. (1991). Childhood and childcare in Japan and the United States: A comparative analysis. *Sociological Studies of Child Development: Vol. 4. Perspectives on and of children* (pp. 51–88). Greenwich, CT: JAI Press.

Bornstein, M. H., Haynes, O. M., Azuma, H., Galperin, C., Maital, S., Ogino, M., Painter, K., Pascual, L., Pecheux, M., Rahn, C., Toda, S., Venuti, P., Vyt, A., & Wright, B. (1998). A cross-national study of self-evaluations and attributions in parenting: Argentina, Belgium, France, Israel, Italy, Japan, and the United States. *Developmental Psychology, 34,* 662–76.

Bredekamp, S., & Copple, C. (Eds.) (1997). *Developmentally appropriate practice in early childhood programs* (Rev. ed.). Washington, DC: National Association for the Education of Young Children.

Center for the Child Care Workforce. (1999). *Current data on child care salaries and benefits in the United States.* Washington, DC: Center for the Child Care Workforce.

Chao, R. (1994). Beyond parental control and authoritarian parenting style: Understanding Chinese parenting through the cultural notion of training. *Child Development, 65,* 1111–19.

Children's Defense Fund. (1998). *The state of America's children: Yearbook 1998.* Washington, DC: Children's Defense Fund.

Christianity Almanac. (1990). [Kirisutokyo Nenkan]. Tokyo: Kirisuto Shinbusha.

Clancy, P. M. (1986). The acquisition of communicative style in Japanese. In B. B. Schieffelin & E. Ochs (Eds.), *Language socialization across cultures* (pp. 213–50). New York: Cambridge University Press.

Cleverley, J., & Phillips, D. C. (1986). *Visions of childhood: Influential models from Locke to Spock.* New York: Teachers College Press.

Conroy, M., Hess, R. D., Azuma, H., & Kashiwagi, K. (1980). Maternal strategies for regulating children's behavior: Japanese and American families. *Journal of Cross-Cultural Psychology, 11,* 153–72.

Coontz, S. (1992). *The way we never were: American families and the nostalgia trap*. New York: Basic Books.

D'Andrade, R. G. (1992). Schemas and motivation. In R. A. D'Andrade & C. Strauss (Eds.), *Human motives and cultural models* (pp. 23–44). New York: Cambridge University Press.

DeCoker, G. (1993). Japanese preschools: Academic or nonacademic? In J. J. Shields (Ed.), *Japanese schooling: Patterns of socialization, equality, and political control* (pp. 45–58). University Park, PA: Pennsylvania State University Press.

DeVos, G. A. (1996). Psychocultural continuities in Japanese social motivation. In D. W. Shwalb & B. J. Shwalb (Eds.), *Japanese childrearing: Two generations of scholarship* (pp. 44–84). New York: Guilford Press.

Doi, T. (1986). *The anatomy of dependence*. Tokyo: Kodansha.

Dore, R. P. (1978). *Shinohata: A portrait of a Japanese village*. New York: Pantheon Books.

Dumoulin, H. (1994). *Understanding Buddhism: Key themes*. New York: Weatherhill Inc.

Efron, S. (1997, February 16). Battle for best schools reaches age 2 in Tokyo: Baby boomers shell out big yen to prep children for careers. *San Francisco Sunday Examiner and Chronicle*, p. C15.

Feiler, B. S. (1991). *Learning to bow: Inside the heart of Japan*. New York: Ticknor & Fields.

Fujita, M., & Sano, T. (1988). Children in American and Japanese day-care centers: Ethnography and reflective cross-cultural interviewing. In H. T. Trueba & C. Delgado-Gaitan (Eds.), *School and society: Learning content through culture* (pp. 73–97). New York: Praeger.

Fukuzawa, R. I. (1994). The path to adulthood according to Japanese middle schools. In T. P. Rohlen & G. K. LeTendre (Eds.), *Teaching and learning in Japan* (pp. 295–320). New York: Cambridge University Press.

Fuller, B., & Holloway, S. D. (1996). When the state innovates: Interests and institutions create the preschool sector. *Research in Sociology of Education and Socialization, 11*, 1–42.

Geertz, C. (1983). *Local knowledge*. New York: Basic Books.

Greenfield, P. M. (1994). Independence and interdependence as developmental scripts: Implications for theory, research, and practice. In P. M. Greenfield & R. R. Cocking (Eds.), *Cross-cultural roots of minority child development* (pp. 1–37). Hillsdale, NJ: Erlbaum.

Haase, B. (1998). Learning to be an apprentice. In J. Singleton (Ed.), *Learning in likely places* (pp. 107–33). Cambridge, England: Cambridge University Press.

Hara, H., & Minagawa, M. (1996). From production dependents to precious guests: Historical changes in Japanese children. In D. W. Shwalb & B. J. Shwalb (Eds.), *Japanese childrearing: Two generations of scholarship* (pp. 9–30). New York: Guilford Press.

Hendry, J. (1986). *Becoming Japanese: The world of the pre-school child.* Honolulu: University of Hawaii Press.

Hermans, H. J. M., & Kempen, H. J. G. (1998). Moving cultures: The perilous problems of cultural dichotomies in a globalizing society. *American Psychologist, 53,* 1111–20.

Hersh, S., & Peak, L. (1998). Developing character in music teachers: A Suzuki approach. In J. Singleton (Ed.), *Learning in likely places: Varieties of apprenticeship in Japan* (pp. 153–71). Cambridge, England: Cambridge University Press.

Hess, R. D., & Azuma, H. (1991). Cultural support for schooling: Contrasts between Japan and United States. *Educational Researcher, 20,* 2–8, 12.

Ho, D. Y. F. (1994). Cognitive socialization in Confucian heritage cultures. In P. M. Greenfield & R. R. Cocking (Eds.), *Cross-cultural roots of minority child development* (pp. 285–313). Hillsdale, NJ: Erlbaum.

Hofstede, G. (1994). Foreword. In U. Vikim, H. Triandis, C. Kağitçibaşi, S. Choi, & G. Yoon (Eds.), *Individualism and Collectivism* (pp. ix–xiii), Thousand Oaks, CA: Sage Publications.

Holland, D., Lachiotte, W. Jr., Skinner, D., & Cain, C. (1998). *Identity and agency in cultural worlds.* Cambridge, MA: Harvard University Press.

Holloway, S. D. (1988). Concepts of ability and effort in Japan and the United States. *Review of Educational Research, 58,* 327–45.

Holloway, S. D., & Fuller, B. (1999). Families and child-care institutions: Divergent research and policy viewpoints. In S. Helburn (Ed.), *The silent crisis in U.S. child care. Annals, American Academy of Political and Social Science* (Vol. 563, pp. 98–115). Thousand Oaks, CA: Sage Publications.

Holloway, S. D., Kashiwagi, K., Hess, R. D., & Azuma, H. (1986). Causal attributions by Japanese and American mothers about performance in mathematics. *International Journal of Psychology, 21,* 269–86.

Holloway, S. D., & Minami, M. (1996). Production and reproduction of culture: The dynamic role of mothers and children in early socialization. In D. W. Shwalb and B. J.

Shwalb (Eds.), *Japanese childrearing: Two generations of scholarship* (pp. 164–76). New York: Guilford Press.

Holloway, S. D., Fuller, B., Rambaud, M. F., & Eggers-Piérola, C. (1997). *Through my own eyes: Single mothers and the cultures of poverty.* Cambridge, MA: Harvard University Press.

Hori, G. V. S. (1996). Teaching and learning in the Rinzai Zen monastery. In T. P. Rohlen and G. K. LeTendre (Eds.), *Teaching and learning in Japan* (pp. 20–49). New York: Cambridge University Press.

Horio, T. (1988). *Educational thought and ideology in modern Japan: State authority and intellectual freedom.* Tokyo: University of Tokyo Press.

Hunter, J. E. (1989). *The emergence of modern Japan: An introductory history since 1853.* London and New York: Longman.

Ishigaki, E. H. (1991). The historical stream of early childhood pedagogic concepts in Japan. *Early Child Development and Care, 75,* 121–59.

———. (1992). The preparation of early childhood teachers in Japan (part 1): What is the goal of early childhood care and education in Japan? *Early Child Development and Care, 78,* 111–38.

———. (1994). *Lower birth rate and children's rights: The present condition of Japanese family.* Paper delivered at the 1994 OMEP World Council and Seminar. Warwick University, UK.

Japan briefing December 1–7: Education Ministry. (1997, December 1–7). *Japan Times Weekly International Edition,* p. 2.

Japan Buddhist Nursery and Kindergarten Association [Nihon Bukkyo Hoiku Kyokai] (1998). *Outline of the Japan Buddhist Nursery and Kindergarten Association.* Tokyo.

Japanese National Committee of Organisation Mondiale pour l'Education Précolaire (OMEP). (1992). *Education and care of young children in Japan.* Tokyo: Kandadera Kindergarten.

Japan's education dilemma. (1998, May 25–31). *Japan Times Weekly International Edition.*

Japan's lingering recession creates generation of lost youth. (1999, February 12). *San Francisco Chronicle,* p. A16.

Joffe, C. (1977). *Friendly intruders: Child care professionals and family life.* Berkeley, CA: University of California Press.

Kağitçibaşi, C. (1990). Family and socialization in cross-cultural perspective: A model of change. In J. Berman (Ed.), *Nebraska symposium on motivation* (pp. 135–200). Lincoln, NE: University of Nebraska Press.

Kim, U. (1994). Individualism and collectivism: Conceptual clarification and elaboration. In U. Kim, H. Triandis, C. Kağitçibaşi, S. Choi, & G. Yoon (Eds.), *Individualism and collectivism: Theory, method and applications* (pp. 19–40). Thousand Oaks, CA: Sage Publications.

Kitagawa, H. M. (1987). *On understanding Japanese religion.* Princeton, NJ: Princeton University Press.

Kojima, H. (1986a). Becoming nurturant in Japan: Past and present. In A. Fogel & G. F. Melson (Eds.), *Origins of nurturance: Developmental, biological and cultural perspectives on caregiving* (pp. 123–39). Hillsdale, NJ: Erlbaum.

———. (1986b). Japanese concepts of child development from the mid-17th to mid-19th century. *International Journal of Behavioral Development, 9,* 315–29.

———. (1988). The role of belief-value systems related to child-rearing and education: The case of early modern to modern Japan. In D. Sinha & H. S. R. Kao (Eds.), *Social values and development: Asian perspectives* (pp. 227–53). Newbury Park, CA: Sage Publications.

Kondo, D. K. (1990). *Crafting selves: Power, gender, and discourses of identity in a Japanese workplace.* Chicago: University of Chicago Press.

Kontos, S., Raikes, H., & Woods, A. (1983). Early childhood staff attitudes toward their parent clientele. *Child Care Quarterly, 12,* 45–58.

Kontos, S., & Wells, W. (1986). Attitudes of caregivers and the day care experience of families. *Early Childhood Research Quarterly, 1,* 47–67.

Kotloff, L. J. (1993). Fostering cooperative group spirit and individuality: Examples from a Japanese preschool. *Young Children, 48,* 17–23.

Kozu, J. (1999). Domestic violence in Japan. *American Psychologist, 54,* 50–54.

Krauss, E. S., Rohlen, T. P., & Steinhoff, P. G. (1984). Conflict and its resolution in postwar Japan. In E. S. Krauss, T. P. Rohlen, & P. G. Steinhoff (Eds.), *Conflict in Japan* (pp. 41–60). Honolulu: University of Hawaii Press.

Kumagi, F. (1986). Filial violence: A peculiar parent-child relationship in the Japanese family today. In G. Kurain (Ed.), *Parent-child interaction in transition* (pp. 357–69). New York: Greenwood Press.

Kuper, A. (1999). *Culture: The anthropologists' account*. Cambridge, MA: Harvard University Press.

Lanham, B. B., & Garrick, R. J. (1996). Adult to child in Japan: Interaction and relations. In D. W. Shwalb and B. J. Shwalb (Eds.), *Japanese childrearing: Two generations of scholarship* (pp. 97–124). New York: Guilford Press.

Lareau, A. (1989). *Home advantage: Social class and parental intervention in elementary education*. London: Falmer Press.

Lebra, T. S. (1984). Nonconfrontational strategies for management of interpersonal conflict. In E. S. Krauss, T. P. Rohlen, & P. G. Steinhoff (Eds.), *Conflict in Japan* (pp. 41–60). Honolulu: University of Hawaii Press.

———. (1992). Self in Japanese culture. In N. R. Rosenberger (Ed.), *Japanese sense of self* (pp. 105–20). Cambridge, England: Cambridge University Press.

LeTendre, G. K. (1996). Shidō: The concept of guidance. In T. P. Rohlen & G. K. LeTendre (Eds.), *Teaching and learning in Japan* (pp. 275–94). New York: Cambridge University Press.

———. (1999). The problem of Japan: Qualitative studies and international educational comparisons. *Educational Researcher, 28*, 38–45.

LeVine, R. A. (1974). Cultural values and parental goals. *Teachers College Record, 76*, 226–39.

Lewis, C. C. (1995). *Educating hearts and minds: Reflections on Japanese preschool and elementary education*. Cambridge, England: Cambridge University Press.

———. (1996). The contributions of Betty Lanham: A neglected legacy. In D. W. Shwalb and B. J. Shwalb (Eds.), *Japanese childrearing: Two generations of scholarship* (pp. 125–38). New York: Guilford Press.

Lubeck, S. (1994). The politics of developmentally appropriate practice: Exploring issues of culture, class, and curriculum. In B. L. Mallory & R. S. New (Eds.), *Diversity and developmentally appropriate practices* (pp. 17–43). New York: Teachers College Press.

Markus, H. R., & Kitayama, S. (1991). Culture and the self: Implications for cognition, emotion and motivation. *Psychological Review, 98*, 224–53.

McKinstry, J. A., & McKinstry, A. N. (1991). *Jinsei Annai, "life's guide": Glimpses of Japan through a popular advice column*. Armonk, NY: M. E. Sharpe Inc.

Miyoshi, M. (1994). *As we saw them: The first Japanese embassy to the United States*. New York: Kodansha International.

Morigami, S. (1993). *Saishin hoiku shiryo shu* [The latest child-care materials]. Kyoto: Minerva.

———. (1996). *Saishin hoiku shiryo shu* [The latest child-care materials]. Kyoto: Minerva.

———. (1999). *Saishin hoiku shiryo shu* [The latest child-care materials]. Kyoto: Minerva.

Mouer, R., & Sugimoto, Y. (1986). *Images of Japanese society: A study in the social construction of reality.* London: Kegan Paul International.

Nakano, M. (1995). *Makiko's diary.* Stanford, CA: Stanford University Press.

Nation of "little emperors" creating chaos in schoolrooms of Japan. (1999, January 30). *San Francisco Chronicle,* p. A11.

Nelson, J. K. (1996). *A year in the life of a Shinto shrine.* Seattle, WA: University of Washington Press.

New, R. S. (1994). Culture, child development and developmentally appropriate practices: Teachers as collaborative researchers. In B. L. Mallory & R. S. New (Eds.), *Diversity and developmentally appropriate practices* (pp. 65–83). New York: Teachers College Press.

Nine percent of moms abuse kids, survey says. (1999, April 16–30). *Japan Times Weekly International Edition,* p. 4.

Okano, H. (1995). Women's image and place in Japanese Buddhism. In K. Fujimura-Fanselow & A. Kameda (Eds.), *Japanese women: New feminist perspectives on the past, present, and future* (pp. 15–28). New York: Feminist Press.

One-third of women are physically abused. (1998, June 1–7). *Japan Times Weekly International Edition,* p. 4.

Peak, L. (1991). *Learning to go to school in Japan: The transition from home to preschool life.* Berkeley, CA: University of California Press.

———. (1992). Formal pre-elementary education in Japan. In R. Leestma & H. J. Walberg (Eds.), *Japanese educational productivity* (Michigan Papers in Japanese Studies, No. 22) (pp. 35–68). Ann Arbor, MI: Center for Japanese Studies.

Philip, L. (1989). *The road through Miyama.* New York: Vintage Books.

Powell, D. R. (1994). Parents, pluralism, and the NAEYC statement on developmentally appropriate practice. In B. L. Mallory & R. S. New (Eds.), *Diversity and developmentally appropriate practices: Challenges for early childhood education* (pp. 166–82). New York: Teachers College Press.

Quinn, N., & Holland, D. (1987). Culture and cognition. In D. Holland and N. Quinn (Eds.), *Cultural models in language and thought* (pp. 3–40). New York: Cambridge University Press.

Reischauer, E. O. (1981). *Japan: The story of a nation* (3rd ed.). Rutland, VT: Tuttle.

Rohlen, T. P. (1983). *Japan's high schools.* Berkeley, CA: University of California Press.

————. (1989). Order in Japanese society: Attachment, authority, and routine. *Journal of Japanese Studies, 15*(1), 5–40.

Rosenberger, N. R. (1996). Fragile resistance, signs of status: Women between state and media in Japan. In A. E. Imamura (Ed.), *Re-imaging Japanese women* (pp. 12–455). Berkeley, CA: University of California Press.

Rosenstone, R.A. (1988). *Mirror in the shrine: American encounters with Meiji Japan.* Cambridge, MA: Harvard University Press.

Sato, N. (1996). Honoring the individual. In T. P. Rohlen & G. K. LeTendre (Eds.), *Teaching and learning in Japan* (pp. 119–53). Cambridge, England: Cambridge University Press.

Sato, M. (1998). Classroom management in Japan: A social history of teaching and learning. In N. Shimahara (Ed.), *Political life in the classroom* (pp. 189–214). New York: Garland Press.

Sayle, M. (1998, June). Japan's social crisis: The bad economic news is a symptom of a worse problem. *Atlantic Monthly,* pp. 84–94.

Shand, N. (1985). Culture's influence in Japanese and American maternal role perception and confidence. *Psychiatry, 48,* 52–67.

Shigaki, I. S. (1983). Child care practices in Japan and the United States: How do they reflect cultural values in young children? *Young Children, 38,* 13–24.

Shimizu, K. (1992). *Shido:* education and selection in a Japanese middle school. *Comparative Education, 28,* 109–29.

Shirakawa, Y. (1996). Culture and the Japanese kindergarten curriculum: A historical view. *Early Child Development and Care, 123,* 183–92.

Shore, B. (1996). *Culture in mind: Cognition, culture, and the problem of meaning.* Oxford, England: Oxford University Press.

Shwalb, D. W., & Nakazawa, J. (1999, April). Japanese mothers' ideas about preschool children: Sources of parenting information, confidence and anxiety. Paper presented at the biennial meeting of the Society for Research in Child Development, Albuquerque, NM.

Shwalb, D. W., Shwalb, B. J., Sukemune, S., & Tatsumoto, S. (1992). Japanese nonmaternal child care: Past, present, and future. In M. E. Lamb, K. J. Sternberg, C. Hwang, & A. G. Broberg (Eds.), *Child care in context: Cross-cultural perspectives* (pp. 331–53). Hillsdale, NJ: Erlbaum.

Shweder, R. A., Goodnow, J. J., Hatano, G., LeVine, R. A., Markus, H., & Miller, P. (1998). The cultural psychology of development: One mind, many mentalities. In W. Damon (Ed.), *Handbook of child psychology* (5th ed.), Vol. 1. (pp. 865–937). New York: Wiley & Sons.

Smith, H. W. (1994). *The myth of Japanese homogeneity: Social-ecological diversity in education and socialization.* Commack, NY: Nova Science Publishers.

Smith, R. J., & Wiswell, E. L. (1982). *The women of Suye Mura.* Chicago: University of Chicago Press.

Spodek, B., Saracho, O., & Davis, M. (1991). *Foundations of early childhood education* (2nd ed.). Englewood Cliffs, NJ: Prentice Hall.

Stevenson, H. W., & Stigler, J. (1992). *The learning gap: Why our schools are failing and what we can learn from Japanese and Chinese education.* New York: Summit.

Sugimoto, E. I. (1929). *A daughter of the samurai.* Garden City, NY: Doubleday, Doran & Co.

Tobin, J. J. (1992a). Introduction: Domesticating the west. In J. J. Tobin (Ed.), *Re-made in Japan: Everyday life and consumer taste in a changing society* (pp. 1–41). New Haven, CT: Yale University Press.

———. (1992b). Japanese preschools and the pedagogy of selfhood. In N. R. Rosenberger (Ed.), *Japanese sense of self* (pp. 21–39). Cambridge, England: Cambridge University Press.

———. (1995). The irony of self-expression. *American Journal of Education, 103,* 233–58.

Tobin, J. J., Wu, D. Y. H., & Davidson, D. H. (1989). *Preschool in three cultures: Japan, China, and the United States.* New Haven, CT: Yale University Press.

Trudeau, G. (1992, June 29). Learning curves [op-ed]. *New York Times.*

Tsuda, A. W. (1994, December). Cultural values in Japanese preschools and international preschools in Japan. Bulletin of Seiwa College, Nishinomiya, Japan.

Tsuda, S. (1966). The idea of *Kami* in Ancient Japanese Classics. *T'oung Pao*, 52, chaps. 4–5, 294.

Turiel, E. (1999). Conflict, social development, and cultural change. In E. Turiel (Ed.), *Development and cultural change: Reciprocal processes.* New directions for Child and Adolescent Development (No. 83) (pp. 77–92). San Francisco: Jossey-Bass.

United States Department of Education, National Center for Education Statistics. (1998). *Characteristics of children's early care and education programs: Data from the 1995 National Household Education Survey* (NCES 98–128), by S. L. Hofferth, K. A. Shauman, R. R. Henke, and J. West. Washington, DC.

Uno, K. A. (1987). *Day care and family life in industrializing Japan, 1868–1926.* Unpublished dissertation, History Department, University of California, Berkeley.

Uno, K. S. (1991a). Japan. In J. M. Hawes & N. R. Hiner (Eds.), *Children in historical and comparative perspective: An international handbook and research guide* (pp. 389–419). New York: Greenwood Press.

———. (1991b). Women and changes in the household division of labor. In G. L. Bernstein (Ed.), *Recreating Japanese women, 1600–1945* (pp. 17–41). Berkeley, CA: University of California Press.

Valsiner, J., & Litvinovic, G. (1996). Processes of generalization in parental reasoning. In S. Harkness & C. M. Super (Eds.), *Parents' cultural belief systems: Their origins, expressions, and consequences* (pp. 56–82). New York: Guilford Press.

Vogel, E. F. (1963). *Japan's new middle class: The salary man and his family in a Tokyo suburb.* Berkeley, CA: University of California Press.

Vogel, S. H. (1996). Urban middle-class Japanese family life, 1958–1996: A personal and evolving perspective. In D. W. Shwalb & B. J. Shwalb (Eds.), *Japanese childrearing: Two generations of scholarship* (pp. 177–200). New York: Guilford Press.

Walthall, A. (1991). The life cycle of farm women in Tokugawa Japan. In G. L. Bernstein (Ed.), *Recreating Japanese women, 1600–1945* (pp. 42–70). Berkeley, CA: University of California Press.

West, J,. Hausken. E. G., & Collins, M. (1993). *Profile of preschool children's child care and early education program participation.* (National Household Education Survey; NCES 93–133). Washington, DC: National Center for Education Statistics, U.S. Department of Education.

White, M. (1987). *The Japanese educational challenge.* New York: Free Press.

White, M., & LeVine, R. A. (1987). What is an "*ii ko*" (good child)? In H. Stevenson, H. Azuma, & K. Hakuta (Eds.), *Child development and education in Japan* (pp. 55–62). New York: Freeman.

Whitebook, M., Howes, C., & Phillips, D. (1998). *Worthy work, unlivable wages: The National Child Care Staffing Study, 1988–1997.* Washington, DC: Center for the Child Care Workforce.

Whiting, B. B., & Whiting, J. W. M. (1975). *Children of six cultures: A psycho-cultural analysis.* Cambridge, MA: Harvard University Press.

Wikan, U. (1991). Towards an experience-near anthropology. *Cultural Anthropology, 6,* 285–305.

Wollons, R. (1993). The black forest in a bamboo garden: Missionary kindergartens in Japan, 1868–1912. *History of Education Quarterly, 33,* 1–35.

Zinsser, C. (1991). *Raised in East Urban: Child care changes in a working-class community.* New York: Teachers College Press.

Zipangu (1998). *Japan made in U.S.A.* New York: Zipangu [on-line]. Available: www.tiac.net/users/zipangu.

INDEX